Workers' participation in industry

Workers' participation in industry

Michael Poole
Department of Sociological Studies
University of Sheffield

Routledge & Kegan Paul
London and Boston

First published in 1975
by Routledge & Kegan Paul Ltd
Broadway House, 68–74 Carter Lane,
London EC4V 5EL
and
9 Park Street,
Boston, Mass. 02108, USA

Set in 11 on 12pt Plantin
and printed in Great Britain by
Ebenezer Baylis and Son Ltd
The Trinity Press, Worcester, and London

ISBN 0 7100 8004 2

For Anne

Contents

Preface

I have endeavoured within the compass of a single volume to draw together material from a wide range of practices designed to extend the control of workers over decisions within their places of employment. It is my considered view that, notwithstanding their disparate origins, these experiments have a certain unity and that the principles which bind them together are made intelligible by reference to deep-rooted causes in economic, political, and social life. If, therefore, a principal aim of this study is to maintain interest in and to create a sympathetic attitude towards developments in this direction, the primary focus is inescapably explanatory.

It was originally my intention to produce a text which was both more theoretical and more empirical in content and, in particular, I would have drawn substantially on the research which formed the basis of my doctoral dissertation. However, in modifying these first tentative proposals I was provided with the twin opportunities of extending my coverage and of subjecting my original thesis to the challenge of new data. Apart from the intellectual enjoyment this afforded the net effect will, I hope, be a book of interest to the general reader as well as the specialist.

In this prefatory note, I should also like to avail myself of the opportunity to record my appreciation of the contributions of friends and colleagues. I owe the greatest debt to my wife, Anne, a fellow sociologist, who was not only an unfailing source of encouragement but who also read through every chapter and made many helpful suggestions. I am also indebted to those workpeople and managers who, in giving of their time, helped in countless ways in the formulation of my ideas but whose anonymity I respect. I must however mention Mr Bill Walker who without doubt taught me far more about industrial relations than I could have grasped from almost any textbook and so I, along with many others, will be forever in his debt. My doctoral dissertation was supervised by Dr David Lee who is now at the University of

Essex and both Annette Kuhn and Bridget Pym read through and made helpful comments on an early draft of the opening chapter here. I should also like to thank in addition, the many secretaries who were involved in one way or another in preparation of the typescript, namely Sylvia Clarke, Beryl Ibbotson, Thelma Kassell, Sylvia Lockey, Margaret Sayles, Margaret Scarr and Renee Shaw. Finally, however, the responsibility for the arguments advanced here is of course entirely my own.

Department of Sociological Studies
University of Sheffield

1 Point of departure

All workers participate in industry by virtue of producing the substance of man's material existence, but since the advent of the industrial revolution all but a few have been consistently denied an effective voice both in the management of the firms in which they are employed and, at a higher level, in the framing of policies on the allocation of resources within the confines of a given social order. In perspective, of course, the subordinate majority have, by consequence of their task-based expertise, acquired a measure of control over the actual performance of work and this, together with other workgroup practices designed to extend their frontier of control over decisions at shop-floor level, has guaranteed the maintenance of rudimentary expressions of participation in most industrial milieux. But the mode of industry today is still incompatible with a condition in which man is reconciled with himself through his work, from which he derives a meaning and a purpose, and through which he can begin to 'regain *control* over essentially man-made institutions and historical situations'.[1]

This property, of course, was somewhat more typical of pre-industrial pursuits, for although the population of those times unquestionably suffered from scientific and technical immaturity and, as a result, were by no means well adapted to their natural and physical habitat, the social organization of activities was perforce highly decentralized. In industrial societies, by contrast, our understanding of natural/scientific laws and thus our power to control the environment have proceeded apace with the result that our material standards of living have been raised to heights undreamed of by earlier generations; but this process has not been matched by a corresponding amelioration of the human social condition. On the contrary, with increasing concentration and centralization of decision-making processes at work, people have become truly disenfranchised, being unable to determine the shape of their own economic existence to the extent that, as C. Wright Mills has so poignantly argued, they now feel their lives to be a series of traps:[2]

They sense that within their everyday worlds, they cannot overcome their troubles, and in this feeling they are quite often correct. What ordinary men are directly aware of and what they try to do are bounded by the private orbits in which they live; their visions and their powers are limited to the close-up scenes of job, family, neighbourhood; in other milieux, they move vicariously and remain spectators. And the more aware they become, however vaguely, of ambitions and of threats which transcend their immediate locales, the more trapped they seem to feel.

Individual passivity is thus an inevitable consequence of lack of autonomy and this is in turn incompatible with the notion of man 'able to realize his full potential and to create a truly human order . . . freed from external constraint'.[3] The problem of control has thus come to represent a critical component of sociological thinking: indeed, there is widespread recognition in the discipline that 'to control a situation is to impose meaning on it by acting upon it',[4] and that, by the same token, to be deprived of any decisive influence within the social environment generates an intense and a seemingly inescapable experience of powerlessness which has consequences more far reaching than at first sight appears obvious. Its repercussions have implications for the formation of attitudes on the nature of man and society and equally have a bearing on those which relate to the minutiae of daily existence. Deprived of any opportunity to participate in decisions which are the substance of their lives, or able to do so only circumspectly, ordinary people are apt to resort to 'world views' of an essentially passive, fatalistic and dependent kind.

But the prospects of a change in this form of consciousness are by no means bleak. To begin with, by virtue of the ability to control, the minority who occupy dominant positions in society have far more faith in the capacity of man to influence his physical and social environment than have the *comparatively* powerless majority. But, more importantly, a great many people who occupy basically subordinate roles have now begun to seek an amelioration of their condition and are evolving a variety of methods through which to participate in, and even at times to win control over, certain decision-making processes in the workplace.

Furthermore, as a by-product of this enthusiasm for workers' participation and control, an appropriately persuasive case has been argued for the democratization of social institutions. This is upheld, first, by an appeal to selected values which are widely advocated in most industrial societies; second, by recourse to a body of ethical principles which strengthen this underlying reasoning and, finally, by reference to abundant, carefully collected evidence, of the substantial socio-economic benefits of effective participation.

In the first place, then, the proponents of participation have been able to found their case on widespread commitment in industrial societies to democratic ideals, one necessary element of which would be the inalienable right of the citizen to a voice in his own concerns. To be sure, the status accorded to participation in democratic thought is open to debate. Indeed, until recently, it appeared that the term had been successfully exorcised from the vocabulary of democracy by the so-called modern theorists for whom, following Schumpeter, 'responsible' government was the essence of democracy.[5] This orientation, incidentally, was in complete contrast to the position taken by those, including Bottomore, who claimed that 'modern democracy has most often . . . been defined as the participation of the mass of people in government',[6] and, what is more, it ignored the retention of this meaning in popular political argument. For our purposes, however, it is sufficient to note that, as a result of changes in thinking in the latter half of the 1960s, participation again came to be represented in the mainstream of social and political thought and, indeed, Blumberg and Pateman in particular have argued for the creation of a genuinely participatory society (based in the first instance on participation in the work situation) as an essential foundation of any successful democratic system.[7]

A belief in the virtues of democratic control can thus be traced to certain fundamental human values which are commonly held and officially sanctioned in most industrial countries. In addition, participation has been hailed on theoretical grounds as the most appropriate solution to the problems of alienation in modern industrial societies, as the best method of facilitating the development of socially aware and public-spirited people, as a stepping-stone to the fulfilment of certain 'higher echelons' of needs which are deemed to be common to all men, and finally, as a means of overcoming major social disadvantages which are consequent upon non-democratic modes of decision-making.

Now, notwithstanding the controversy surrounding the concept, the conviction is widely shared that alienation, embodied in the estrangement of men from the products of their creation, is endemic in our era. To be sure, this tendency had been recognized in the early phases of the industrial revolution,[8] but awareness of the problem has been particularly acute and widespread in recent years. So much so, indeed, that as Barakat has remarked: 'We are repeatedly told that alienation of man from society, social organization and/or himself is one of the dominant conditions and modes of life of modern times.'[9] An involvement in decision-making processes and greater control by workers over their work environment has been frequently offered as a partial solution to this problem.

The value of participation had, of course, been argued by a number of early political theorists as a means of optimizing individual freedom and self-determination within a collective context. The very act of participation would, it was suggested, increase the willingness to participate on future occasions, and the ultimate ideal to be furthered by active involvement was a society in which social awareness and public spiritedness were the norm rather than the exception in human behaviour.[10]

These ideas have recently been reinforced by the contributions of a group of social psychologists, including Maslow, Likert, and McGregor,[11] who are of the opinion that much of human motivation can be explained by the existence of a hierarchy of needs, the ultimate of which is 'self-actualization'. And although this analysis may be culturally specific (in other contexts 'collective actualization' might be a more appropriate term) it would seem reasonable that, having satisfied their primary physiological, economic and social needs, people will intensify their search for self-expression, self-actualization and creativity within their work environment. It would, moreover, be logical to hypothesize that with the progressive evolution of industrial societies and the consequent gratification of primary require-ments, certain emergent needs, which are satisfied in participatory environments, would take on a new significance. And, while they might place greater emphasis on values than on needs in determining the relative importance of any given criterion,[12] sociologists, in their turn, would be inclined to accept that the fulfilment of basic physical requirements will have positive implications for the *value* that is attached to creative and unalienating work.

Furthermore, it has always been recognized that undesirable social consequences can ensue from the concentration of decision-making power. This, in its most general formulation, has been best expressed by Lord Acton ('power tends to corrupt, and absolute power corrupts absolutely'), but more specifically it has been argued that, under com-petitive conditions, these problems are magnified by the danger and, indeed, the likelihood of unscrupulous men reaching controlling posi-tions. This is 'because of the way in which the processes of selection for positions of authority favour ruthless power seekers'[13] since, with competition, 'those with too many scruples' are effectively excluded leaving the prizes to be won by the most ruthless and least humanitarian among men.[14]

This situation is potentially exacerbated because the upwardly mobile are not averse to geographical as well as to social mobility, a process which could have a number of important consequences.[15] First, the highly mobile would tend to place only limited value on stable friendship and kinship patterns; second, whenever there was a conflict between achievement and satisfactory human relationships the highly mobile would tend almost inevitably to choose the former; and finally, their association with others and, by corollary, any commitment to humanitarian goals, would tend to be essentially calculative with the result that they would have a 'capacity to give up existing social relationships and to form new but superficial (and more profitable) ones at a higher social level'.[16] It is a salutary thought, then, that the chance of selecting leaders with genuinely humanitarian sympathies becomes particularly remote in societies in which recruitment to élites is to any significant degree on a competitive basis, so that the need for genuine participation and active involvement by the majority becomes absolutely essential if untoward human and social consequences are not to ensue in these circumstances.

The impressive *a priori* case which may be advanced for the extension of participation has been amply supported on empirical grounds as well, though naturally not all the studies in question have been wholly consistent. The aims of the investigators, the research methods used, the samples selected and even, at times, the results, have been by no means identical but the overwhelming trend in the evidence has given almost unqualified support for the case in favour of democratic control. And, indeed, after an exhaustive review of these findings Blumberg was able to argue that 'there is scarcely a study in the entire literature which fails to demonstrate that satisfaction in work is enhanced or that other generally acknowledged beneficial consequences accrue from a genuine increase in workers' decision-making power', and to make the further point that such a degree of unanimity in findings is rare in sociological research.[17]

Thus, despite certain minor inconsistencies, it is possible to make a number of definitive judgments about the effects of various 'experiments' in participation. First, in so far as the ordinary worker is concerned, participation at shop-floor level has had impressive results; second, representative systems involving participation in decisions of a policy nature have been by no means unsuccessful and, third, the attitudes of workers towards industrial participation tend to be positive though they may well at times still place other satisfactions higher on their list of priorities.[18]

The evolution of these ideas has been paralleled, too, in the formulation of government policy so that, in the last few years, statutory means have been frequently employed in the furtherance of participation; indeed, most industrial countries now have some *legal* provision for workers' representation in decision-making processes within the firm. Moreover, member states of the EEC, in an endeavour to systematize procedures in this field, have adopted two principal sets of proposals, the first being the statute for the European company (put forward in June 1970) which ensured a separation of management functions from those of supervision or control in all enterprises within the community. Then, in September 1972, the draft Fifth Directive of the EEC Commission called for the establishment of co-determination in all constituent countries; this would secure not only a two-tier or double-decker system of formal authority within the firm but would also guarantee the rights of workers to representation on the senior tier. These schemes, incidentally, were modelled primarily on the German system, though the practice in Holland (where the supervisory board is appointed by the general meeting of shareholders but the works councils have rights of nomination and veto) was a pertinent example too.[19]

Now in supporting co-determination the EEC Commission was not being conspicuously innovatory but was merely sanctioning a practice which had already been adopted by a number of states; indeed, among the current participants in the EEC, Great Britain and Eire are the only countries in which, for example, works or employee councils are not yet mandatory. Elsewhere, in Austria, Belgium, Finland, France, the Federal Republic of Germany, India, Luxembourg, the Netherlands, Tanzania and Tunisia, such forms of representation were already in general use. Furthermore, workers' representation on the boards of enterprises has for some time been obligatory in a number of states such as the Federal Republic of Germany, Austria, France, Spain, the Netherlands and Norway. Again, selected Eastern European socialist countries have developed, in addition to works councils and other co-operative machinery at factory level, the most extensive legislation to date by which to encourage actual self-management on the part of workers. Yugoslavia is the classic example of this radical approach to workers' participation but similar arrangements have been introduced (if only for brief periods) in both Poland and Czechoslovakia and, further afield, in Algeria.[20]

For their part, in response to these changes, the main political parties in Great Britain have now taken up their positions on this matter and their respective policies must surely at some time be reflected in at least a nominal transformation of the rights of workers to participate in the decision-making processes in the companies in which they are employed. Unfortunately, at the time of writing, the Conservative Party's Green Paper on this subject is still awaited, but there have already been some preliminary indications from the party's headquarters and research department of what is in store. There is, for instance, evidence of a widely-held view that some legislative action is needed if an extension of workers' rights is to be achieved, especially in the case of managements who are continually obstructive in their struggle 'to retain rights and privileges which have no part in a progressive industrial society'.[21] In detail, it is suggested that works or employee councils be obligatory, unless, after a ballot of employees, two-thirds of those actually voting express their opposition to such an arrangement. On the question of wide-ranging legislation on representation at board level, however, there is somewhat less enthusiasm, though this is supported in the case of workers' representatives who seek to further the interests of the company as a whole, and not merely the workers' 'section' of it. There is, on the other hand, a general feeling emanating from the Conservative political centre that flexibility and choice should be maximized in this sphere.[22]

On the face of it, the British Labour Party has been broadly committed to industrial democracy for a longer period than any of its rivals, since Clause Four of the party's constitution calls not only for the common ownership of the means of production, distribution and exchange, but also for 'the best obtainable system of popular administration and control of each industry or service'. But while in office, for reasons which will be examined later, it has advanced workers' participation and control only circumspectly, largely by extensions of bargaining and consultative machinery in nationalized industries. However, after 1967, a far more positive interest in participation could be detected, and since then the party has been committed to the implementation of the Industrial Representation Act. In brief, this proposes a system of joint control by unions and management at all levels of decision-making, using existing trade-union machinery and shop stewards' organizations: 'The aim is to extend into the workplace the constructive power the unions now have in national economic planning. It will mean a new positive role for the shop steward or plant official.'[23] The party is also anxious to relieve job monotony by extending the scope of the decision-making power of operatives at workgroup level, although again—and this is the critical difference between these proposals and those of, say, the Liberal Party—this would be grounded in and not an alternative to the established structure of trade unions.[24]

The Liberal Party, too, has for a number of years, expressed its enthusiasm for various forms of workers' participation, its earliest proposals being directed towards profit-sharing and other employee asset-formation schemes. These ideas have since been supplemented, first, in the run-up to the 1970 general election by the notion of mandatory works councils and, second, by that of board-level representation which would bring British arrangements into closer correspondence with those operating in other EEC countries. The Liberals now envisage a comprehensive system of employee participation (on the shop floor, on works councils and on company boards) and are of the view that works councils and departmental meetings are 'the foundations of industrial democracy'.[25] They, too, like their Labour Party counterparts favour the fifty/fifty representation of employees and shareholders on a supervisory board, but differ from Labour on the question of union membership. Under the Liberals' plan, the employee representatives on supervisory boards would be elected through the works council and, in principle at least, it would be irrelevant whether or not those selected were in fact trade-union officials. They are opposed, too, to the Dutch system of veto which they regard as an abuse of power, but would particularly like to see the establishment of a two-tier board system, for, in their view, the single board 'has failed to promote adequate direction to British industry and has equally failed to provide democratic control over directors'.[26]

Outside the official party system, there has seldom been consistent support for workers' control since the argument was advanced so forcibly and so cogently in the early decades of this century, but a sizeable group of trade unionists and other labour activists are committed in principle to the idea, which for many years has been propagated by the Institute for Workers' Control. Again, most socialist groupings to the left of the British Labour Party are now firmly convinced of the need for workers' control to supplement the nationalization of all existing industry, though the precise weighting to be given to central planning on the one hand and local control on the other is a matter for perennial debate.

But if the case for participation is so impressive, why, it may reasonably be asked, has not industrial democracy proceeded further? In reply we would contend that the critical role of power in industrial life has simply been ignored or at best treated cautiously by those who are most active in its cause but whose reasoning at times, therefore, has fluctuated between the naïve and the Utopian. Our contribution here, then, will be explanatory; we shall concentrate on participation as a dependent rather than as an independent variable and by so doing provide a rather more reliable guide than has hitherto been available to the proposals most likely to achieve viable democratic institutions in the workplace. To this end, in chapter 2, we seek to clarify the nature of power and its relation to the issues of participation and control. The central proposition to be developed here is that workers' participation and control is a function of certain underlying or latent power forces and a climate of values which may or may not be conducive to evolution along these lines. Evidence from all manner of schemes for participation by workers in industry will then be cited in support of this contention. The order of treatment of selected examples of the various practices is here dependent on the source from which they emerge, namely, management, workers, trade-union officials or government. But having thus classified the wealth of material pertaining to participation and control we could not fail to recognize the potency of certain phenomena which with almost monotonous regularity were observed to provide the impetus for, and determine the viability of, any venture. Thus, we hope that it is, above all, in the identification of these forces that the main value of this study lies and that this represents a real contribution to our understanding of the workings of industrial relations, and a pointer to those forms of consciousness which are fundamental if political, economic and social institutions are to be adapted for the betterment of mankind.

2 Power in industrial relations

Introduction

In any significant debate concerning the form and content of workers' participation in decision making, there must arise broader issues about the exercise of power in industry and society at large. Indeed, as early as 1912, Graham Wallas, in his address to the annual meeting of the Sociological Society on the question of syndicalism, made the point that:[1]

> industry was now organized on a scale and with an intensity without precedent in the history of the world, and perhaps the most important question before the Sociological Society was what forces or body of men should control this vast organization.

As a sequel to this, it is not surprising that such issues as the nature of power in industry and the patterns of formal control in organizations have emerged frequently in the subsequent literature, with the result that power, at least, has increasingly become something of a hybrid concept. It is not inappropriate in this chapter, therefore, to say something—if only rather briefly—about its principal meanings and to relate the more specific debates about workers' participation and control firmly into this broader theoretical canvas.

The main argument of this chapter is that participation and control are important *manifestations* of fundamental processes involved in the exercise of power in society. To be sure, the more ardent apostles of participation have usually regarded it as an especially critical component of power, principally because in their view it is through participation in decision-making (and especially in an industrial context) that basic lessons about man's essential subjectivity can be learned, and also, by virtue of being so central, it can significantly affect other questions in social life such as what is to be produced in society and on the basis of what principles the fruits of labour should be distributed. However, without in any way wishing to challenge significantly the validity of such assertions we would regard participation as only one manifestation of power, albeit an important one. Moreover—and this is fundamental to our own inquiry—participation is in our view very much the offspring of deeper, *latent* power processes which operate in society and the *values* about participation which obtain at any given point in time in particular societies and organizations.

There has, as it happens, been a growing measure of agreement among sociologists that new socio-cultural forms are only generated when concomitant changes take place in the power structures of particular societies and social organizations. To be sure, power is frequently envisaged as both a cause and a consequence of such changes, but like energy in the physical world, 'it pervades all dynamic social phenomena' and may be observed in 'every instance of interaction and every social relationship'.[2] However, perhaps in part because of this ubiquitous character, it has been taken for granted in a great many sociological investigations of industry and, more importantly, its precise impact on social attitudes and behaviour has been insufficiently documented. Up to a point, this problem can be attributed to the development of certain socio-linguistic forms within the discipline which, notwithstanding their implicit recognition of the exercise of power within organizations, serve largely to label, describe and even justify specific patterns of domination and, in so doing, prevent more basic issues concerning the exercise of power in social life from being brought into focus at all.

This has been especially evident when the question of the distribution of power in industry has arisen in discussions of bureaucratic and other formal organizational structures. Thus, for example—although, to be sure, many of the earlier studies of bureaucracy were grounded in Weber's classic work on this subject—the concept and the terms associated with it were abstracted from Weber's wider discussions on the nature of power, and from his analysis of certain predominant modes of domination and their legitimation in social and organizational life. The result was that terms such as 'hierarchy of authority', 'system of rules', 'span of control', 'chain of command' and so on came to be used *in vacuo* and, even though Weber himself considered that they merely reflected *particular* configurations of power and a specific historical relationship between economy and society, they were seldom understood in this way. Similarly, in modern organizational analysis, although the language has become even more complex, repeated references are made to 'specialization', 'standardization', 'formalization', 'centralization' and so on, but these terms remain unconnected—at least in any systematic manner—with the broader, implicit issue of the exercise of power in industrial relations. In short, because power is recognized as central to social and industrial life, its existence is taken for granted and, hence, its effects have been left largely uninvestigated.

But among those who have actually taken more systematic account of the concept of power there has been a major division between those who view its exercise in industry in an essentially positive light (non-zero-sum theorists)[3] and those who have emphasized its more negative consequences (zero-sum theorists).[4] The principal case of non-zero-sum theorists is that power can be best understood as a 'circulating medium', similar to money in the economic system, which can have major social and economic benefits. In particular, it facilitates the co-ordination and integration of the capacities, talents and work of very large numbers of people and, in so doing, gives those societies, institutions, and groups which are prepared to maximize this potential, immense evolutionary advantages in the struggle between different social orders and social systems. Again, turning more specifically to the principal organizational developments of modern industrial societies, non-zero-sum theorists have suggested that these permit what Parsons has referred to as the 'miracle of loaves and fishes'[5]—that is to say, particular circulations of power occurring in modern organizations have major and even potentially unforeseen positive social effects. Thus, for example, present-day manufacturing industry, by generating immense productive capacities from what must be regarded historically as a proportionately small part of the population of a given society, has enabled about a quarter of the world's population to have a standard of living undreamed of by earlier generations of men and women.

By way of contrast, zero-sum theorists have emphasized entirely different problems and issues. To be sure, they have acknowledged that modern organizations have the capacity to create great productive wealth but, in its distribution at least, it must in their view obey the laws of a zero-sum game where the gains of one party or group inevitably involve losses for another. Moreover, any accretions in material wealth (which may in any event be temporary) have to be weighed against certain further social consequences brought about by immense concentrations of power. Thus, in characteristically graphic manner, C. Wright Mills was to argue that, in the modern era, 'if men do not make history, they tend increasingly to become the utensils of history makers'.[6] In other words, the passivity of the majority of the human population as far as crucial decisions affecting the future of mankind are concerned, are the very consequence of those movements in history which non-zero-sum theorists are most ready to welcome. Again, zero-sum theorists would never regard power as a potentially value-neutral circulating medium. Rather, on their assumptions, the directions taken by particular organizations either must obey certain external laws which are thereby alien to man or must reflect the values and decisions of those in key controlling positions. And, on either view, not only do the majority exercise only limited impact on their own futures but also there inescapably arise fundamental structural conflicts in society between those who occupy dominant positions and those over whom power is exercised.

Theories of power

But while non-zero-sum and zero-sum power theorists have both come to grips with certain fundamental problems associated with the exercise of power in social and industrial life, they have seldom developed adequate definitions of the concept, nor have they really related these problems very closely to the wider issues of participation and control. It is apposite at this point, therefore, to review briefly the principal dimensions of the concept since, as we shall see, this helps to clarify not only our own position on the question of workers' participation and control but also many of the previous theoretical discussions on this subject.

There have, of course, been major debates about the meanings of all key concepts in the social sciences and therefore it is no real surprise that power has been unexceptional in this respect. But since it is not particularly fruitful to engage in endless and sterile conceptual controversies in an applied study of this kind, it would appear to be preferable to draw up a list of principal dimensions of power, which, while being sensitive to the main theoretical issues raised here, have the added advantage of clarifying the more specific arguments on the nature of workers' participation and control.

In the literature to date, three main dimensions of power may be identified; first, *manifest power*; second, *latent power* and, third, *values and ideologies* as principal components of the legitimation of particular power distributions. These will be examined in turn.

(1) Manifest power

A great many interpretations of power have focused on its more obvious manifestations in given social relationships and social structures. At root, most may be traced to Weber's classic definition of the concept as 'the probability that one actor within a social relationship will be in a position to carry out his will despite resistance, regardless of the basis on which this probability rests'.[7] To be sure, sociologists of this school would exclude the actual use of force as a criterion of power, but, in so doing, they would not wish to underplay the importance of force in social life nor to suggest that there are other than a wide range of manifestations of power.

Thus, to begin with, many writers have regarded particular distributions of income and wealth as crucial indices of the existence of major inequalities of power in particular societies. This is even hinted at in functionalist writings. Thus, for Davis and Moore, the highest-ranking positions in society are also seen to be the most *important* (i.e. powerful) positions and in turn to convey the best rewards.[8] Similarly, a frequently-used index of the power of trade unions is their ability to gain particular economic rewards for their members despite managerial hostility. Again, it is common to adduce differences in power between classes, groups and individuals from indices of the distribution of wealth and property ownership; the concentration of property ownership, in particular, has been taken as evidence of the persistence of the power of the property-owning classes and the dominance of capitalist economic formations in modern western industrial states. And, in this respect, Worsley has argued (so far as Great Britain is concerned) that 'the uninterrupted, albeit modified, dominance, of the property-owning classes, in a society which has long been the most highly "proletarianized" in the world, is surely one of the most striking phenomena of modern times'.[9]

A second area of focus has been the study of the social origins of the members of the main social, political and economic élites. The principal assumption here has been that if particular élites continue to attract members from among those of privileged birth, this may be taken as some indication of their significance in the power structure of any given society. Thus, the respective importance, in terms of power, of the Higher Civil Service,[10] industrial and commercial élites,[11] the military,[12] the landed aristocracy, the Church[13] and the higher education establishments[14] has been a perennial subject of debate.

A third manifestation of power is the formal pattern of control within particular societies, communities and organizations, and this of course brings us closer to the question of *workers'* participation and control of these formal structures. Control over production systems is thus seen by many as the fundamental basis of class rule:[15]

Whatever the decision-makers decide upon has to be actualized in the sphere of production because the manner of distribution depends on that of production. Without control over the production process, no decisions can be made, no class can rule. Control of production is exercised by control of the means of production, by ideology and by force. But property, ideology, and force alone can produce nothing. It is upon productive labour that the whole edifice rests.

Rather more simplistic notions about manifest power, however, have equated formal organizational position with power, their only redeeming characteristic being that power is at least viewed in structural terms distinct from the incumbents of particular positions. None the less, few sociologists have been satisfied with restricting their analysis to such formal structures alone, for although critical decisions may be *ratified* by those occupying senior positions in an administrative hierarchy, they may emanate from different levels entirely. This was certainly Galbraith's view which he developed in *The New Industrial State*, the so-called 'technostructure' rather than the board of directors being regarded as increasingly significant to the power structure of the modern corporation.[16] Moreover, other writers in this vein have tried to measure the amounts of power possessed by 'lower participants' in organizations,[17] and, even when research findings have tended to confirm the importance of formal administrative position, investigators have still—rightly—seen this as problematic. Many studies of community power have in fact rested on Hunter's so-called 'reputational' approach to power measurement.[18] The basis of this method is to ask respondents in a local community to rank those local leaders whom they consider to be most powerful. Their replies are then combined in order to provide indices of *reputations* for power in a given community. This technique has, of course, been heavily criticized, particularly on the grounds that the ability of a person or group to realize certain goals, if necessary against the opposition of others, cannot be judged by such subjective criteria alone.[19] Moreover, there are certain inherent biases in the approach which in any event will tend to encourage respondents to equate power with social position, for they are, after all, asked to make judgments about the respective importance of local leaders *identified in positional terms*. None the less, despite its defects, this technique provides another important example of manifest power understood in terms of particular patterns of domination in organizations, communities and societies.

The range and scope of issues over which interested parties exert influence and control provide further manifestations of power. Indeed, many political scientists have gone so far as to regard these as sufficient indices of the distribution of power in social life as a whole, with the consequence that the so-called 'issue approach' to power measurement has become an important technique for continually monitoring the exercise of power in local communities. This method can be traced particularly to Dahl's classic study of New Haven, in which three main issue areas were chosen for measuring the influence of social and economic notables on public life—the nominations of the two political parties, urban redevelopment and public education. Using this technique, he argued that the main social notables had very little influence on key positions in these areas, while the influence of the economic notables (mainly local businessmen) was largely confined to urban redevelopment.[20] Thus, by selecting rather different *manifestations* of power, quite distinct conclusions about its concentration in society could be drawn by contrast not only with those employing the reputational approach to power measurement, but also, more generally, with those who would regard wealth and property ownership as *the* crucial substantive aspects of power.

Finally, there are those who would argue that variations in the distribution of power between given parties cannot be judged except when actual power conflicts take place and the results of these are satisfactorily measured. This is partly because of the so-called 'rule of anticipated reactions' which both Friedrich[21] and Simon[22] in particular have suggested can be expected in normal decision-making processes. That is to say, decisions are usually taken on the basis of *subjective estimates* of the strength of another party and therefore certain ones will not be taken if it is *anticipated* that in a trial of strength the outcome will be unfavourable. Thus, for example, management will hesitate, say, to pursue a particular dismissals procedure if costly strike action is perceived to be the inevitable consequence. But because the 'rule of anticipated reactions' rests so much on subjective estimates of an opponent's power, it is not necessarily a very good guide to the distribution of power itself. Hence, it may be only during actual manifest conflicts that the 'realities' of power become readily identifiable. Moreover, although most manifest power theorists have tended to place little emphasis on the role of force in social relations, this is not the case among this last group of scholars who regard it as potentially decisive in predicting the outcome of a given conflict situation.

Thus, the first dimension of power involves equating the concept with certain of its more probable manifestations—notably, the distribution of income and wealth, the social origins of members of key élites, formal positions within particular societies and organizations, the scope and range of issues controlled or influenced by particular parties and, finally, success in a given power conflict. Many of the writers in this school have been nominalists who find it impossible to divest the concept of power from its manifestations in actual social life. Moreover, most have been highly sensitive to the problems of measurement as well as meaning and this former consideration has very much influenced their overall approach to this issue. And finally, questions of participation and control have arisen particularly from this manifest tradition of defining and measuring social power.

(2) *Latent power*

And yet, notwithstanding the problems of measurement, there are many power theorists who have not been content to restrict the concept to its more obvious and concrete manifestations in social life. These so-called *latent power theorists* have sought not only to define the concept in a different way but also to focus primarily on the power *bases* or *sources* at the disposal of particular parties. That is to say, they have endeavoured to obtain some guide to the *underlying* power of particular groups and to their *potential* for achieving given ends, if necessary at the expense of those of conflicting groups.

Indeed, it is the general view of latent theorists that no group or class has the capacity to exercise power unless it first develops certain power bases or sources which are potentially available to it, and they have been anxious to ensure that the actual exercise of force should never be confused with the concept of power. Bierstedt, in particular, as a well-known representative of this school, has argued that power 'is the predisposition or prior capacity which makes the application of force possible . . . the ability to employ force, not its actual employment, the ability to apply sanctions, not their actual application'.[23] Nor should such arguments be regarded merely as exercises in semantics, for they have helped to open up a separate dimension of power which, as we shall see, is a principal component in the controversy on power in industry and society and in the more specific argument over workers' participation and control.

Of all the classical sociological theorists it was Marx, above all, who was the main exponent of the latent approach, for although he was highly sensitive to the role of force in social transformation and of the importance of consciousness in social action, a great deal of his work was designed to uncover the latent power bases of particular social classes. And in this respect, of course, he argued that the power of given classes rested primarily on the nature of, and developments in, the underlying material forces of production (consisting primarily of technical and economic factors) and of the social relationships associated with these. Moreover, it was precisely certain *evolutionary* developments in the material base of capitalist society—notably, increasing industrial concentration, which would reduce the number of employers and increase the number of propertyless wage-earners, the decline of certain older classes (the landed aristocracy and peasantry), the multiple crises of capitalist economies and the ultimate polarization of classes in society—which heralded, for Marx, substantial changes in the latent power of the main contesting classes and ultimately, in turn, the revolutionary transformation of society and the birth of a new social order.

Now it is not our intention here to enter into any lengthy debates on the accuracy of his predictions, but it is worth mentioning that Marx was aware of other developments in the material base of society which could operate against the predictions contained in the mainstream of his thesis. He certainly recognized the growth of joint-stock companies and the possible consequential spread of capital ownership[24] and, further, he was clearly cognizant of certain technical changes which could bring about the emergence of the so-called new middle class of salaried employees, thus:[25]

> What [Ricardo] forgets to mention is the continual increase in numbers of the middle classes . . . situated midway between the workers on the one side and the capitalists and landowners on the other. These middle classes rest with all their weight upon the working class and at the same time increase the social security and power of the upper class.

But what is important to note in the Marxist framework of ideas is the germ of a theory about the distribution and nature of power in industry and society and the way in which this can be substantially affected by economic and technical change. Moreover, not only is the significance of the interplay between economy and society raised here, but it also provides the starting point for an analysis of social power based on latent factors and the foundations of a genuinely causal theory.

These virtues have been far less evident, however, in the work of many other latent theorists who have usually restricted their analyses to descriptive categories. This tendency, moreover, has been so marked that Lockwood in particular has criticized many of their ideas on the grounds that they focus on the anatomy of power rather than on its physiology and thereby fail to 'get to the problem of how, through time, power is actually employed to alter or to maintain a given institutional allocation of rewards, facilities and personnel'.[26] Among these latent theorists, then, power has been measured in

terms of numbers, organization and resources.[27] The first two categories are self-explanatory but resources have been understood to
cover a wide range of potential bases of power such as 'money,
property, prestige, knowledge, competence, deceit, fraud, secrecy',
and so on.[28] Now although each of these may be important in particular power contexts, latent theorists have not really come to grips
with the factors which predispose any one of these bases (or any group
in conjunction) to be particularly salient, nor have they developed
their possible causal significance in accounting for particular manifestations of power which were examined in the previous section.
And this is undoubtedly unfortunate because these categories are
rather more meaningful than Lockwood would appear to suggest.
Thus, by way of illustration, if Marx's ideas are reinterpreted in these
terms, it was precisely the growing numbers of propertyless wage-
earners brought about by economic change that affected the balance
of power between the main social classes; it was the consequence of
organization which merited the encouragement of trade-union and
political-party action; and it was the problem of resources—both
physical and mental—which stimulated the recognition of the role of
consciousness in transforming a class 'of itself' to a class 'for itself'.
In short, numbers, organization and resources—as the key latent
elements of power—may have been used too descriptively in the
literature to date, but there is no fundamental reason why they should
not be principal components of a more genuinely explanatory power
analysis, and, indeed, it will be one of the aims of this study to show
how this possibility may be realized.

(3) Values and ideologies

We have already touched briefly on the role of consciousness in social
action and, doubtless, it could be argued that the following discussions would be better included in a section on latent power, for, after
all, values and ideologies are principal components of the mental
resources at the disposal of particular groups, parties or classes.
None the less, they may also—although this is ultimately an empirical
question—form a critical link between the other latent or potential
aspects of power and their actual realization in those specific contexts
outlined in our earlier section on manifest power. Moreover, in any
sociological analysis of power, the role of values and ideologies in the
process of legitimation of patterns of domination would inevitably be
fundamental and does, therefore, merit special consideration at this
point.

The role of values in social action is a central issue in the social sciences, partly because of the dominance of 'idealistic' philosophical notions in western sociology, but also because it reflects a basic concern about the possibility of men actually shaping their own environment in the light of their powers of reason, rather than this being largely determined by forces of social evolution over which they have limited control. It also highlights the problems of subjectivity within the social sciences, since, if man can be clearly distinguished from the physical and natural world by his possession of independent powers of reason (which give him a measure of free will to 'make his own history'), subjective elements must always be central rather than peripheral to social-scientific investigations and this in turn must sharply differentiate the basic methodologies of the natural and social sciences. Moreover, turning more specifically to the question of values as a component of power, these must be significant in this context, since it is precisely the human powers encapsulated in values and consciousness which form the mainspring of man's essential humanity and which underlie his evolutionary advantage over other species.

It is scarcely surprising, then, that the role of values and ideologies as components of social action have provided a focal point for theoretical discussions not only within sociology generally, but more specifically whenever the question of power has been brought into sharper focus. Moreover, in so far as discussions on power are concerned, the main emphasis has been on the effects of values in legitimizing the authority of a dominant group or class or in permitting any subordinate group to challenge successfully the hegemony of the dominant grouping. Thus, the question of consciousness was fundamental in the work of Marx who not only saw it as decisive in converting a class in itself to a class for itself, but who also, with respect to trade unions, criticized a great deal of working-class action for its limited scope which resulted in trade-union power being largely latent and trade-union action being confined to 'resistance against the encroachments of capital', rather than to the search for simultaneous changes in the existing system of production and productive relations.[29] For Dahrendorf, too, it was only when the occupants of subordinate roles in specific organizations became aware or conscious of their particular interests and hence developed clear 'political' structures, that loosely cohering quasi-groups became fully fledged interest groups capable of taking effective action.[30] Again, for Parsons, the commonly-shared values of the members of a given social system not only formed the crucial basis of its solidarity but also under-

pinned his by now familiar non-zero-sum conception of power.[31]

Nevertheless, it was Weber, of course, who provided the best-developed contribution to the debate on values as a component of social power. To be sure, he was concerned largely with the role of values in *maintaining* given patterns of domination and in bestowing to these a measure of *stability, persistence* and *endurance,* and a rather more general account would have considered how values lead to effective challenges by any grouping subordinate to the rule of a dominant class. But, at the same time, it is difficult to minimize Weber's contribution to this question.

Now Weber's views on patterns of domination were firmly grounded in his conception of the nature of power. He thus clearly regarded domination—'the probability that certain specific commands (or all commands) will be obeyed by a given group of persons'[32]—as only one aspect of the exercise of power or influence over other persons. Moreover, he was keen to point out that 'not every case of domination makes use of economic means, still less does it always have economic objectives',[33] to ensure compliance, though it generally required the existence of a so-called 'administrative staff' who could 'normally be trusted to execute the general policy as well as the specific commands'.[34] But every form of domination also necessitated 'a minimum of voluntary compliance' on the part of subordinates which depended on their perceived *interest* in carrying out specific directives or decisions. The most obvious bases of such an interest would be economic, affectual or ideal in character, but as Weber pointed out—and this was crucial to his general position on the question of *legitimate* domination:[35]

> Experience shows that in no instance does domination voluntarily limit itself to the appeal to material or affectual or ideal motives as a basis for its continuance. In addition every such system attempts to establish and to cultivate the belief in its legitimacy.

Moreover, it was precisely the principal variations in 'claims to legitimacy' which provided the basis for classifying different aspects of domination structures:[36]

> But according to the kind of legitimacy which is claimed, the type of obedience, the kind of administrative staff developed to guarantee it, and the mode of exercising authority, will all differ fundamentally. Equally fundamental is the variation in *effect.*

And then, finally, Weber arrived at the most familiar part of his thesis, that there are three pure types of legitimate domination (authority), the validity of their claims being based on (1) rational grounds, (2) traditional grounds and (3) charismatic grounds.[37]

In a subsequent section we shall see how two of these grounds in particular have been developed by management as a means of supporting their domination over the lives of others in work contexts. Moreover, we shall observe that workers' participation and control does offer a major challenge to managerial hegemony and to the kinds of arguments which have normally been deployed to protect the existing systems of social control in industry. But there are certain problems in Weber's contribution to the debate on values as integral components of power which merit further consideration at this point.

The most obvious—as we have mentioned earlier—is that the foundations of Weber's argument lie in the role of values as a means of supporting or maintaining given patterns of control; he does not give any guide to the origins and nature of rather different values and ideologies which favour the interests of subordinate groups. A great deal of information is thus provided on the methods used by dominant groups to cultivate a belief in the legitimacy of their rule, but there is virtually nothing on the genesis of counter-values and ideologies which serve to challenge existing control structures. Moreover, the language he employs tends to be *dichotomous* in nature. That is to say, structures of domination, whatever their basis of legitimacy, tend to be of an inherently order-giving, order-receiving form: there is therefore little room in the model for any participation or control by subordinates over the decision-making processes in any organization. And while historically this may represent the most common social pattern, this in no sense implies its inevitability, nor that power in social life must invariably be possessed by one class, party or group. On the contrary, even if in most formal patterns of domination it is easy to identify superordinate and subordinate roles and to classify the incumbents of these roles on the basis of whether they issue commands, directives or decisions or receive them, there is usually *some* reciprocal influence by the subordinate not only on the outcome of particular decisions but also on their genesis as well. Moreover, it is this reciprocity that Wrong has in mind when he argues convincingly that:[38]

> People exercise mutual influence and control over one another's behaviour in all social interaction—in fact, that is what we *mean* by social interaction. Power relations are asymmetrical in that the power holder exercises greater control over the behaviour of the power subject than the reverse, but reciprocity of influence—the defining criterion of the social relationship itself—is never entirely destroyed

except in those forms of physical violence which, although directed against a human being, treat him as little more than a physical object.

Thus, although we would in no way wish to suggest that power equality has ever been the main pattern of distribution, it is equally erroneous to imply the inevitability of dichotomous decision-making processes.

Finally, with respect to the broader question of values as an aspect of social power, it is easy to develop a rather one-sided idealist analysis in which ideas are stripped from their origins, in particular structural contexts, and in which the interplay between other bases of power and values becomes a secondary theme. But as we shall see it is precisely when the question of values and processes of legitimation are linked to wider questions of the underlying power of particular classes and groups that the greatest explanatory advantages with respect to the questions of workers' participation and control are to be gained.

Power, participation and control

So far, then, we have argued that the more specific question of workers' participation and control inescapably raises broader issues about the nature of power in social life as a whole. None the less, as we have also mentioned, sociologists have not necessarily agreed on the meaning of this key term or on the types of behaviour to which the concept can legitimately be applied. And yet, despite these points of difference, it was possible to observe three principal approaches to this problem: namely, a focus on the principal manifestations of power (such as the distribution of income, wealth and property, patterns of domination in organizations, the outcome of power conflicts and so on), a concentration on the latent or potential strength of particular classes, parties and groups which has been measured principally by means of their numbers, organization and resources, and finally, an account of the role of values and ideologies in which are rooted essential questions about man and his relation to the natural and physical world. These also form part of the processes whereby particular patterns of domination are maintained and new possible relationships come into being.

It is our intention in this study to use these approaches in combination in order to explain the origins, patterns and success of specific forms of workers' participation and control, but first the question of the relationship of participation and control to the wider issues of power must be satisfactorily understood.

Advocates of workers' participation in decision-making have usually had in mind a conception of power based on two of its principal manifestations: namely, the formal patterns of control within organizations; and the scope and range of issues over which particular parties have some influence.

Indeed, workers' participation is viewed as the principal means of obtaining greater control by workers over several aspects of their working lives and in so doing augmenting their power *vis-à-vis* that of management. Thus, to begin with, in terms of the formal patterns of control within organizations a number of levels have been identified which broadly correspond to the formal patterns of decision-making within the firm. The first level concerns individual 'on the job' decision-making where the worker is viewed as having some right to organize his activities within certain discretionary limits. Technological factors, however, are very important at this level, as we shall see, for, in general, the higher the degree of skill of the worker the less easy it is to measure directly his work activities and the greater will tend to be his freedom from managerial supervision. By contrast, in a technology where the level of skill required of an individual worker is not of any great magnitude, the easier it is for management to control the worker's activities and to introduce such schemes as measured day work and productivity bargains, which are specifically designed to reduce the worker's own initiative and autonomy.

The second level comprises the workgroup or workteam. Again the decisions here may cover production questions and, indeed, are likely to do so whenever group activities are involved in the actual production process itself. However, at this level there are a number of further possible decision-making areas which may involve the workers actively but which, as a rule, management has sought to determine unilaterally and to define as its 'prerogatives'. These may include hiring and firing, starting and stopping times, the distribution of wages, hours of work, overtime working and so on.

It would in general not be unreasonable to argue that the higher the level of decision-making the less likely it has been for workers to have any direct determining influence on the outcome of events, and the more vigorously managerial 'prerogatives' have been defended. Between the levels of plant and workgroup there are admittedly a number of sectional and departmental levels but these have not involved workers very greatly at least in any formal or official sense. Moreover, moving to the highest decision-making levels there have again been a number of potential and logically separable foci of decision-making, namely plant, enterprise, industry and economy.

As far as these ultimate levels are concerned, it has not been unusual to make the distinction between processes of industrial *government* and those of industrial *management*. Chamberlain, in particular, considered this necessary in order to differentiate broad policy-making bodies from their executive organs, to distinguish, in other words, between decision-making processes about the aims or ends of particular organizations, and the means of achieving them.[39] And although it is not always easy to achieve such a separation in practice, it is theoretically useful not only in differentiating ends and means, but also, with a consideration of levels, it forms the basis for a classification of participation, as developed by Child in Table 1.

TABLE 1 *Forms of workers' participation and control: scope of decision-making*

focal level	*goals* + *means* ('*democratic*')	*means only* ('*conservative*')
whole organization	A	B
small group	D	C

Based on J. Child, *The Business Enterprise in Modern Industrial Society*, p. 89.[40]

Type A here includes most forms of workers' self-management and control as well as co-determination experiments; type D involves some of the many attempts at workgroup autonomy; types B and particularly C, however, derive largely from the human relations tradition and are really techniques for ensuring that certain general decisions (which are not open for negotiation or debate) are carried out in practice.[41]

But not only can participation clearly entail a number of distinct decision-making levels, but also the *scope* of actual influence by workers over any given issue may vary enormously from the most minimal forms of consultation to outright control. In order to account for these variations, several writers have developed continua of workers' participation, probably the most sophisticated of which is that of Shuchman who distinguished between 'co-operation' and 'co-determination'. The former relating to those schemes in which workers influence decisions but are not responsible for them, contrasts with the situation of the second in which workers have actual control and authority for particular decisions. Table 2 (p. 26) lists the various elements of each of these basic types.[42]

Clearly, a continuum of this kind has important merits; it helps the analyst to avoid *lengthy* definitional problems which have, it must be said, been only too apparent in the literature on this subject, while still incorporating the distinction between influences over decisions by

TABLE 2 *The scope of issues involved in workers' participation and control*

co-operation	co-determination
(1) right to information	(1) right to veto
(2) right to protest	(a) temporary
(3) right to suggestion	(b) permanent
(4) right to consultation	(2) right to 'co-decision'
	(3) right to decision

Based on A. Shuchman, *Co-determination*, Washington, 1957, p. 6.

working people and their actual involvement in the formulation and execution of a given decision itself. Again, it encompasses a wide range of possible models of participation including the right of either temporary or permanent veto as well as the more familiar gradation from information, through consultation, co-determination and finally control. None the less, without wishing to be unnecessarily pedantic about meaning, there has been a growing consensus in this context that situations where management effectively exerts control cannot be synonymous with fully-fledged participation in decision-making and, similarly, that participation must itself be incompatible with genuine workers' control. Thus Verba, not unreasonably, has found fault with a collection of schemes on the grounds that they offer merely '*pseudo-participation*' and involve no genuine control, even of a partial kind, by workers in the actual processes of decision-making.[43] There are, for example, certain supervisory styles, which are usually labelled as participative, in which in fact the final decision-making prerogative rests entirely in the hands of the supervisor. And, while these devices may well be conducive to more harmonious industrial relations and to increases in industrial efficiency, this is peripheral to the question whether the role of workers is decisive rather than purely marginal in the formulation of policies which are significant to them. Moreover, and this is a subject to which we shall return when the issue of industrial ownership is raised, there is a great deal of difference between workers, say, jointly controlling with management a given process of decision-making within the private sector of the economy and actually controlling it within the framework of publicly-owned industry. Moreover, many theories of workers' control have presupposed the creating of *acephalous* organizational forms in which management ceases to exist in any meaningful sense. And these conceptions are rather different from those normally understood when the issue of workers' participation in decision-making is brought into sharper relief.

It is evident, then, that certain problems of definition are unavoidable in any analysis of the scope of workers' participation. To some extent the same applies when we come to highlight the *range* of issues involved here; there are thus numerous potential areas over which workers may—and indeed do—have a measure of decision-making control, from technical 'on-the-job' problems to questions covering welfare and safety, wages and working conditions, and wider production, commercial and economic issues. These can be clarified conceptually and the classification used most often here is, again, based on the work of Shuchman who endeavoured to relate these areas of workers' participation to the levels in which they are confined. Unfortunately, he included 'enterprise' and 'supra-enterprise' in this context and in so doing omitted individual, workgroup and departmental levels, those very areas which involve the ordinary worker most and in which his most notable contributions might be made. However, this does not entirely detract from the importance or the utility of his contribution which may be summarized as in Table 3.

TABLE 3 *The range of issues involved in workers' participation and control*

enterprise		supra-enterprise	
(1)	personnel	(1)	manpower
(2)	social	(2)	social welfare
(3)	economic	(3)	economic
	(a) technical		
	(b) 'business'		

Based on A. Shuchman, *Co-determination*, Washington, 1957, p. 8.[44]

Thus at enterprise level, the main areas of workers' participation may focus on; first, personnel decisions, such as the hiring, firing, promotion and transfer of workers; second, social decisions, including such matters as health and safety, the form and administration of pension funds and so on; and third, a range of economic questions including (*a*) technical aspects, such as new methods of production and the introduction of new machinery; and (*b*) 'business' issues which refer more to marketing and financial questions; the latter usually involving the uppermost decision-making layers within the enterprise. But the special virtue of Shuchman's classification is that supra-enterprise considerations supplement plant-related issues and this underpins the rights of workers in policy-formation at regional and national level. The momentous consequences of this involvement have been emphasized in the Report of the Club of Rome.[45]

There can be disappointments and dangers in limiting one's view to an area that is too small. There are many examples of a person striving with all his might to solve some immediate, local problem, only to find his efforts defeated by events occurring in a larger context. A farmer's carefully maintained fields can be destroyed by international war. Local officials' plans can be overturned by a national policy. A country's economic development can be thwarted by a lack of world demand for its products. Indeed there is increasing concern today that most personal and national objectives may ultimately be frustrated by long-term, global trends.

Thus, it is clearly not enough to restrict workers' participation and control to more limited objectives, since, although these may be most meaningful to the individual worker, their outcome may, in fact, be decided by more general trends over which he has almost no control. Again, these general issues do not necessarily involve global questions; they may include currently fashionable 'manpower' policies, and notably those relating to the transfer and mobility of workers from one geographical area to the next, social welfare programmes, and of course the business of control over the economy as a whole. And once again, such issues, which are usually left out of discussions concerned specifically with workers' participation at enterprise or plant level, set major limitations on the ultimate possibility of effective domestic and local participation.

Workers' participation in decision-making therefore involves a number of distinctive levels of potential operation, a considerable variation in the scope of actual control of workers over any given decision, and a range of areas in which participation can, in fact, take place. Thus, from a classificatory point of view any study which purported to highlight variations in workers' participation experienced within given organizations or societies would have to take some account of all these variables.

But, returning now to our general theme, it is important to reiterate that participation may be regarded as one of the principal manifestations of power. Nevertheless, because advocates of participation have generally taken their arguments much further than this, it is worth briefly examining, and in some instances re-examining, their case at this point, in so far as it relates to the wider consideration of power and its exercise in industrial relations. Fundamentally, four propositions have been put forward about the effects of participation on the exercise of power in industry and society: first, that occupancy of a given position enables an extension of the scope, range and even level of issues over which control can be exercised; second, that participation has dynamic effects upon values and consciousness and thereby leads to increasing expectations of, and demands for, participation; third, and rather more generally, that it is only through participation in decision-making processes in the industrial field that essential lessons about man's relation with the physical and natural world can be learned and the problems of alienation satisfactorily solved; and finally, that workers' participation in decision-making at workplace level is an important basis for extending democracy within society as a whole.

Briefly, the first argument is that the more workers are involved at the actual focal points of decision-making, the more they are able to extend their influence and control over other areas; or, expressed more theoretically, other aspects of manifest power may be extended by virtue of workers' participation. They may be able to affect the distribution of income and wealth by influencing 'cash-flow' within the firm and by reducing dividend payments and may furthermore induce changes in the process of selection of key personnel and in the formal organization of the firm to the benefit of workers; they may extend, too, both the range and scope of their influence and, indeed, augment their chances of success in power conflicts by gaining more information about the operation, attitudes, and behaviour of management—all as a consequence of membership of key decision-making bodies. Of course, such views must be somewhat Utopian, particularly in societies in which market forces have a major external influence on decision-making processes, and again, must be substantiated by careful empirical investigation, but they none the less represent significant theoretical claims about the relationship of participation to the wider theme of power. After all, from this standpoint, workers' power in society as a whole can be significantly advanced, even by what at first sight appears to be rather small-scale modifications of the existing authority structure of the enterprise. In short, participation is viewed here not as *one* aspect of power; rather it is recognized as its central component.[46]

The second claim is that participation has a major effect on *consciousness*, serving to modify general values about work relationships and leading not only to increases in the desire for participation among workpeople but also to its acceptance as a 'normal' means of reaching decisions within society as a whole. This is partly associated with the greater *effectiveness* and *ability* to participate which accompanies sustained periods of involvement; in other words, certain dynamic repercussions of participation extend to fundamental changes in consciousness, and hence in our third dimension of power—the value and ideological framework.

Moreover, this argument has been taken somewhat further by those who suggest that participation in decision-making processes in the economic system of a given society enables people to become conscious of their essential subjectivity and of man's relationship with the natural and physical world. Again, by the same token, it is precisely because the majority of men and women participate at best only ineffectively and intermittently in such processes that they experience a sense of alienation *vis-à-vis* the material and natural world. Partly as a result of this, but also because market criteria are so significant in the allocation of resources, man's economic activities have, it is argued, increasingly developed along paths which now give so much cause for concern. Hence, although the scientific and technical revolutions which were brought about in the wake of industrialization undoubtedly led to a major development in human understanding of natural and physical laws, the social relationships existing in modern industrial organization—by contrast with the pre-industrial era when man's relationship with nature was much more self-evident—have served to strip the majority of men of this crucial subjective consciousness. And the consequence is, therefore, that the majority of people in industrial society feel, as Mills argued, that their lives are a series of traps,[47] and that their destinies are determined entirely by external forces over which they have limited control.

Lastly, the advocates of participation argue that the democratic character of a society as a whole is profoundly influenced by the nature of social relationships in the industrial sphere. Almond and Verba, in particular, have proposed that political *efficacy* and political consciousness are largely developed in the work context.[48] They have not suggested, of course, that childhood and family experience are entirely irrelevant here—quite the contrary—but they would regard the opportunities to 'participate in decisions at one's place of work' as of 'crucial significance' to the development of political sagacity in a wider social context. Again, it may well be that authoritarian relationships within the work context have consequences which are far greater than at first sight appear obvious and, in particular, that they form the basis for authoritarian family relationships. For when a worker has little autonomy and opportunity for self-direction in his own work tasks and is subjected to arbitrary and inconsistent managerial behaviour, this may well provide the critical learning environment for the internalization of modes of domination in interpersonal life which then spills over, above all, into his family life and to the patterns of authority deemed to be appropriate here.[49]

It is not our intention at this point to assess the merits of these claims about the dynamic effects of participation, although these indeed will be more closely analysed in the following chapters, but what is essential to recognize is that many proponents of participation have been concerned only marginally to justify it as a practice on its merits alone. For them, workers' participation is the major point of access to key decision-making processes in society at large and an indispensable foundation for the exercise of power in social life. None the less, there are other writers who, while being broadly sympathetic to a greater measure of power-sharing in social and industrial life, have come out against workers' participation largely because they have a rather different viewpoint about the nature of power and its operation (at least within the industrial sphere). It is not unreasonable, therefore, to examine certain of these contributions rather more closely at this juncture.

Opposition to participation: the case of Clegg, Dahrendorf and Mandel

In the literature to date, the most influential and sustained theoretical critique of workers' participation was advanced by Clegg in his now familiar 'new approach' to industrial democracy.[50] Actually his main conclusion—that collective bargaining rather than participation was the key to industrial democracy—had been anticipated by the Webbs more than sixty years previously in their classic work on this subject,[51] but what was more novel about the approach was its relationship with ongoing debates among political scientists about the essential characteristics of democracy. Up to that time, most classical theories of democracy had recognized participation by the people in the processes of government as a centrepiece of any genuine democratic system; but by the mid-1950s, the so-called modern theory of democracy had begun to dominate theoretical work in this area, and here the emphasis was on opposition rather than participation.[52] Clegg transposed these terms from the political to the industrial sphere and made the case for a strong and independent oppositional body to management (i.e. the trade unions) since, in his view, this provided the means for developing and sustaining the power of resistance among working people and hence was the mainspring of industrial democracy. But Clegg took the argument further, postulating that workers' participation in management was not only irrelevant to the question of industrial democracy but could actually be harmful to workers' interests and to the extension of 'democratic' social relationships in industry, principally because of the problems of role conflict experienced by workers on decision-making bodies but, second, because of the inherent danger that they might acquire managerial definitions of the proper functions of the enterprise.[53]

Clegg thus developed three main principles of industrial democracy: first, that unions must be independent of both state and management; second, that only trade unions can represent the interests of industrial workers; and third, that the ownership of industry is irrelevant to 'good' industrial relations.[54] The main theoretical case against participation was clearly, therefore, a logical consequence of the first principle, since trade unions could not, at least in Clegg's view, operate as an effective opposition if they in any way became part of management, or their activities were shackled by governmental decision.

But the oppositional concept—and, hence, Clegg's more general theory—has been criticized on a number of important counts.[55] To begin with, since the main premise rests on a theory of democracy which is not in accord with the way the term has been traditionally understood, it only requires a restatement of classical principles (in which, once again, participation is a crucial component) for there to be many serious semantic objections to the theory. Second, it is quite possible, of course, for there to be democracy in the classical sense without opposition, and this is the case, for example, in smaller trade union branches. Third, 'opposition' itself does not arise in a social vacuum; rather it is located structurally in configurations of interests which characterize specific types of society, and in the absence of these structural divisions the need for organized opposition—to prevent the total domination of one section of society over another—would lose its primary rationale. Fourth, even if we have in mind a definition of democracy based on the modern theory, there are certain major differences between the political and industrial fields in Clegg's formulation, notably that the opposition party in industry (i.e. the trade unions) can never in fact replace management and form a government—they are doomed to the exercise of only a rather negative kind of power and, because of this, find difficulties in attracting high-calibre personnel and in gaining widespread public support. And finally, it is in any event rather a dubious policy to countenance the existence of organized opposition merely as a necessary precondition for democratic social relations, for in this formulation the problem of accountability on the part of leaders of any organization to their 'electorate' is simply not catered for at all.

However, although such criticisms are now familiar in the literature and, indeed, highlight many important semantic and empirical difficulties in Clegg's thesis, most of their authors have failed to recognize that Clegg's conception of power rests implicitly in the latent rather than the manifest tradition. In other words, it infers that interests will be accommodated in society largely in proportion to the latent strengths of contending parties or classes. And here Clegg's arguments are rather more convincing than those of certain of his critics, for while it is clearly nonsense to argue that workers *cannot* participate in managerial decision-making, to pursue such a strategy at the cost of union organization could leave workers extremely vulnerable in the event of unfavourable economic circumstances or hostile enactments by government. Moreover, as we shall see, it is precisely when the latent power of workers has increased for some reason or other that participation has been a very common consequence. In any event, by simply participating in management rather than building up their latent strength, working people may fail to have any perceptible effect on the power of capital, for if the question of union organization is seen as secondary to participation, this may indeed result in a reduction in the influence of working people in the long term. Ironically, since there is, as we intend to demonstrate, a relationship between the latent power of workers and participation, this policy could even have the effect of lowering the levels of effective participation in the future, unless, that is, the 'dynamic' effects of participation can be seen substantially to outweigh any loss of latent power. Therefore, despite the many weaknesses of his theory, the strategy of increasing workers' organizational power which Clegg would appear to favour is by no means unreasonable if one is genuinely seeking an effective form of workers' participation in decision-making.

Clegg is not alone in his rather pessimistic approach to workers' participation in management, for Dahrendorf's conclusions are similar and, since his case is sociological in nature and rests firmly on his general understanding of the issues of power and authority, it is relevant to our discussions here.[56] By contrast with Clegg, who epitomizes an essentially latent view of the exercise of power in society and in social organizations, Dahrendorf's main starting-point for an analysis of power is the formal authority division within particular enterprises. The basis of Dahrendorf's claim, therefore, is that in all organizations there inescapably arises a demarcation between those who are vested with the powers of decision-making in that organization and those who have to submit to those decisions.[57] Encompassing Weber's concept of 'imperatively co-ordinated association', he thereby postulates that there are always two fundamental organizational positions: one of superordination and one of subordination. Moreover, these positions, representing the so-called plus and minus sides of what is inevitably the zero-sum nature of the distribution of authority, form the basic lines of social cleavage and the fundamental origins of social conflict in organizational life. Again, since there are but two basic organizational divisions there are essentially only two conflicting groups.[58]

Now, for Dahrendorf, and here his argument begins to show at least certain points of affinity with that of Clegg, the optimal strategy for those occupying subordinate roles is to become aware that their interests are distinct from those in superordinate positions (in this case in industry) and to develop fully-fledged interest groups to bargain with the employers. Industrial democracy therefore consists of a number of 'structural arrangements'[59] based ultimately on the recognition of conflicting interests of subordinates and superordinates within workplaces. Oppositional parties emerge to represent the interests of subordinates, they thus criticize and oppose management but take no part in the process of decision-making itself. Moreover—and this is a central aspect of Dahrendorf's case in this context —workers who participate in management, and especially worker directors, belong not to the group whose interests are in opposition to the prevailing system but rather 'to the ruling quasi-group of those whose objective role-interests aim at the maintenance of existing conditions'; indeed, he suggests that the labour director of West German enterprises in the coal and iron and steel industries is simply 'an entrepreneur'.[60]

Despite starting, then, from a somewhat different notion of power and its exercise in organizations, Dahrendorf's conclusions are essentially similar to those of Clegg. But it is important to challenge in both arguments the inherently élitist assumptions about the exercise of legitimate authority. Indeed, at root each has a quite unfounded conception, possibly about the exercise of power, and certainly about the distribution of authority within social life, for as Wrong observed, power and authority tend to be distributed *asymmetrically* rather than *dichotomously*, and what this means of course is that subordinates with organizational life have almost invariably possessed at least a certain residuum of power.[61] They may have been dominated by superordinates but not totally controlled; and even in those circumstances (such as the early phases of the industrial revolution) where the power of the employer was of such an order to rank close to the dichotomous point on the power continuum, this would not in any event have prevented the *possibility* of greater egalitarianism in the distribution of power in different economic and political circumstances.

Moreover, and this is crucial to the debates on workers' participation in managerial decision-making, what is true of the distribution of power is also the case for the distribution of authority. Thus most workers have always had a certain discretionary element in decisions of an on-the-job kind and in general the more highly skilled the task the more noticeable this has been. Again, under favourable circumstances they have been able to extend the 'frontiers of their control' over workplace decision-making processes, with the consequence that a large number of practices become accepted by management (if only tacitly) as workers' rights, as reflecting, in other words, the legitimate exercise of workers' authority over particular decision-making areas. To be sure, these have fallen far short of the dreams of industrial democrats, and, in so far as high-level policy decision-making is concerned, workers have seldom had any fully-established powers in this context, but the existence of even the most minimal forms of workers' decision-making rights is itself sufficient to nullify these élitist and inherently static assumptions about the distribution of workplace authority, the boundaries of which are in fact continually open to redefinition. Indeed, to make any claim to the effect that workers *cannot* participate in management is not only unsound theoretically by virtue of treating power and especially authority as inherently dichotomous in nature; it is also quite nonsensical from an empirical point of view, since there have been so many examples of workers' participation in decision-making at workplace level.

Nevertheless, it is important, at the same time, to recognize that although it is thus unreasonable to argue that workers' participation *cannot* come about, such developments may not, in the event, be seen to be in the long-term interests of workers; certainly this would reflect the view of Mandel whose Marxist interpretation may be usefully examined at this point:[62]

> One can sum up the basic difference between the ideology of 'participation' and 'co-management' on the one hand, and the demand for workers' control on the other, in the following ways. Workers' control rejects the idea that the unions and/or workers' representatives should share in the management of capitalist industry; it demands for the workers a power of veto in a whole series of spheres relating to working conditions on the job, etc. Workers' control rejects the idea of secrecy, with the account books being opened only to a handful of carefully chosen union officials. On the contrary, it demands the widest, most total publicity for all that the workers may discover, not only from their examination of the employer's accounts and the way the firm's money is handled, but also, more important, by comparing those accounts on the shop floor with the economic reality they are supposed to reflect. Workers' control rejects all institutionalization, all

notion of becoming, even provisionally, party to the functioning of the system; for its protagonists realize that any such integration would inevitably mean its becoming a tool of class conciliation instead of one for an intensified class struggle.

But Mandel would not only wish to delineate sharply between programmes for participation which, in his view, tend to work against the long-term interests of workers and those of control which may help to promote them. He would also wish to identify a number of short-term problems inherent in workers' participation itself. These include, first, that if workers are integrated into the management and board structures of the firms in which they are employed, 'they cannot help making the "firm's interests" their own' and, hence, take on an essentially competitive world view *vis-à-vis* other firms and *their* workers and worker directors; second, the majority of workers will tend to be confined to immediate and short-term demands; third, some worthwhile experiments in self-management may peter out in the context of a macrostructure of competition and lead to disenchantment; and fourth, a great deal of workers' agitation—and especially that of the more militant among them—may be channelled into production and productive issues, which not only lead to competition with fellow workers in other factory locales but also involve them in taking up questions 'where their inferiority is most evident'. This can in turn lead to further disillusionment with the prospects of workers ever seriously determining the crucial parameters of their own working lives.[63]

These clearly are the most telling arguments against participation which we have examined so far. They highlight certain dangers in even quite extensive participation programmes, and express the concern particularly that workers may forsake the 'natural' co-operation inherent in union activities, only to replace it by an essentially competitive *weltanschauung* and thereby to lose the foundations of a more genuinely 'co-operative' society. Nevertheless, the risks may be somewhat fewer than Mandel fears, since it is by the development of their own independent power that workers acquire the right to participation and control. In other words, participation is only likely to occur on any scale when workers' organizations (and the high level of co-operation inherent in 'union' activities) are also at an advanced stage. It is appropriate at this point, therefore, in the final section of this chapter, to move on to lay the foundation of an explanatory model which will bring our analysis 'out of Utopia' by uncovering some of the principal determinants of the most widely ranging of workers' participation and control programmes.

A model of workers' participation and control

Following the analysis developed by Bain in a rather different context[64] it would seem useful to summarize the key independent and dependent variables involved in the development of workers' participation and control by a three-equation model which, in turn, conveys the central propositions of this inquiry:

$$P = f(L, V)$$
$$L = g(E, T, G)$$
$$V = h(P, L, G, I)$$

where P = workers' participation and control
   L = latent power
   V = values
   E = economic factors
   T = technological factors
   G = governmental action
   I = more general ideologies

The first equation summarizes the basic argument of this study that workers' participation and control are functions of the latent power of particular industrial classes, parties or groups and the value 'climate' which may or may not be favourable to participation experiments. These values thus form an important mediating influence between certain *structural factors* associated with latent power and their realization in the form of workers' participation and control. Now the principal structural factors associated with the latent power of the main industrial classes, parties or groups are *economic factors*, such as the levels of employment, the profit margins of particular companies, the levels of competition, the degree of industrial concentration and periods of economic 'disintegration'; *technological factors*, such as the approximation of the technology of a company to a given point on the 'technical scale', and the degree of complexity and education involved in any given task; and finally, various forms of *government action* such as legislation on 'labour' issues, its intervention in the workings of the economic system and so on. These combine to give the second equation, that latent power is a function of economic factors, technological factors and government action. Finally, more specific values may be underpinned by broader *ideological* considerations, such as religious, managerialist, socialist, democratic, libertarian and humanitarian ideals. And values concerning participation and control may thereby be influenced, not only by such general ideologies, but also by the existing levels and development of workers' participation and control (these refer to the dynamic components of participation): *latent* elements of power such as educational resources and the levels of 'needs' already fulfilled by subordinate classes, parties and groups as a result of this power; and finally, *government action* which may be conducive to participation experiments and their acceptance within a given society. Therefore, the third and final equation that values about participation and control are functions of the existing levels of workers' participation and control, latent power, government action and ideologies. These should be developed more fully at this point.

Proposition *1* Workers' *participation and control are functions of latent power and values*

It is our main aim to demonstrate, therefore, that developments in workers' participation and control, their ebb and flow in particular historical periods, their variations in significance in specific industries and factories and even their main international variations, can largely be attributed to differences in the latent or underlying strength of the main industrial classes, parties and groups, although the question of values is a central part of the equation. When, that is, the underlying power of workers as a whole, of their specific organizations, or at the still more local level of particular workgroups, has for some cause or other been enhanced this has usually been expressed *at the manifest level of power* in given developments in participation and control. As we shall see the possibilities of variation are multiple and, recalling our previous discussions on the meaning of participation, the levels at which workers have had an influence over decisions have differed greatly as have the range and scope of control over particular areas, but any lasting development along these lines has, we suggest, been dependent on certain external factors which have enhanced the power of workers (or particular groups among them) *vis-à-vis* management. Yet these changes in latent power, while necessary conditions, are not the sole impetus for extending the scope of workers' influence. There have been many occasions, indeed, when the latent power of workers would appear to merit their greater participation in decision-making but this has not taken place, or has occurred only circumspectly, because particular values—whether of workers or management— have been indispensable intermediary influences. But by the same token, as we shall see, values *on their own* are not the crucial determinants and cannot explain the development of *effective* participation and control without the question of latent power being taken into account. For participation schemes which have been instigated as a result of value considerations alone have been at worst shortlived or at best shaped very much in the interests of the initiators concerned.

Proposition 2 Latent power is a function of economic factors, technological factors and government action

The first proposition, however, conveys nothing about the causal model it is intended to develop here and, left on its own, would remain largely descriptive. The main components of both latent power and values have, therefore, to be outlined as well.

In so far as latent power is concerned, the strength of workers *vis-à-vis* management is closely affected by a number of economic factors. To begin with, periods of full employment doubtless signal an increase in the latent power of working people. Their numbers, of course, grow in such circumstances, but, in addition, the development of effective opposition is fostered in the absence of any serious threat from non-unionized and unemployed labour. Moreover, resources are likely to be enhanced in these conditions; with the growth in the pecuniary power of unions it is possible to support correspondingly more officials from union funds; victimization and other arbitrary acts of management are less likely to occur than in periods of depression and this enables highly talented and educated workers to represent their members at local level without any great fear of loss of livelihood; and finally, locally-based representatives have sufficient time, free from any such threats, to gain valuable experience in union affairs.

But other economic factors have an important influence on the potential or latent power of workers. A number of market criteria—and notably, the profit margins of particular companies, the degree of competition experienced in a given industry, and whether an industry is an expanding or a contracting one—may all affect the underlying strength of particular sections of working people. After all, bargaining, not just on wage questions, but also on a wide range of other issues, must be facilitated, for instance, in a highly profitable section of industry which is comparatively free of external competition, and in the mainstream of a growing sector of the economy.

Moreover, the increasing scale and concentration of industry is also of importance in this respect, after all, industrial concentration is associated with increasing bureaucratization and the consequent elimination of paternalistic practices which may operate in smaller firms to the detriment of unionization. There are, indeed, several

4

reasons why industrial concentration favours union growth,[65] the most obvious being that large aggregates of workers are prone to perceive common interests *vis-à-vis* their employers, and this facilitates joint action and, hence, union organization. Similarly, promotion within the firm increasingly depends on technical criteria and less on 'affectual' ties and, therefore, those workers who perceive their opportunities for individual advancement to be inescapably limited, tend to see union organization as their only effective means of improving their wages and conditions. Management, too, may gradually wish to deal with their employees on a relatively more systematic and regular basis and this enhances the prospects of their recognizing particular unions. And finally, union agents are likely to seek recruitment in highly concentrated firms, partly because here the 'objective' conditions for unionization are in any event favourable, but also their costs per worker recruited will be somewhat lower by comparison with a comparable recruitment programme among a much more scattered workforce. Again, while having an indirect effect on workers' latent power, concentration may directly favour participation since, as Banks has argued: 'The very magnitude of the social problems involved in large-scale collective co-ordination has resulted in some participation by workers with managers in the conduct of day-to-day production affairs.'[66]

Although, on balance, periods of depression will tend to reduce the latent power of workers, this may not be the case during violent economic upheaval and, in particular, in times of actual economic disintegration. For, after all, in such periods of chaos, the legitimacy of a whole social order may be brought into question and workers, having of necessity to be concerned with day-to-day survival, may take control over production processes at all levels, this having been particularly evident during the present century on the cessation of wars.

But technical factors also impinge on the opportunities for workers' participation by affecting the latent power of workers *vis-à-vis* management. It was Sayles who pointed out, of course, that the latent power of workgroups, as well as the social characteristics of their members, could be profoundly influenced by the technical organization of work itself.[67] Indeed, contributions such as this from the so-called 'technical implications' school have become familiar in industrial sociology. The main exponents of this view have not only sought to relate variations in workers' latent power to different technological structures but have been at pains to demonstrate the variety of managerial characteristics and forms of managerial organization which stem from these very differences in underlying technology.[68] More specifically, for instance, with respect to the question of alienation and the influence of work processes on the chances of workers having a significant degree of control over task-based decision-making, it is usual to posit that an inverted 'U' curve may be observed as the technical scale is ascended.[69] In craft-type industries, the diversity of work and the high levels of skill among workers not only have certain direct implications with regard to the discretionary power of workers over task-based decision-making, but also, while craft workers are able to control the supply of labour into their occupations, such workers are difficult to replace, and this furnishes them with an important additional resource of power which is not shared by their less-skilled colleagues. By contrast, in the intermediary ranges of the technical scale—and especially in assembly-line industries—the prospects of workers having any significant measure of 'on-the-job' control are slight, the opportunities for direct mensuration of work are maximal, and workers are reduced to more negative forms of influence over their tasks, such as absenteeism, labour turnover, and industrial sabotage. On the other hand, because, increasingly, the proportion of costs attributable to 'labour' tends to decline and those of capital machinery to escalate with every advance in technology, the economic damage that workers can inflict by direct action multiplies accordingly. Finally, in more fully-automated industries, where workers' productive functions have been taken over by machinery, the need for 'intellectual' labour and for highly-skilled maintenance craftsmen is accelerated so that, once again, technology can be seen substantially to affect power relations between management and men. To begin with, because of their high levels of skill, it is difficult for managements to monitor all workers' tasks directly and, although they may be able to negotiate productivity deals to ensure greater task flexibility, they cannot easily control the on-the-job, decision-making environment of the individual operative. At the same time, 'labour' costs as a proportion of total costs tend to be small, while with the unrelenting demand for highly-trained 'labour', the development of fully-automated industries could provide the technical basis for integrating intellectual and manual working people, though, equally of course, there could emerge a tiny aristocracy of such highly-skilled workers alongside the growth of an impoverished proletariat, unable to find any employment in basic manufacturing industries at all. But, whatever the outcome of these developments, there will undoubtedly be major repercussions with regard to management–worker relations as an offshoot of these fundamental changes.

And yet, neither economic nor technological variables exhaust all possible latent factors, for certain wider political questions are salient in this context as well. We are not referring at this point, of course, to the many governmental enactments on the specific question of workers' participation and control. On the contrary, these, as we shall see, very much reflect what is possible within the constraints of given socio-economic and political systems, and although this is not to argue that governments can never exercise a certain measure of choice in these respects, it is to suggest that such decisions are inescapably circumscribed by other important influences. Thus, where governments can be more or less influential is in affecting the latent power of the main industrial classes, although once again, there are major restrictions to possible government action here. Nevertheless, with respect to the organizational strength of workers, government action may be of positive benefit: first, by guaranteeing minimal rights of workers to belong to trade unions; second, by putting pressure on employers to recognize trade unions; and, finally, by its own policies with regard to unionization in the publicly-owned sector of the economy. Again, as Bain has argued with respect to white-collar unionization, government action has been critical in ensuring the ultimate success of workers in certain major recruitment battles, and because nationalization acts have given positive encouragement to union formation, there is a considerable disparity in the organizational strength between white-collar workers in the private and publicly-owned sectors of the economy.[70] Furthermore, in states where two-party systems of government operate—even when both the parties have only limited formal connection with the indigent labour movement—if 'the maintenance of full employment is a precondition of gaining and retaining political power, then the voting power of the post-Keynesian wage earner is a political resource that indirectly affects his bargaining power in the labour market'.[71]

It is evident, therefore, that political action can affect the latent power of the labour movement to a not inconsequential degree and this can be observed especially clearly by a consideration of negative aspects of governmental intervention. Totalitarian regimes, for instance, have generally sought to eradicate trade unionism, or to control it closely, or, at the very least, to inhibit 'free' collective bargaining, and this has clearly constrained even the most rudimentary forms of workers' action at local levels. But, of course, these actions are not confined to such regimes. In almost all Western industrial societies the influence of government on the wages and salaries front has been increasing, with the result that many pay 'battles' have been between government and workers rather than employers and trade unions. Moreover, the Industrial Relations Act in Great Britain represented a major legislative attempt to reduce the powers of shop stewards and other locally-based organizations and to outlaw as well as to define a host of actions as 'unfair' practices, many of which are important trade-union tactics. On the other hand, the clearly limited effectiveness of this Act is a reflection of the difficulty governments face when operating outside limits set by the *latent* power of the main industrial-relations classes.

Proposition 3 *Values concerning workers' participation and control are a function of the existing levels of participation, latent power, government action and ideologies*

If we turn finally to the role of values as regards developments of workers' participation and control these, too, may be traced to a number of antecedent conditions.

We have already referred to the probable dynamic consequences of the establishment of given participation and control programmes and these therefore need not detain us greatly here; nevertheless it is worth pointing out that there is probably some *reciprocal* influence between values and workers' participation, with the result that the development of a given participation programme may not only serve to reduce the level of opposition to future extensions in participation by virtue of making it a 'normal' practice for resolving problems, but it may also increase the desire for, and efficiency of, participation from the standpoint of members of subordinate groups.

Similarly although, as we have argued, values may intervene between particular latent power distributions and their reflection in participation and control practices they, too, may be modified by latent power. More especially, since the latent power of workers may be expected also to lead to rises in their material standard of living, this may have future consequences for their general attitudes and values, as Maslow postulated.[72] In brief, he argued that man is basically a 'wanting animal' with an ascending scale of needs: the first is physiological and includes the need for food, shelter, clothing, etc.; the second is social; and the third is the need of the ego for self-actualization, self-realization and so on. These 'higher echelons of needs' not only lead one to a desire for more interesting and fulfilling work but also, more importantly in this context, to seek greater participation and control over decisions which affect one's livelihood. To be sure, this hierarchy may be substantially affected by further values

—and notably materialist ones—which tend to restrict demands to a lower level of 'needs'. But there are increasing signs that expectations of a greater sharing of power and control are growing, 'thereby confirming the Maslovian prediction that the needs at the top of the hierarchy will become increasingly important',[73] even if these are not desired *at the expense of* further material gains. Moreover, it is probable that the consequent 'revolution of rising expectations' is of fundamental importance (taken in conjunction with a number of latent variables) in explaining the desire for, and emergence of, workers' participation programmes in almost every European country during the late 1960s and early 1970s. Nor, in view of the Maslovian hierarchy, is it at all surprising that demands for greater participation have been especially evident among the affluent middle classes.

Now, although it is our view that government action has, on balance, been far more instrumental in advancing participation by way of affecting (if only slightly) the latent power of the main industrial classes than by the deliberate promotion of participation itself, the merits of these more direct lines of action may be considerable if taken in the context of their impact on the values of the community as a whole. That is to say, government action may help to set a threshold of expectations with regard to participation which thereby forms an anticipated minimum of behaviour not only within factory contexts but also in other organizations and in society at large. But once again, therefore, it is the indirect rather than the direct consequences of government action which are most important to identify with respect to workers' participation and control.

Finally, values towards participation are profoundly influenced by more general ideologies about human social organizations and the nature of man. On the negative side, whenever the predominant ethos of a society has been authoritarian and whenever the main assumptions of the leaders of given organizations have been based on their belief in man's essential evil rather than good, the prospects of enhancing human freedom by way of participation—where the people as a whole are able to control their own destinies within the context of a genuinely 'human' social order—have been inescapably limited and circumscribed. More specifically, we may recall that Weber's three main bases for the legitimacy of 'authority', legal/rational, traditional and charismatic grounds, have all been used at one time or another to protect decision-making powers and to resist any encroachments on 'prerogatives' by workers and their trade unions. But ideologies have had positive effects as well: indeed, participation has been a mainspring for many broadly humanitarian philosophies, whether socialist, democratic, libertarian, humanistic, religious, or whatever. In order to make sense of some of these variations, the best classification of ideologies for our study was developed by the Webbs in their classic statement of the methods of empirical sociology, *Methods of Social Study*.[74] Indeed, there is still no better textbook on methods of social investigation of the empiricist kind. Referring, then, to the effects of general ideas on human behaviour, they argued:[75]

> Into this social atmosphere, with momentous and almost incalculable effects on the behaviour of men in their various groupings, we see entering successive waves of thoughts and feelings, which spread over entire communities, and, with increasing inter-communication, increasingly over the whole world.

Moreover, with respect to their effects on social institutions, the Webbs distinguished between those arising from (1) religious 'emotion'; (2) humanistic ideals; and (3) deliberate planning for efficiency in carrying out social purposes.[76] And in the context of workers' participation and control, as we shall see, there have been certain experiments originating as a result of religious faith, while others (and notably those deriving from socialist, democratic and libertarian creeds) have been based on humanistic ideals. Finally, as has become increasingly evident and fashionable, there are those developing because participation is seen as the best means of optimizing industrial efficiency. And whatever their essential philosophy all these general ideologies have had some bearing on the prospects of workers' participation in industry.

Summary

To recapitulate, then, the main themes of this chapter, our principal aim has been to argue that workers' participation and control may be best understood as a major *manifestation* of the exercise of social power. To be sure, there are other obvious signs—notably the distribution of income, wealth and property, the patterns of recruitment into particular élites, and the outcome of specific conflicts in which parties may resort to the use of force—but participation does encompass two main aspects involved here, namely, the formal patterns of control in particular societies, communities and organizations, and the range and scope of issues over which decision-making power is exercised. But there are other important dimensions of power as well, and especially the *latent* power of particular classes, parties or groups —which is usually measured by means of their numbers, organization, and resources—and *values*, which affect not only the processes of legitimation of given authority structures but also the prospects of subordinate groupings challenging the hegemony of the more dominant. Moreover, these two dimensions help to span the classical sociological contributions by Marx and Weber on the question of social power.

Turning more specifically to the relationship between power, participation and control, not only did we discuss the probable conceptual relationship between them but also, from a descriptive point of view, we endeavoured to map out the main parameters of participation. In this respect, distinctions were made between the levels at which participation takes place and whether the decisions concerned ends as well as means, the scope of workers' decision-making rights from that of information to outright control and, finally, the range of issues or areas over which workers exercise a measure of influence, such as personnel, social and economic questions. Moreover, although in chapter 1 the case for participation has been outlined in some depth, we observed here that advocates of participation had also attempted to argue that it formed a particularly significant aspect of power; first, because it was viewed as enabling an extension of the issues over which control can be exercised; second, on account of its 'dynamic' effects on values and consciousness; third, as a consequence of the possible effect it may have on man's recognition of his subjective 'powers' and his relationship with nature and the physical universe and, finally, on the basis of its probable contribution to the extension of democracy in society as a whole.

At this point, the arguments of a number of opponents of workers' participation in decision-making were developed, principal among these being the respective contributions of Clegg, Dahrendorf and Mandel. Moreover, notwithstanding the elaborate criticisms of their theories, the important point here in terms of power was that each had a rather different understanding of the concept and, in particular, emphasis was placed on the significance of its *latent* component. Thus, rather than participation being seen as extending the power of working people, these writers were of the opinion that the oppositional strength of workers could be put at risk by this very process and, for Mandel at least, workers would thereby inescapably develop competitive world-views and lose both the practical and theoretical bases for developing more co-operative social relationships which at present exist in the trade unions.

None the less, it is our view that the attainment of participation and control is consequent upon the growth of workers' latent power; it therefore remained to develop the main elements of a causal model for accounting for the origins of particular experiments in this respect. These were summarized in three central propositions, that workers' participation and control are functions of latent power and values, that latent power is a function of economic factors, technological factors and government action, and finally, that values concerning workers' participation and control are a function of the existing levels of participation, latent power, government action and ideologies. These propositions thereby encapsulate the main dependent and independent variables relating to this inquiry.

It is now our intention to demonstrate the validity of these propositions by examining a wide range of different experiments in workers' participation and control. In chapter 3, some of the main forms initiated by management will be examined; this will be succeeded by an outline of those originating on the basis of workers', trade unions', and governments' initiatives. And in each case we shall see the great extent to which either the latent power of particular groups or their values (and not infrequently the two in conjunction) influenced these experiments, not only in their origins, but also in the subsequent success or otherwise that any given experiment enjoyed.

3 Proposals by management

In view of the extremely wide range of forms of workers' participation in decision-making and of the great many interpretations of this particular term, it is clearly not unreasonable to attempt to clarify an otherwise rather confusing picture by means of classification. But there are, to be sure, many potential means of classifying any given phenomenon, and therefore, unless the basis of selection is to be purely arbitrary or idiosyncratic, certain distinctions should be made at the outset which have some association with the main purposes of this inquiry. To begin with, then, it would seem to be essential to identify the principal *initiators* of the different programmes, partly because it requires a certain measure of *power* to bring any specific scheme into effect, but also for the reason that the *values* of given classes, parties and groups can be easily recognized by this method. However, in so far as forms of participation initiated by management are concerned, it is also particularly important to make the further distinction between *direct* participation on the one hand and *indirect* or *representative* participation on the other, for, by so doing, different

TABLE 4 *Forms of participation initiated by management*

Direct participation

(1) Piecemeal attempts by management to raise production and efficiency while reducing conflict and increasing workers' satisfaction on the basis of work-group participation, 'total participation' exercises
(2) Joint consultation in primary working groups
(3) Job rotation, job enlargement, job enrichment
(4) Suggestion schemes, employee shareholding and other profit-sharing schemes, co-partnership, 'commonwealth' ventures

Indirect participation

(1) Joint consultative committees
(2) Specific committees covering productivity, welfare and safety, the administration of various trust funds, and so on
(3) Productivity bargaining

levels of decision-making within the managerial hierarchy may be fairly readily identified. These distinctions thus form the basis of the following classification (see Table 4).

Managerial ideologies and values

We shall examine each of these main forms during this chapter, but at the outset it is appropriate to say something about managerial ideologies and their relationship to workers' participation as well as discussing some of the underlying conditions which have led particular managements to seek changes, however minor, in the more traditional authority structure of the firm.

As a general rule, ideologies would appear to become increasingly important in any power struggle whenever the latent power of conflicting classes, parties or groups becomes less unequal, and conversely, the more unequal the distribution of power, the more likely it is for dominant groupings to use force rather than ideological devices in order to maintain their position of hegemony. Thus, during the nineteenth century, in most industrial countries, it was common for attempts to be made to suppress embryonic and extremely weak unions by means of force and it was not until the twentieth century—and then not universally—that trade unions became an accepted part of the industrial landscape, bounded more and more by ideological and legal restrictions on their activities. Nor should Great Britain be regarded as an exception to this rule. On the contrary, the early political and industrial acts of working people in Britain were not untypically met with violent reprisals. Thus, in 1812, the Duke of Wellington put into the field more troops against the Luddites than he had commanded in the Peninsular War, and in 1848, soldiers were again sent in, this time to confront the Chartists at Kennington Common.[1]

Admittedly, the trade unions in Great Britain had achieved a measure of legal protection by the 1870s and from this time onwards the role of ideology became noticeably more pronounced, while physical force was marshalled less in the relations between government, management and the trade-union movement. By far the best example of this trend was provided in 1919 by Lloyd George in his dealings with the Triple Alliance.[2] Recognizing the enormous latent power at the disposal of these unions he evolved a forceful and oft-repeated argument against its use, namely that 'if a force arises in the State which is stronger than the State itself, then it must be ready to take on the functions of the State, or withdraw and accept the authority of the State'.[3] And in every confrontation with governments since that time, the trade-union movement has, on the whole, always accepted the *ultimate* authority of parliamentary institutions and has never itself sought to *control* the industrial and political framework.

Parallel developments may be observed in the increased attention paid to managerial ideologies within the industrial system. Throughout the nineteenth century the power of the employers was of such an order that to develop any coherent ideologies in support of their position of dominance would have seemed superfluous. Workers were treated merely as a factor of production and their labour was bought and sold like any other commodity largely on the employers' terms. And this practice—as well as the inescapable human misery it entailed —was supported so much by the social conventions of the day that it was accepted as the normal and even natural order of affairs. None the less, in so far as it was possible to recognize the formation of any coherent ideologies during this period, the most prominent focused firmly on ownership rights. In Weberian terms, that is, the view prevailed that tradition alone was sufficient justification of employer domination. Since then, however, following on the growing power of working people, ownership 'rights' are now by no means regarded as sacrosanct, although, to be sure, it is still true that, in relative terms, the distribution of income and wealth has changed but fractionally this century, with the property-owning classes being as supreme as ever even in highly proletarianized states, the concentration of industrial capital having reached gargantuan proportions, and the great extremes of wealth and poverty being no less outrageous. But on the other hand, there have been noticeable shifts in the arguments used to justify social inequalities on this scale.

Thus, the most important managerial ideology to emerge in the twentieth century was based on the so-called 'managerialist' thesis, which, in terms of power, contains three assumptions of great significance: first, that a divorce of ownership from control of the means of production was rapidly taking place in all advanced industrial countries; second, that in view of this the new controllers of industry would become largely non-propertied, technically proficient and highly professional; and third, that a very different distribution of social rewards would now be forthcoming. The legitimacy of managerial domination was thus gradually transferred from traditional (property ownership) to legal-rational grounds, resting on the expertise of key industrial administrators. In consequence, too, a belief was fostered that industry would be controlled by those most fitted in terms of natural and acquired abilities. Achievement rather than family connection would be the basis for acquiring managerial posts in the first place, industry would reach undreamed-of levels of efficiency and therefore any attempt to curb managerial powers would be socially and economically short-sighted.

At this point in the thesis there were some differences of opinion as to the additional effects of these developments, two principal variants being recognized here. In one view, a non-zero-sum power situation would obtain and management would therefore exercise its decision-making powers in a socially responsible way to the resultant benefit of all members of the population. But in the other, which rested more on a zero-sum power conception, any accretions in managerial power brought about by such developments would inevitably take place to the detriment not only of older entrepreneurial classes but also of all other classes. Again, the more meritocratic societies became, the greater would be the tendency, since lower social classes would be robbed of effective and talented leaders.

But the assumptions and key arguments of all versions of the managerialist thesis are meretricious in the extreme. The persistent inequality in the distribution of social rewards, the inescapable market restraints on the behaviour of key industrial decision-makers whatever their social origins and attitudes and the fact that only certain members of the population are likely to be beneficiaries of decisions taken in these circumstances, are all sufficient to suggest certain serious weaknesses in such a framework of analysis. Moreover, even if we were to leave aside such fundamental objections as these and to confront the 'managerialist' thesis on its own terms, the evidence by no means suggests that a new non-propertied, technocratic and professional élite now runs industry. On the contrary, Nichols has effectively marshalled the empirical material of relevance to each of these main issues in so far as British management is concerned and has drawn rather different and quite contrary conclusions.[4]

Thus, while the case for the emergence of a new managerial élite is undoubtedly strongest on the question of capital ownership, even this is not sustained, for while it is true that there has generally been a diminution of directoral shareholdings as a proportion of total shareholdings, and, to that extent, the 'capitalist' may be said to have gone out of 'capitalism', the majority of directors none the less do own shares in the companies they work for; indeed, 'a specified minimum holding is usually a legal qualification for office'.[5] Moreover, some directors have substantial holdings and it is quite clear from evidence on the distribution of income and property ownership that the modern controllers of industry belong to the tiny wealthy stratum of western industrial societies.[6]

Turning more specifically to the question of the technical quali-fications of modern managers, it is absolutely clear, as Nichols has argued, 'that the majority of directors are not, in any meaningful sense of the word, "technocrats" '.[7] To begin with, about eight out of ten directors do not even have university degrees and of those who do many have graduated in Arts subjects bearing little if any relation to their responsibilities. As Nichols has pointed out:[8]

> There is scant evidence to suggest that many directors hold *either* a university degree *or* any other kind of formal qualification. Barritt has shown that 74% of directors in companies with assets of £500,000 and over had no qualifications at all. And the three studies by the Institute of Directors found approximately 60% of directors were not 'qualified'—even when an Arts degree was counted as a qualification.

But while such data offer little or no support for the emergence of a highly-qualified managerial élite, the empirical material bearing on the professional competence of modern management is similarly damaging. After all, among the common criteria for designating profes-sional status are that particular skills are acquired which are based on an established body of knowledge, and that a system of norms and ethical practices governs relations between professionals and derives from a source independent of their income. But while management education has been a major growth point in recent years in all indus-trial countries, acquired skills of this kind have not become a mini-mum qualification for office and, in so far as relations among managers themselves are concerned, the absence of any generally accepted normative code is so familiar that, as Durkheim correctly pointed out, these relationships form a *locus classicus* of particularly entrenched, pathological anomie. Again, large numbers of managers still, at best, pay only lip service to the possibility of building up a managerial science, preferring instead to rely on far more emotive and 'rule of thumb' methods, and at worst try to discredit such a notion in its entirety.[9]

And yet, if it is difficult to find empirical support for the view that a new kind of manager has emerged to replace the old-style entre-preneur, this of course has in no way limited the effectiveness of such an ideology with regard to developments of workers' participation in decision-making processes. Thus, while in the nineteenth century it was generally thought unnecessary to offer any justification for domination by management—and exceptions to this rule usually involved applying traditional criteria based on ownership rights—in the years following some explanation for this order of things in which workers are denied an effective voice in decision-making processes has become imperative and has come to rest on organizational position and the *assumed* competence and expertise associated with it. But while a development along these lines is doubtless consequent upon the growth of bureaucratic administrative forms, more importantly in our context, it substantially affects and indeed is far more antithetical to genuine workers' participation than traditional organizations which have regard only for profit-making criteria. After all, since it can be shown so easily that profit and efficiency are almost invariably enhanced by workers' participation in decision-making, this provides sufficient reason in itself for the apostles of capitalism.

However, inasmuch as modern managers have internalized an ideology which defends their decision-making authority on the basis of expertise, they will be unwilling to threaten this by encouraging participative and democratic practices: indeed, we would predict that the more a given manager approximates or considers himself to approximate to the stereotype encapsulated by the managerialist thesis, the more vehemently will be his opposition to workers' participation and control, and that conversely it will be the profit-oriented managers who will be most supportive of limited experiments along these lines.

To be sure, as Clarke *et al.* suggest, it is by no means impossible that new criteria, relatively more consistent with workers' participation in decision-making, will ultimately be found in managerial circles:[10]

> Looking to the future the desirable form of the industrial enterprise
> would seem to be one in which that autonomy, which in the
> nineteenth century was considered justified by ownership and which
> in the first half of the twentieth century was seen as a right exercised
> by managers because they were the appointees of the owners who
> were the sole judge of their ability, as well as the sole source of their
> right to manage, will increasingly be seen to spring from an objective
> and accepted appraisal of functional requirements in which all
> concerned are recognized to have a legitimate interest.

But, at all events, what is important to note in so far as managerial attitudes to workers' participation in decision-making is concerned, is that the main managerial ideology of the twentieth century has worked strongly against developments in this direction.

Not surprisingly, therefore, the most common and generally preferred solution to the expansion of the latent power of working people has been for management to develop paternalistic practices for which the 'human relations movement' provided the main rationale and personnel management the most obvious institutional form. The growth of humanitarian policies may be viewed as a direct response to changing economic, political, and technical circumstances which altered the balance of latent power between the main industrial relations classes. Thus, during the post-Second World War period—and especially in the 1950s—there were actual labour shortages in most advanced industrial countries and as a result the recruitment and retention of an adequate labour force was imperative to management. This therefore provided a fertile ground not only for the development of a number of welfare practices, such as sickness and pensions schemes, but also for the growth of personnel departments at workplace level to deal with the problems of individual workers. Moreover, the easy availability of employment undoubtedly increased the bargaining power of workers and this was manifested principally in the emergence of domestic bargaining arrangements based on the shop-steward system. The post-war period, too, saw the growing intervention by government in labour–management relations and this, in turn, led to a host of legal measures which required more systematic attention by employers to 'human relations' practices than was the case in the inter-war years. And finally, although certain technical changes have led to an erosion of job opportunities in traditional manufacturing industries and, to that extent, have reduced the workers' bargaining strength in this context, on balance, many new developments have helped to further the latent power of working people. Thus, as a result of technical integration of productive processes in large-scale companies, many workers have found themselves in particularly strategic positions to inflict major economic costs on their respective employers; the growing scale and concentration of industry are undoubtedly favourable to union growth and to collective action by the employees of these large combines. And, with the increased demand for highly-skilled maintenance workers as the 'technical scale' is ascended, there is little chance of replacing such workers and this again has the effect, of course, of changing the balance of latent power to the benefit of the workers concerned.

Thus, although none of the arguments above should be taken to imply that workers are now in any sense stronger than their employers, the main point here is that in the post-Second World War period certain forces have been in operation which have served to advance the position of working people and, further, that the most common managerial response to this situation has not been to encourage workers' participation in decision-making but rather to develop more paternalistic human relations and personnel policies. Moreover, even when managements recognize conflicting interests at workplace level they still *prefer* to hold on to a 'unitary conception of the organization', i.e. 'to favour the view which sees it as having but one proper source of authority and one focus of loyalty'.[11] For management, then, socially-oriented policies may be viewed as 'the most *practically* effective courses of action in modern socio-economic conditions'[12] since they may lead to a reduction of the demands of working people to a point where changes in the authority structure of the firm are not contemplated and where the managerially-valuable, 'unitary conception', is not significantly brought into question. For, after all, as Fox has argued, such a conception is also an ideology which serves three purposes: 'It is at once a method of self-reassurance, an instrument of persuasion, and a technique of seeking legitimation of authority.'[13] And, to the extent that this is a fair judgment, there are clearly important grounds here for managements who seek to retain such a view of the authority structure of the enterprise to make social welfare policies *a function of management* and thereby to deny workers effective autonomy to control such issues themselves. None the less, there have been occasions when management has, in fact, sought to give workers a greater share in the decision-making processes of the firm, but before we turn to examples of these, it is worth identifying a number of general matters raised here.

To begin with, in the majority of schemes initiated by management it is evident that the scope, level and range of issues over which workers have a voice have typically been restricted. Thus, in so far as the scope of workers' influence on any given decision is concerned, management has been inclined towards *consultative* rather than *participative* institutions and, as Clarke and his colleagues have argued, it still remains true that[14]

> on the whole, employers and their spokesmen have evinced deep mistrust as to the value of participation, particularly in integrative forms, such as the appointment of workers' directors though they reflect a widespread belief in prior consultation with workers on matters which concern them.

Then again, in terms of range of issues, certain social, personnel and, to a point, technical decisions, have at times been opened to wider discussion, but critical commercial and business items which concern the long-term development of the firm have on the whole remained

5

exclusively in managerial hands. And finally, decision-making opportunities have generally been confined to the shop-floor level and to
the implementation of policies already decided upon unilaterally by
managements.

In general, therefore, managements have only sought to institute
broader programmes when the power of workers has been sufficiently
strong, or when they have been obliged to do so as a consequence of
government legislation, or when they have internalized certain general
ideologies different from the main ones examined so far in this chapter
—chief among these being humanist, religious or an overriding
commitment to industrial efficiency.

There has always been a minority of employers who have objected
on broadly humanitarian grounds to the predominant modes of the
social organization of work in industry, but because of the importance
of market rather than ethical criteria in determining economic success, the evolution of industrial organization is punctuated by the
graveyards of some of the boldest, most imaginative, and humanitarian attempts to develop rather different work relationships. Not
infrequently, the secular humanism implied here has been buttressed
by certain religious convictions—and this has been especially true of
Quaker employers—but at the ideological level the two can be
effectively separated. It is important to note, however, that such
broad ideologies have, in a limited way, had some influence over
managerial values towards participation and, for instance, served to
encourage a number of interesting experiments in this field. More
commonly, however, an overriding concern with industrial efficiency
has been the principal ideological stimulus behind the acceptance of
new forms of organization of work. Participation has been seen to
facilitate this in the following ways: it enables the skills and abilities of
workers to be effectively tapped, it reduces workers' resistance to
technological change, it spurs management to increase efficiency, it
raises the level of workers' satisfaction and thereby makes for a more
contented workforce, and finally it is viewed as an important means
for improving industrial relations. Naturally, assumptions such as
these are open to empirical investigation, but our concern here is the
ideological basis for changing assessments of the utility of employee
participation.

Direct participation

Turning more specifically now to the managerially-initiated programmes for involving working people in decision-making, we shall

begin our analysis with an examination of the most important forms of direct participation. These involve practices in which all the members of a given workgroup, or workteam, are able to influence decision-making processes; they do not therefore have to rely on their representatives alone. However, not surprisingly, as we shall see, the majority of these practices are restricted to very low levels of decision-making and, further, they are largely confined to issues of an 'on-the-job' character. Therefore, even if they may have had important effects in so far as industrial 'efficiency' is concerned, it is doubtful whether they imply any significant erosion of managerial 'prerogatives' and, as a result, to many critics they are examples of 'pseudo'-participation.

(1) *Piecemeal attempts to raise efficiency by means of workgroup participation*

Ever since the Hawthorne experiments began to have an impact on managerial and academic thinking during the 1930s, it has been understood that workgroups can have a particularly important influence on industrial efficiency. On the one hand they may develop various practices which prevent competition between members and thereby restrict individual output to a common group norm; on the other hand, the workgroup itself may figure as a powerful vehicle for enhancing output and productivity.[15] Moreover, for the latter situation to obtain, a critically important component is the development of 'workshop democracy'. Thus, in the classical relay assembly test-room experiment—in which output of the group was observed to rise progressively week by week despite major changes in the physical environment of work—the most important social factor appeared to be the almost total disappearance of externally-imposed discipline and supervision. As Blumberg has argued: 'In brief, the entire system of industrial authority which these workers had been accustomed to labouring under was transformed during the experiment, as the test-room workers developed into an almost self-governing body'.[16] Therefore, although, to be sure, the level of decision-making implicated here was largely confined to the workgroup, the relevance of autonomy to workers' satisfaction and raising industrial efficiency had begun to be recognized.

Following the Hawthorne experiments there have, of course, been many extensive and detailed studies of workgroup behaviour although the majority have been related in only a rather peripheral way to the issues of power and participation. But there have at the same time been some attempts to bring these themes into closer apposition. Thus, in the USA, the Scanlon Plan provided for developments in participation based on working groups as a stimulus to industrial efficiency[17] and two further studies are noteworthy at this point because they highlight the more general explanatory themes of our own study exceptionally well.

The earliest and best-known attempt to measure the effects of participation on workers' output and satisfaction was carried out by Coch and French in an American clothing factory in which production methods were changing in order to cater for civilian rather than military markets after the close of the Second World War.[18] The details of the study are too well known to merit a lengthy treatment here, but its most important aspects were as follows. In the main experiments, three groups of workers were set up: first, a control group for whom there was *no participation* in decisions relating to the prospective changes; second, an experimental *participation through representation* group; and third, certain experimental, *total participation* groups, in which all members were involved in designing the changeover in production. The results of this study have formed the basis of many of the most optimistic projections as to the consequences of participation by workgroups. Thus, in the control group, for whom no participation in the changes was possible:[19]

> Resistance developed almost immediately after the change occurred. Marked expressions of aggression against management occurred, such as conflicts with the methods engineer, expressions of hostility against the supervisor, deliberate restriction of production, and lack of cooperation with the supervisor. There were 17% quits in the first 40 days. Grievances were filed about the piece rate, but when the rate was checked, it was found to be a little 'loose'.

But the situation in the other groups was markedly different. The attitude of the representative group was 'co-operative and permissive', the group adapted well to the changes and their output soon reached a level higher than that obtaining before the experiments were set up. There was only one recorded act of aggression from this group and no one left the workteam as a result of the changeover. Moreover, the total participation groups adapted most speedily of all to the changes, their 'efficiency ratings' showed sustained progress 'to a level about 14% higher than the prechange level'. There were no indications of aggression to management and supervision and, again, no labour turnover within the group.[20] Thus, the positive effects of participation on output, satisfaction and labour–management relations appeared to be confirmed.

However, notwithstanding the more obvious criticisms of these experiments in so far as the distribution of power in industry is concerned—and notably, that participation took place at a very low level, that the decisions which the workers influenced focused on means towards ends already established by management, and that these decisions were largely confined to task-based problems—there are certain further points of interest which should be raised here. To begin with, such forms of 'participation' are of course likely to be preferred to higher-level programmes by management because they demand so little change in the traditional authority structure of the firm and therefore fit reasonably well into the so-called 'unitary conception' of authority within the enterprise. Indeed, in view of the positive effects of these experiments, it is somewhat surprising that they are not already the most common means for dealing with managerial problems of this type. The probable explanation for this situation, therefore, is that authoritarian methods are generally preferred to democratic ones by the great majority of managements and that their objections to participation are frequently based on ideological considerations in which concern for industrial efficiency is of a lower order than the maintenance of a particular pattern of domination. And this would certainly be predicted on the basis of any internalization by management—whether conscious or unconscious—of the main tenets of the managerialist thesis.

But what is particularly intriguing in the study by Coch and French is that the workers concerned should have shown so little resistance not to the changeover in production but to the specific forms of managerial initiative involved in this experiment, and the principal reason for this was almost certainly the low levels of latent power obtaining among these employees. Such a conclusion is certainly justified if we consider the equally well-known attempt to replicate this study in a Norwegian factory.[21] Once again, the details of the experiment are not especially important for our purposes, but it is of fundamental significance that the researchers had *to refine their theory of participation* by demonstrating that increased participation affected production, labour–management relations, and job satisfaction:[22]

> only to the extent that four conditioning variables were present: (a) the decisions were important, (b) the content of decisions was relevant to the dependent variable, (c) the participation was considered legitimate, (d) there was no resistance to change (i.e. no negative reaction to the *methods* of managing the change).

Fundamental to the outcome of these experiments was the level of unionization of the workpeople in each factory, as French, Israel and Ås pointed out:[23]

> The Norwegian workers had a stronger tradition of being organized in a union than had workers in the American factory. This in turn can produce an attitude that the legitimate pattern of participation is through union representatives rather than direct participation.

But we would wish to take this argument somewhat further by postulating that the higher level of organizational power of workers in the Norwegian factory almost certainly necessitated the introduction of the four conditioning variables. That is to say, it was precisely the power of these workers that enabled them to insist that the decisions they took were important, that they were relevant to the dependent variable concerned (e.g. job satisfaction), that prompted them to regard certain forms of participation as *illegitimate* (because they were perceived either as manipulative or to clash with their own representation). Finally for this reason, too, the Norwegian workers were able and willing to resist certain *methods* of managing the change.

Moreover, to the extent that these interpretations are valid, there are certain general conclusions to be drawn concerning the relationship between power and participation. To begin with, although it clearly requires a modicum of latent power, together with appropriate values, to establish a given participation programme in the first instance, the latent power and values *of the other party* are clearly critical in affecting the degree of success recorded in any particular scheme. Thus, whereas in the American factory very modest erosions of managerial prerogatives were sufficient to ensure major changes in workers' attitudes and behaviour, this was clearly less true in the Norwegian works. And second, it would appear that not only does the latent power of workers substantially affect their demands for taking decisions on matters which are important to them, but this also forms a basis for developing certain values towards participation in which a distinction is made between certain managerially-initiated programmes which *may* be regarded as illegitimate and those, based on their union organizations, which are recognized as the most appropriate means for handling problems. Values towards participation are therefore affected by latent power. And finally, if our assessment is correct, this also suggests that the success of small-scale, managerially-initiated programmes depends to a great extent on the latent power and values of the workers. When workers are poorly organized, the best results from a managerial point of view are likely to ensue, since major benefits may be expected to accrue from small changes in the authority structure of the firm; but, by way of contrast, certain programmes may be rejected outright by workers in highly unionized firms, unless they are conducted through the union channels which are regarded by the workers as the legitimate means for handling labour-relations issues. And, in any event, workers in such highly unionized firms may characteristically demand rather more control over decision-making processes than management might wish to concede.

This judgment tends to be ratified further by the experience of certain 'total involvement' exercises carried out during periods of dramatic technical change. A particularly well-researched example is the case of ICI at its Gloucester nylon-spinning plant where not only shop-floor discussion groups were set up to involve all the workers in the changes, but also a joint management–union working party including the shop stewards was established together with a joint negotiating party to sanction any proposals and suggestions emerging from the groups and the working party.[24] Clearly, therefore, a much broader framework of participation was appropriate on account of the strength of workplace union organization.

Furthermore, although top management may welcome such changes on the grounds that they are concerned largely with means for implementing managerial policy decisions, the consequences may be particularly severe for lower and middle management in terms of both decision-making authority and ideology. Indeed, in the ICI study by Cotgrove and his colleagues, enthusiasm for the scheme among supervisory personnel was much less marked than among top management, workers and shop stewards. Thus, although efficiency and 'happiness' among workers were undoubtedly encouraged by such developments:[25]

> The adoption of a supervisory style based on participation was not easy. For all supervisors, it meant a threat to their status and security; for some, the fundamental changes in behaviour required were more than they could manage. Some had left, and others had experienced severe strain in adjusting to the demands of the new style, with its shift in emphasis from authority and directives to participatory leadership.

(2) *Joint consultation in primary working groups*

Not surprisingly, then, because supervisors have been less than happy with the consequences of direct participation, management has on the whole shown a more pronounced preference for consultative rather than more clearly participative practices. One symptom of this has been its encouragement of joint consultation in primary working groups. To be sure, in some measure this may be best regarded as a response to the problems involved in formal consultative systems but the great advantage of all forms of consultation from the managerial viewpoint is that they are defined in such a way as to involve no reduction of its decision-making powers whatsoever. They are limited to the inclusion of workers in discussions over issues which affect them, prior to a decision being made by management alone. Employees therefore *influence* but in no way *determine* managerial policy and practice. Of course, none of this should be taken to suggest that the line between consultation and decision-making can be so easily drawn, or that workers share these managerial definitions and assumptions, or again, that, if they are strong enough, workers cannot effectively ensure that decisions are taken along only certain lines. But it is to argue that, whereas for the majority of managers participation has been strongly rejected because it demands some sharing of decision-making powers, joint consultation is more favourably viewed, at least in principle, because it in no way disturbs an authoritarian conception of the authority structure of the enterprise or severely curtails management's right to decide.

The development of joint consultation in primary working groups is, however, no universal phenomenon. But it has been encouraged in the electrical supply industry of Great Britain in particular, partly because of the difficulties encountered in formal consultative machinery in establishing close links with the main body of employees, but also because of the profound changes which have taken place in this industry, and notably the commissioning of new stations which has, of course, had a radical effect on the life-span of older ones. Thus, in the words of Sallis:[26]

> In such circumstances, it was important that a good many employees should know what was going on since, to put it at its best, they would otherwise be bewildered by change and, to put it at its worst, be quite unready to meet it. And the Division knew that, with the tremendous increase in demand for electricity, which was showing itself at that time (and has since materialized), the tempo of change would shortly be accelerated, particularly with the building in the West Riding of vast new power stations. Positive efforts had therefore to be made to see that technological change did not outstrip the capacity of the employees to adapt themselves to it.

But how far, it may be reasonably asked, does joint consultation in primary working groups compare with other forms of workgroup participation and in what respects can it be explained by the broader theme of power which was outlined in chapter 2? To begin with, there are clearly certain points of similarity with other practices. Workers are invited to participate only at a low level in the decision-making process; they are concerned at best with implementing means, the ends having been already established by management; and the programmes have evolved not because they are necessarily desirable in themselves but rather may reflect management's fear of the consequences of introducing changes without *any* prior consultation with the workers. But this resemblance apart, there are several respects in which joint consultative procedures at workgroup level deviate from other participation schemes. In terms of the scope of decision-making power, for instance, consultative practices are, on the surface at least, less beneficial to workers than more genuine participatory programmes. And yet at the same time the range of issues covered during regular consultation within primary working groups is probably more extensive, for they are not necessarily confined to specific problems associated with a particular technical change.

Finally, forms of consultation can be seen as reflecting the latent power and values of the workers in any given firm. When relationships between management and employee are particularly asymmetric there is, in fact, no real necessity for management to consult with workers at all, even if this is beneficial in terms of efficiency. But in circumstances where the power of workers is greater, joint consultation has been commonly developed by management, sometimes to anticipate trade union formation, but more especially to prevent damaging conflicts which would inevitably ensue from the more arbitrary use of its power.

(3) *Job rotation, job enlargement and job enrichment*

There have been many other attempts by management, however, to overcome some of the emergent problems it faces as a consequence of the growth in the latent power of working people. Three of these will therefore be examined at this point: job rotation, which refers to the practice of changing workers from one job to another; job enlargement, which involves some extension of the range of jobs undertaken by a particular operator; and finally, job enrichment, which entails giving far greater responsibility to workers and enabling them to take 'decisions that were formerly the prerogative of supervisors'.[27]

For the great majority of employees, of course, work has always been an alienating experience: indeed, this has been so marked that the concept of work has come to be interpreted in explicitly alienative terms. Moreover, certain technical developments have, if anything, considerably aggravated this problem with the result that, in the so-called middle range of the technical scale (epitomized by the assembly line), even management will acknowledge that working conditions are of an extremely unsatisfying nature. To be sure, many of the workers who are actually in such employment may be atypical of working people as a whole and, in particular, they may have marked 'instrumental orientations' which enable them—so long as they are satisfied with their rates of pay—to accept rather more readily than their colleagues the major disincentives of their work environment.[28] But, in any event, monetary rewards only partially ameliorate this industrial problem which has been exacerbated by technical changes, which, concurrently with other factors, have stimulated the latent power of working people. Symptoms of alienation have multiplied in the great majority of industrial countries in the post-Second World War period; rates of absenteeism, labour turnover, sickness, and accidents have shown a marked deterioration, while many small strikes and stoppages are almost certainly attributable to alienative environments, a few being explicitly so. Moreover, colourful examples of alienation have been provided by the numerous acts of industrial sabotage and restrictive practices. Again, most symptoms of alienation follow a distinctive weekly cycle in which the rate is highest on Mondays but declines progressively as the week advances, a pattern to be expected in alienative environments since, during the early part of the week, the workers' perception of the disrewards of work are likely to be particularly intense. However, this experience would be expected to subside somewhat as the prospect of enjoying 'free time' over the weekend becomes less distant.

Of course, from a managerial point of view, these indices of alienation have begun to reach unacceptable proportions. In the electronics industry, labour turnover alone has been calculated to cost about £13 million a year and has generally been adduced to the dreary and depressing nature of the work.[29] It is scarcely surprising, then, that efficiency-oriented managements have vigorously sought means to minimize these problems and some have begun to accept that the erosion of certain decision-making prerogatives is an acceptable price to pay if this offers some solution. None the less, it is worth mentioning that still only the relatively advanced managements are *acting* along these lines.

As it happens, job rotation and job enlargement have comparatively little impact on the hierarchy of authority in the firm. Indeed, under certain circumstances they may be interpreted by workers as effecting a diminution in their job interest and autonomy since, when rotation, for example, is imposed by management, informal workgroup norms which help to reduce the worst consequences of alienation for the individual worker may also break down. To be sure, as Daniel and McIntosh have argued, these problems can be avoided:[30]

> As far as job rotation and enlargement are concerned, management must create the conditions where this can naturally come about, through the style of supervision, the level of manning and the physical layout of the work area, rather than by imposing preconceived systems of rotation and enlargement on the workgroup. Though the intention may be to increase the workers' job interest and autonomy the effect is likely to reduce them because of closer supervision and loss of social satisfactions through the break-up of established group relationships.

Indeed, because under certain circumstances job rotation and enlargement may involve a slight but scarcely perceptible increase in a worker's ability to take decisions of a technical nature to the detriment of his control over a number of social decisions, they may involve no net gain in the power of the employee whatsoever. It is only job enrichment, therefore, which significantly affects the decision-making powers of working people and this accordingly merits more thorough consideration at this point.

There have now been a number of detailed investigations of job enrichment schemes and in most cases the positive benefits in so far as productivity, flexibility, work satisfaction and industrial relations are concerned have been amply demonstrated. The three best-documented programmes have been those at ICI, the American Telephone and Telegraph Company and at Philips. Paul and Robertson have reported that jobs were restructured at ICI in order that given workgroups might achieve more responsibility and autonomy.[31] Particularly, spectacular results were forthcoming from among the salesmen whose sales not only increased substantially but whose level of job satisfaction showed major gains as well, but in all groups the effects of these experiments were positive in terms of industrial efficiency.[32] Considerable improvements in efficiency were also consequent upon the restructuring of decision-making in a subsidiary of the American Telephone and Telegraph Company. Here, following the reorganization, orders were almost invariably completed on time, the quality of work improved considerably, and, in so far as few grievances can be taken as an index of greater job satisfaction, there were also important gains in this direction.[33] Furthermore, the experiments at Philips are of interest, principally because here an attempt was being made to combat chronic labour shortages. Once again, therefore, an improvement in the relative strength of workers *vis-à-vis* management may have important repercussions for day-to-day relations in the workplace. Indeed, the Philips management introduced several changes in production methods, the most significant for our purposes being the comparatively autonomous production teams which were set up, enjoying considerable decision-making powers which were once the prerogative of middle management and supervisory staff. Again, there were substantial benefits recorded on the efficiency dimension: quality and output increased while labour turnover and absenteeism declined and the workers' attitudes to management became far less antagonistic.[34]

But, by and large, job enrichment programmes of this nature clearly suggest a zero-sum game in so far as decision-making powers at shop-floor level are concerned. Thus, the greater the power which accrues to working people in this respect, the less is available for middle management and first-line supervisors even though the power of top management may remain largely unaffected. Thus, among their colleagues, middle management and supervisors have been found to be most hostile to these changes and, in view of the conclusions of Daniel and McIntosh, this is scarcely surprising:[35]

> The one essential characteristic of any really effective change in the direction of job enrichment is the delegation of greater responsibility to individual workers and workgroups, so that some shop-floor decision-making passes from supervisors to the workgroup. But this immediately changes the position of the supervisor and there will be uncertainty for all at this level. This does not necessarily mean that fewer first-line managers or foremen will be needed or that their span of control will be increased but rather that the numbers at intermediary levels, such as assistant foremen, will be reduced or even eliminated. The jobs of those remaining will be very substantially changed. Indeed they may well feel that their last remaining vestige of status and responsibility has been stripped from them.

As a consequence, managerialist-oriented employers will judge such moves as a betrayal of the ethic which sustains their decision-making authority and an abrogation of responsibility towards their junior managerial staff. But sentiments of this kind are unlikely to prevent the multiplication of schemes along these lines, not only because managements will in any event progressively seek to reduce

the extremely costly consequences of widespread industrial alienation, but also for the reason that those failing to do so will almost certainly find themselves outstripped by their competitors who are
prepared to support programmes such as these. Again, the more
incontrovertible becomes the evidence that workers' satisfaction as
well as efficiency is enhanced by increasing workgroup autonomy and
responsibility, so we would anticipate that the climate of opinion will
favour participation and thereby stimulate further moves in this
direction.

But of particular interest in so far as managerial ideologies are concerned is the effect of any general development of workgroup
autonomy over *technical* decision-making processes. We have already
mentioned that managements, on the whole, have preferred consultative to genuinely participative practices because these are seen as
having no real effect on the ultimate decision-making responsibilities
of management. And although it is true that job-enrichment programmes are largely concerned with means rather than ends and
involve no serious inroads into the policy-making decisions of top
management, they do present a substantial threat to any ideology
which justifies the authority of management on the technical criterion
of expertise, and this is of course especially true for members of the
lower echelons of the hierarchy.

(4) Suggestions schemes, employee shareholding and other profit-sharing schemes, co-partnership and 'commonwealth' ventures

Turning now to our final category of direct participation initiated by
management, this again involves a progression from rather limited
accretions in workers' decision-making powers to programmes of a
much more ambitious character. Taking *suggestions schemes* first of all,
then, these only allow for a measure of participation by individual
workers in facilitating rather specific technical changes at shop-floor
level or in altering work practices which carry the risk of accidents or
sickness. They are, however, a fairly familiar landmark in the British
industrial-relations landscape; indeed, in their study of workers'
participation in management in Great Britain, Clarke and his colleagues discovered that 40 per cent of the companies they contacted
had suggestions schemes and that, in large firms, they were especially
common.[36] In certain rare cases in which technical changes instituted
as a result of suggestions schemes have induced substantial savings for
particular managements, not inconsiderable financial rewards have

been given to the individual workers concerned. None the less, it is far more common for awards to be quite small and, indeed, only nominal where suggestions relate to improvements in safety and health. Moreover, the decision to make an award or otherwise is usually taken by the departmental manager acting on the advice of a number of technical specialists, and although this decision may be subject to further negotiation with a worker's shop steward or joint consultative committee representative, ultimate authority over issues such as these resides clearly in managerial hands. In this sense, then, suggestions schemes are a form of pseudo-participation, for although they may be justified *by management* on the grounds of providing an opportunity for increased participation by employees and of having further bene-fits in so far as morale is concerned, if workers are deprived of the right to any effective voice these schemes are little different from human-relations exercises.

But, all the same, such a conclusion may be unduly harsh since suggestions schemes do have some additional effects on management–worker relations at shop-floor level, and although these experiments have positive benefits so far as efficiency is concerned, they may actually increase the degree of hostility and conflict between manage-ment and men. The level of awards is, of course, a persistent source of friction, for managements usually ensure that no more than 50 per cent of any savings in production costs are passed on to the worker concerned and the proportion is not infrequently very much less than this. Again, conflict is likely to be particularly sharp on suggestions which tend only to benefit shop-floor workers and, notably, improve-ments in safety, since from a managerial point of view, these may actually entail increases in direct costs. And although this is not to say that workers do not generally approve of suggestions schemes, it is better to point out that some disharmony may well arise from their introduction and that, in these circumstances, the organization power of workers at shop-floor level will be decisive in accounting for whether a particular award is finally made.

Suggestions schemes have an important bearing, too, on relations at workgroup level, on trade union negotiations and on the decision-making power and authority of foremen and other lower managerial personnel. The complaint is often heard, for example, that suggestions schemes are potentially damaging to morale within the workgroup. Indeed, at worst, suggestions schemes can encourage competition between members of particular workgroups and lead to substantial differentials in financial rewards. Nevertheless, these consequences may be overdramatized: indeed, in a case study by Gorfin of the operation of a suggestions scheme not only did workers generally approve of the scheme itself—particularly because they viewed it as a recognition that the man working on a given piece of machinery, not infrequently, knew rather more about the job than his supervisors— but also, they made charitable remarks about their colleagues who had actually received awards.[37] Indeed, dissatisfaction about the operation of the scheme was more evident among those who had actually made suggestions than among those who had never participated in the scheme at all.[38]

Again, because the effects of suggestions schemes are seldom dramatic it is easy to overstate trade union objections to them. How- ever, they clearly imply some by-passing of union channels since they create a system of *individual* rather than *collective* rewards and also because, unless the amount of money involved is itself a source of conflict, union officials and shop stewards are rarely implicated. Thus, although the majority of active unionists may still be broadly favourable to schemes of this kind, there is almost certainly some loss of union authority—albeit unremarkable—on questions of remuneration.

But perhaps the most interesting consequences of suggestions schemes are for the power and authority of lower managerial per- sonnel. As Gorfin has pointed out, the successful participation of those below the supervisor can mean that the perceived difference between his skills and those of shop-floor workers becomes pro- gressively narrower, and indeed, in those cases where rewards are really substantial, the position of the supervisor may suffer a marked deterioration. Moreover, this is clearly exacerbated whenever super- visors are expected to be technically more proficient than workers on the shop floor and especially when their authority is based largely on such criteria.[39] There is a close parallel here with certain of the effects of job-enrichment programmes in so far as the power and authority of those in supervisory ranks are concerned, though because sug- gestions schemes are less extensive their consequences are accordingly less pervasive.

Moving at this point to yet another attempt by management to offer financial inducements for greater productivity and output while at the same time involving workers more closely in the affairs of the firm, it is again rather doubtful whether the majority of *employee shareholding* and *profit-sharing schemes* have in fact had quite the decisive impact for working people assumed by their most ardent supporters. Indeed, certain practices of this kind differ little from traditional bonus incentives. They do, however, contrast with suggestions schemes in at least four main ways: the rewards are collective in nature; the whole workforce rather than a considerably smaller proportion of employees are involved; dividends are paid regularly, usually on an annual basis; and, not infrequently, individual employee shareholders have actual voting rights and can on the face of it, therefore, influence managerial policy.

Employee shareholding is in fact far more common than is generally appreciated. In a survey carried out in 1954, the Ministry of Labour found that about 500 companies practised some form of profit-sharing. Moreover, in a study by Copeman, a rich variety of forms of employee shareholding was discovered and Copeman consequently thought it fitting to identify at least nine types of scheme. But the most usual were the straightforward uses of profit-sharing; the employee himself investing some of his savings in the company in return for an extra-high yield on this investment; the creation of an employee share trust which denied the employee full shareholding rights; and access to ordinary stock which the employee could purchase at a price below market value.[40]

Enthusiasm for schemes of this kind has rested on a belief that a permanent change in the status of workers would be brought about and that this would eventually replace the continual struggle between capital and labour which has had deleterious consequences for certain companies. Copeman, among others, writing at the time when the Soviet Union was engaging in early exploration of space, saw employee shareholding as a point of contact between the two sides of industry and an important means of surmounting international competition in a changing political climate.[41] Nevertheless, such unbridled optimism was doubtless misplaced, for it is unlikely that the traditional authority structure of the firm can be substantially altered by movements in this direction. Indeed, Sawtell found no correlation at all between the levels of participation obtaining in the companies he studied and the existence of profit-sharing schemes.[42] Again, in those cases where full shareholding rights are denied to employees, such arrangements amount to little more than bonus incentives and yet suffer with respect to these from being less immediately relevant to an individual worker or group of workers. In other words, the efforts of some employees may be offset by less enthusiastic colleagues, managerial incompetence, or unfavourable market circumstances, all of which are beyond the control of any particular group of workers. Moreover, even in those schemes which allow for voting rights, the fears of certain managers and non-employee shareholders that workers might eventually hold the majority of shares and thereby control the appointment of directors, are largely groundless. In 1955, the chairman of ICI, in answer to a question bearing on this ultimate possibility, estimated that in thirty years' time it was most unlikely that the employees would hold more than 15 per cent of the shares.[43] Unless, therefore, very much more ambitious schemes for employee shareholding are envisaged, the status of employee shareholders (assuming they can be regarded as a homogeneous body) is little different from that of the small investor, whose impact on company policy is undoubtedly marginal. Furthermore, since market criteria determine much of company policy, the leverage of even a controlling group of employees would be by no means substantial. Under such circumstances, then, it is scarcely surprising that large numbers of employees who have received shares in schemes of this kind have simply sold them and have had no illusions whatsoever that employee shareholding is a step to exerting a significant measure of control over the policies and practices of their particular firm. As Sawtell points out: 'The most that can be said is that the employee shareholder will be more interested in, and better informed about the company's activity than the employee with no shares.'[44]

But *co-partnership* represents an advance on employee shareholding, being a more genuine attempt by management to divest some of its decision-making prerogatives. Moreover, the genesis of such programmes is a very different managerial ideology from those we have examined so far in this chapter. Thus, while in the main we have identified efficiency-conscious employers who have relinquished certain of their decision-making rights (and especially those of their colleagues at supervisory level) in exchange for greater co-operation from workers during periods of technical change, for higher output and productivity, and for improved labour–management relations, co-partnership programmes have only arisen when key directors have been guided by broader ideologies—sometimes of a religious kind—to sacrifice rather more of their personal authority.

By way of illustration it is useful here to concentrate on one firm, the John Lewis Partnership, in which the efforts of one such man, the son of the founder of the firm, were fundamental in shaping the nature of the resulting experiment.[45] The main aim of this organization is to bestow the benefits of ownership on all employees and to ensure the sharing of knowledge, gain and power.[46] Great emphasis has been placed on an extensive internal press which conveys items of information to the membership. The sharing of gain is facilitated largely by profit-sharing, the most important form being the partnership bonus

6

which is wholly additional to normal pay. And finally the sharing of power is made possible by means of a rather complicated system of representation. Thus, while the direct participation of all employees takes place in terms of the sharing of profits, representative institutions have been developed in this latter respect and therefore, for the first time, the distinction between direct and indirect participation is difficult to draw, principally because of the composite, all-embracing nature of this particular experiment. The main elected body is the central council which consists of about 140 members, and although the chairman can appoint up to one-third of the council, in general the proportion is usually rather less than this, partly because a great many managers are, in any event, elected on to the council itself. There are, in addition, several standing committees of the central council, including general purposes, ways and means, central claims, pay and allowances and unassured pensions. Moreover, these central arrangements are supported by a system of branch councils which are far less managerial in composition.

Such a fundamental change in formal organizational structure could not have been expected without the guidance of a coherent and influential ideology. Indeed, in the Partnership, this has been developed in a number of important publications[47] and is based on the premise of common ownership. Moreover, the ideology itself is so pervasive and its impact on managerial values so significant that the commitment of key managerial personnel can be observed to be commonly of a moral rather than of a calculative kind.

But while the Partnership itself is an outstanding commercial success, and the majority of its employees consider their working conditions to be significantly better than is usual in industry as a whole, there are some doubts as to whether rank-and-file workers have been very much affected by this ideology, and above all, so far as our general theme is concerned, whether they have genuine participation *in practice* in the decision-making processes of the Partnership. To be sure, the opportunities may be there, but whether these are taken up or not by individual workers depends on other important considerations and, indeed, as Flanders and his colleagues have pointed out:[48]

> Our attitude survey suggested that, for most rank and file workers, the general ethos of employment relations within the Partnership is not essentially different from that which prevails in employing organizations of a more usual kind. The facts of common ownership and accountability, and the ideology associated with them, are not powerful enough to break through the barrier of custom and beliefs which surround employment relationships in our society at large.

Again, as these authors have argued, the emphasis of the ideology is very much on 'government of the people' rather than 'government by the people', and the result is, of course, that there is a danger of paternalism here. Again, although many employees would prefer to work under conditions of benevolent paternalism than of arbitrary managerial authoritarianism, this can work against the development of 'pressure-group' democracy from below. So that, while Flanders and his colleagues judged it to be unreasonable to accuse the Partnership of any actual hostility to unionism, developments of this kind can have the effect of acting as a disincentive to employees setting up independent organizations.[49]

Moreover, in so far as managerial ideologies are concerned, the requirement that management must be accountable to the Partnership as a whole, in one view, may be a source of managerial strength. For if a manager can survive a more open environment, in which his authority is never buttressed by arbitrary decision-making powers over employees, his confidence in his own abilities may become correspondingly greater. Flanders and his co-investigators, writing of an emphasis on the high quality of managers, noted, too, the development of 'superiority complexes' among a number of senior personnel,[50] although to be sure, these feelings may themselves have served as mechanisms for the partial resolution of the conflict inherent in a manager who exercises power in an organization committed to power sharing.

Nevertheless, the difference between the moral commitment of management to the principles of the partnership and the more calculative orientation of the majority of employees does suggest certain implicit limitations in any participation programme, however well-intentioned and far-reaching it may be, that are based on value considerations alone. To be sure, it is clear that powerful ideologies among key members of organizations can lead to major changes in values towards participation and consequently to fundamental alterations in the formal structure of decision-making within the firm. But unless this is backed by the second element in our equation, namely the latent power of employees, its effects are likely to be rather more paternalistic than participative in character.

In principle at least, *commonwealth* schemes go somewhat further than co-partnership systems by ensuring both common ownership and the more direct participation of the workforce in decision-making processes of a policy kind. But the differences between such programmes may be exaggerated and, certainly, both clearly depend on the adherence to strongly-held convictions by their instigators. From the time when Robert Owen first set up his New Lanark community in 1816, there have been many isolated attempts to establish in industry principles of ownership and control which depart from the predominantly capitalist type. Nevertheless, being obliged to operate within an alien economic environment, many of these experiments have been short-lived. For, after all, unless the members of any given commonwealth operate within the terms of a market economy and, by so doing, of course, severely modify the principles on which their new work relationships are founded, it is very difficult to survive competitive pressures, however well-intentioned the experiment and enthusiastic its participants.[51]

A great many commonwealth experiments owe their origins to fervent religious beliefs although it is true that the predominant religious creeds of North America and Western Europe have been of little assistance to the cause of democratic work relationships. Protestantism, above all, has had a profound impact on industrialization and industrial development, but its special emphasis on individual achievement and self help has worked very much against the development of collective and co-operative industrial relations. Moreover, since the established Church has normally been content 'to render unto Caesar' and by so doing, by default, to accept and not infrequently to support the existing structure of ownership and control within industry, the general relationship (if one exists at all) between religious doctrine and secular behaviour has scarcely been favourable to workers' participation. But if this is the general pattern, there have also been many Christian social reformers who have called for changes 'in industrial ownership which will give workers the right to share in some measure in the fruits of their labour and to exercise some measure of control over the enterprises for which they work'[52] and the contribution of a number of Quaker employers has been especially noteworthy in this respect. In other words, on certain occasions, religious ideologies have been sufficiently strong to affect substantially the general climate of opinion at workplace level and to stimulate key managers to introduce major structural reforms in the nature of ownership and control.

The Scott–Bader commonwealth is a particularly cogent example, for, according to Blum, it owed its existence to the 'deeply religious inspiration' of Ernest Bader, a convinced Quaker and pacifist, whose beliefs led to the formation of specific attitudes about the nature of work relationships. By the same token the objections he raised to many of the fundamentals of the capitalist organization of work were, as related by Blum, as far reaching as those of any socialist:[53]

The reduction of all products, people and of nature itself to marketable objects; capital accounting rather than merely monetary accounting became dominant and the principles of sound finance ruled over all human considerations; the transformation of all flesh, mind, heart and soul into prices and costs; the subordination of one group under another group thus making people means for the purposes of other people; the neglect of the ethics of interpersonal relationships and hence the separation of people from each other and from any humanly meaningful purpose—rule of impersonal market forces over all and of personal authority over most people; finally a division of labour without balance and consideration of human values.

Poverty amidst plenty, communal impoverishment and public squalor amidst private affluence resulted from such a situation. Being was transformed into saleable commodities and true Becoming was stunted.

Against such a backcloth and to avoid the problem of 'participation in the administration of evil', Bader sought to establish a different order in which ownership and control were viewed as equally important. The commonwealth envisaged in 1951 incorporated common owner-ship, the development of new channels of participation, the divest-ment of the right to dispose of profit, the gradual transference of power to members of the commonwealth and a division of power into legislative, executive and judicial organs. The main legislative body was the *general meeting* and all members of the commonwealth could participate in administrative and judicial areas as well. Nevertheless, notwithstanding the provisions in the constitution for direct parti-cipation by employees, the founder members retained 10 per cent of shares and ultimate veto rights. Again, although there were many further opportunities to participate—especially in departmental meetings—it was clear that 'people with managerial responsibility or people from the laboratory participated more actively than factory and maintenance people'.[54] And this was particularly important in view of the fact that the greater security enjoyed by members of the commonwealth, by comparison with their colleagues in industry at large, militated against unionization. Moreover, in the interviews with rank-and-file employees, it was clear that the main advantages of the commonwealth were seen in terms of job security and only secondarily in the opportunities it provided for workers' participation in decision-making.

In 1963, however, Bader, who had initially opposed the idea of the commonwealth members having the right to appoint directors, was prepared to divest his authority further so that ultimate power would rest with members of the commonwealth and a wider body of trustees. This does suggest that, given a sufficiently strongly-held conviction in the idea, it is not impossible to promote a major transformation in the formal organization of work. But the outstanding obstacle to ventures of this kind is always their existence as 'islands in the sea of capitalism', for the danger lies in the neglect of technical–market criteria which can in turn herald a premature decline and closure of an otherwise valuable scheme. Moreover, to the extent that such a demise is not forthcoming, as in the successful Scott–Bader commonwealth, this implies some commensurate abrogation of principle. Blum, indeed, recognizes this: 'The central value of the organization—a concept of productivity defined in technical–market terms continues to exist but the implementation of the new purposes will at least make a dent in this concept.'[55] And this is a conspicuous departure from the early intention to effect a transformation in capitalist values and modes of organization in industry.

Furthermore, in so far as the ordinary members of the commonwealth are concerned, their ability to participate effectively may have been restricted by an absence of their own independent organizations. The tendency for members of the higher grades of commonwealth staff to participate particularly efficaciously in decision-making processes, and for the majority of 'employees' to view the benefits of the commonwealth in terms of job security would seem to provide some indications of this. In addition, as was the case with the John Lewis Partnership, the great enthusiasm for the project among senior management did contrast somewhat with the perceptions of the commonwealth among the rank and file.

Nevertheless, although this would seem to confirm that it is only when there is some consonance between latent power and values that truly effective participation can take place, supporters of the commonwealth could claim that certain dynamic aspects of participation are facilitated by schemes of this kind and that these substantially outweigh any losses for working people of their own independent organizational power. In particular, it may be reasonably argued that a management which freely conceded participatory rights, without an embittered power struggle, will in no way wish to frustrate the democratic process in practice; on the contrary, it will do everything to sustain and foster it. Then again, it may be pointed out that 'political efficacy' is enhanced through active involvement and that therefore it is better to set up participatory programmes of this kind and to reap the benefits of the 'dynamic effects of participation' rather than to await a time when workers are both strong enough and sufficiently concerned to seek active involvement themselves. In support of such claims, it is worth mentioning that Blum did indeed argue that certain *holistic* aspects of participation could be increasingly recognized in the commonwealth.[56] Thus, participation in the actual processes of decision-making was seen as one essential aspect of participation, but also important were relations with fellow workers, the wider work environment, the organization of work, the purposes for which this is organized, and the means used to achieve the goals of the organization.[57] In short, participation in a commonwealth venture may encourage a much broader subjective consciousness on the part of the employee and a fuller understanding of his own work role in relation to the wider purposes of the organization as a whole.

If this case were to be conceded *in toto*, it would of course provide the first serious challenge to our explanatory model of the genesis of effective participatory and control practices, since it would infer that 'idealistic' factors alone can account for the emergence of particular programmes, albeit rather untypical ones. Nevertheless, although cumulative effects can be expected from any developed participation programme (and this is accounted for in our model) there is still in our view sufficient evidence that participation is greatly affected by formal status within the occupational and administrative hierarchy to maintain our original confidence in the utility of our own theoretical analysis.

Indirect or representative participation

But at times, managements have turned to less direct forms of workers' participation which are equally applicable to our investigation into the exercise of power in industry at large. Moreover, since somewhat higher decision-making levels are entailed here than in direct participation, most managements can be seen to have sought even greater restrictions on the scope and range of issues discussed. Thus, they have generally been keen to ensure that ultimate powers of decision remain in managerial hands and have not infrequently demanded an embargo on a number of sensitive issues, notably on commercial, business and wages questions.

(1) *Joint consultative committees*

This has typically applied in the case of joint consultative committees which have been a characteristic feature of formal management–worker discussions in a great many British companies. Indeed, in several instances management has drawn a clear distinction between consultation and decision-making, the former involving frank and open discussions within advisory committees and the latter being the prerogative of management alone. Of course, these points of demarcation may be blurred in practice, and in any event are not adhered to by workers' representatives on such committees, but their existence seems to demonstrate that, on balance, the values of management are in general antithetical to participation especially at higher levels.

The history of joint consultation in Great Britain is by now well documented and it would be superfluous to attempt any lengthy review here. The following points are worth making, however. First, most formal consultative schemes are instigated by management: indeed, an investigation by the National Institute of Industrial Psychology revealed that nearly three-quarters of the joint consultative schemes had been set up by management alone.[58] Second, there is nevertheless a great variety of types of committee ranging from the purely advisory with agendas deliberately designed to avoid discussions of wages and related issues, to those in which shop stewards' organizations form the nucleus of workers' representatives and in which almost any matter may be brought up and concluded. Moreover, the nomenclature of such committees also varies, although works councils or joint consultative committees are commonly used. Third, joint consultative committees have been particularly prominent during periods when the organizational power of workers has been well developed and the climate of opinion favourable to co-operation rather than conflict. Thus, although a number of firms can trace their joint consultative machinery back to the nineteenth century, the most notable advances have followed the Whitley Committee recommendations in 1917 when the First World War was being fought; similarly, the growth of joint production, consultative and advisory committees was stimulated by the Second World War. It is worth mentioning, too, that unionism also flourished during these periods of international conflict, partly as a function of full employment but also because of the need for governments to court the union movement in a period of crisis. Joint consultation, however, suffered a major decline in the 'inter-war' period and, although post-Second World War conditions were favourable to the development of latent power among working people, and in particular to the extension of their rights to participation, the most important channel to emerge was the shop-steward system, since this was more suited to deal with conflicting interests at workplace level.[59]

It is therefore relatively easy to account for the principal trends in consultation in Great Britain during the present century in terms of changes in both the organizational power of working people and in prevailing values pertaining to social relations at work. But at the micro-level, it is also clear that the nature of joint consultative machinery is a particularly sensitive barometer of the organizational strength of workers and to the values which inform management–worker relations. Thus, although the relationship between collective bargaining and the shop-steward system on the one hand and joint consultation on the other is more appropriately dealt with in chapter 4, it is worth tracing certain of the main elements of the association between power and consultation at this point.

Now, if the term 'joint consultation' is interpreted narrowly as discussions of 'common interest' questions prior to a decision being made by management, it is clear that such committees cannot effectively survive strong shop-floor organization and workers' militant attitudes. Indeed, understood in this sense, joint consultation is in any event founded on a paradox, as, indeed, McCarthy has pointed out:[60]

> It is assumed that management should only agree to share
> responsibility on controversial and conflicting subjects, like wages; on
> non-controversial and common interest issues, like manning, it
> cannot do more than consult. So we reach a position in which it is
> suggested that agreements are only possible when the two sides are
> basically opposed; when they are really united there cannot be any
> question of agreement.

Moreover, from an empirical point of view, the association between the demise of the consultative committee and the organizational power of working people has been the subject of a number of studies. Derber, for instance, postulated that three factors affected the status of joint production consultative and advisory committees: union strength, the attitudes of management to personnel work and 'the extent of mutual confidence and goodwill'. Thus, the machinery was used least when unions were weak and when management paid little attention to personnel work. On the other hand, negotiating machinery was prominent when unions were strong, management production-minded and the relationship between senior stewards and top management antagonistic. Finally, advisory machinery was in operation when management was personnel minded.[61] Moreover, in the specific instance of the engineering industry, as Marsh has pointed out, the decline of joint production consultative and advisory committees is directly related to the rise in number and importance of shop stewards.[62] Again, in their study of workers' participation,

Clarke *et al.* found that the greater the degree of unionization, the greater the extent of joint decision-making. Managements in strongly unionized firms were ready to enter into consultation and negotiation with their employees, while in companies with low levels of unionization they tended to look to formal consultation as an alternative to negotiation.[63]

None the less, the relationship between power, values and joint consultation is probably rather more complex than at first sight appears obvious from the findings of the above studies. Thus, to begin with, the climate of values is shaped by members on both sides of industry and, therefore, although a personnel-minded management might be expected to encourage joint consultation, the preferences of workers for particular institutional arrangements are important considerations as well. Again, the fairly subtle relationship between social structural variables (and especially the latent power of workers) and aspects of social consciousness have seldom been satisfactorily developed in this context.

Turning, therefore, to a largely unpublished study of the relationship between power, consultation and participation in a number of Sheffield workplaces,[64] two further points may be made. First, the organizational strength of workers (and particularly the existence of joint shop stewards' committees) largely determines the *limits* of effective participation by employees at workplace level. But second, this aspect of latent power is not sufficient to ensure the transformation of joint consultative to negotiational bodies, for the degree of militancy among shop stewards is also of great significance. Thus, in only one out of four workplaces studied intensively had the classic pattern of 'the decline and transformation' of consultative machinery as a result of the emergence of shop stewards been evident. In this factory, a fully-fledged works committee (on which any issue could be brought up and concluded) had replaced the earlier JPAC. Moreover, the stewards here were particularly well organized, for, not only did a favourable ratio of stewards to members obtain, but a joint shop stewards' confederated committee had been established which had the effect of substantially reducing inter-union friction and rivalry. The stewards were strong at the value level as well: they were on the whole hostile to management, prone to interpret their role in activistic terms and to wish for a far greater say in decision-making processes.

In a second works, these developments were in progress, for a works council based on the shop-steward system had replaced an earlier consultative committee, but management still insisted on a ban on wage discussions and formally maintained the distinction between consultation and decision making. Interestingly enough, too, the stewards here were militant but operated in the face of organizational divisions among them which had the effect of reducing their latent power. In a third factory, where stewards suffered from weakness of organization and values, even though among hourly paid employees 100 per cent unionization obtained, a joint consultative committee was the workers' only channel of representation. This would suggest, then, that at certain levels of shop stewards' power, joint consultation may be actively fostered since management will probably seek some opportunities for dealing with emergent problems, but equally the stewards will be unable to insist on any other arrangements which are more suited to their particular interests. And finally, in the fourth workplace, joint consultative proceedings were more important than negotiational issues even though a dual system of representation had been established to cover both these contingencies. This was principally because, although the stewards were well organized, very few interpreted their duties in activistic terms. Indeed, only a minority wanted any further say for employees in decisions made by management (the only workplace where this was the case) and *no one* described his own duties in terms of active opposition to the employer in pursuit of workers' interests.[65] The status of joint consultative committees would seem, therefore, to depend on a rather subtle relationship between latent power and values in which neither, by itself, is sufficient to ensure a transformation of formal consultative structures. Once again, then, it is the interplay between social structure and social consciousness, between objective and subjective factors, and between latent power and values, which is so crucial to understanding and explaining particular 'participation' practices.

(2) *Specific committees covering productivity, welfare and safety, the administration of various trusts and funds, and so on*

One of the consequences of the development of human relations techniques in modern industry is that in some respects the relationship between management and worker has become more complex. Certainly the range of issues dealt with in many work contexts has grown substantially during the past quarter of a century and will continue to do so for as long as companies take over functions which might otherwise be performed by public bodies and institutions. But this means, of course, that the opportunities for workers' participation in these new areas have been extended as well, and, even if these have only a marginal impact on company policy as a whole, they are not necessarily without interest to the workforce itself.

Individual committees may pre-date the establishment of personnel functions with the firm. Thus, production and safety committees, which are usually made up of management and workers' representatives, have been a familiar if peripheral part of workplace industrial relations for a great many years. But a host of diverse arrangements only began to emerge as management began to take human relations policies rather more seriously; committees evolved to attend, among other things, to welfare, canteen and transport facilities, accident prevention and the administration of various trusts and funds.

To elaborate on the connection between the power of employees and the genesis of committees of this type would be to labour the point. After all, we have already seen that human relations policies generally and personnel work more specifically have tended to develop alongside increases in workers' power, and that therefore these various committees are very much a reflection of the general tendencies we have traced throughout this chapter. Nevertheless, productivity bargaining is a particularly interesting case in point and merits more detailed attention.

(3) Productivity bargaining

In some respects it is paradoxical to include productivity bargaining among managerial efforts to further workers' participation. After all, this form of bargaining offers management the possibility of reclaiming authority over areas which came under the control of particular groups of workers when their latent power markedly increased following certain economic developments in the 1950s and early 1960s. But from the workers' standpoint, certain advantages have accrued from this form of negotiation with management: the scope of some forms of representative participation, for example, has been extended, as has the stature of shop stewards on the plant. And yet productivity bargaining has been detrimental to workers' control over a number of shop-floor issues; its net effect has been a diminution in workers' participation and control of industry.

Interest in productivity bargaining became very marked in the late 1960s following the important lead given by management at the Esso refinery at Fawley, Southampton. Indeed, between 1967 and 1969 a total of over 4,000 agreements covering over 8 million workers were approved by the Department of Employment and Productivity.[66] Essentially, the main aim of such bargains is to ensure large increases in earnings in exchange for a more efficient utilization of labour. To this latter end, major relaxations of job demarcations, the withdrawal of craftsmen's mates, additional forms of shift working, and generally greater freedom for management in the use of its supervisory powers have all been characteristic components of any given productivity 'deal'.[67]

But while necessarily resulting in greater managerial control over the behaviour of workers and workgroups at shop-floor level, these bargains indirectly enhance the power of shop stewards too. Thus, taking the example of the Fawley productivity agreements, major changes in work practices had certain unforeseen consequences from a managerial viewpoint and especially the greater formality and lesser flexibility of the rules governing management–worker relations which prevailed after the agreements, and the growth in shop stewards' influence on union negotiations. In the first place, then, there was a marked disposition on the part of stewards to insist on the *letter* of particular agreements:[68]

> The unions were saying in effect 'a bargain is a bargain'. They adopted a measured attitude towards their obligations under the agreements and refused to give anything away they had not signed for. At the same time they were not averse to exploiting any loopholes in the working of agreements, and began to query customary practices accepted without demur before.

The greater formality of workplace labour relations which were consequent upon the introduction of this particular productivity bargain were in fact both a cause and a consequence of shop stewards' power. The existence of such agreements helped to foster the power of shop stewards since workpeople continually sought their advice on the implementation of particular rulings, but equally the stewards themselves were able to insist on such formality given their own bargaining strength. But the power of shop stewards was also heightened by virtue of their influence on union negotiations. Thus, prior to the agreements there was a clear-cut division between the provinces of shop stewards and full-time officials in their negotiations with the Fawley management. And although the former controlled the distribution of overtime, for example, and in annual wage negotiations their views may have been taken into account, full-time officers undoubtedly controlled the situation from the union side. However, since the agreements had the effect of linking pay with working practices, the effect was, of course, that the stewards began to have far more control over negotiations than had previously been the case. Moreover, because of the differential influence of this particular productivity bargain on individual workgroups, there was clearly a major realignment of forces at shop-floor level and, in the nature of things, workers affected adversely by comparison with their colleagues would seek the help of their stewards in an effort to rectify the situation.[69] And this, too, of course, served to promote the standing of shop stewards in relation to the processes of decision-making within the plant.

In many respects, however, it is the factors underlying management's ready countenance of these agreements in the last years of the 1960s, rather than the resulting modifications of workplace labour relations, which is of interest here. For, during the 1950s, most managements had tacitly accepted a great many informal workgroup practices which had effectively extended the workers' frontier of control over production processes and had, by default, presided over the growth of the shop-steward system and domestic bargaining more generally. But in so far as British industry is concerned, it is quite clear that the 1960s witnessed an acute decline in rates of profit and this therefore almost certainly provided the overriding stimulus for an offensive by employers on many hitherto accepted workgroup procedures.[70] Indeed, not only did productivity bargaining become important at this time but a number of simultaneous developments, such as measured daywork, reflected the increasing determination of managements to control effectively once more the processes of production at shop-floor level. That they were generally unable to do so, in any significant measure, helped, as we now know, to prepare the ground for the creation of the Industrial Relations Act, and when this in turn was found wanting, whenever workers were prepared to use to the full their considerable powers of numbers and organization, a new-found willingness among employers and government to involve workers far more in the decision-making processes of the firm was to emerge.

4 Workers' initiatives

So far, the evidence presented on a variety of experiments in participation has shown consistent support for the view that workers' participation and control ultimately develop from particular configurations of what may be termed the 'latent' power of the main industrial classes which, together with the values of those concerned, bear on whether there is a genuine match between these underlying conditions and the actual determination of decisions at workplace level. In this chapter it is hoped to extend this argument by examining a rich and interesting diversity of forms of workers' participation and control which have, by way of contrast with the examples studied above, originated largely from the initiatives of employees. Many of these practices have been established only after major struggles with the employing classes who have generally been hostile and antipathetic rather than merely indifferent to them. But once again, for classificatory purposes, it is useful to retain the distinction between direct and indirect or representative participation here and to summarize the main examples in figurative form (see Table 5).

TABLE 5 *Forms of participation and control initiated by working people*

Direct participation and control

(1) Control by craft-groups over hours and conditions of work
(2) Demarcation and control over 'job rights'
(3) Workgroup practices
(4) Producer co-operatives

Indirect participation and control

(1) Workers' control, syndicalism and industrial unionism
(2) Guild socialism
(3) Shop-steward movements and other plant-based systems of worker's representation
(4) Factory occupations, work-ins and take-overs

Workers' ideologies and values

Nevertheless, before examining these arrangements and the factors accounting for them, it is worth pursuing the issue of workers' ideologies and values in some detail not only because these relate to the central themes of this study but also because this has been the source of keen argument within the discipline of sociology itself. After all, it is recognized that one of the principal advantages of all dominant classes is their capacity to foster a climate of opinion which supports their hegemonic position. Moreover, even if for one reason or other those in subordinate roles are less than completely convinced by the resulting ideology and thus only partially legitimize the power of the dominant class, they are still a far cry from developing counter-ideologies and values which help to promote rather different interests and ideals.

The origins of values among working people are, of course, central to analyses of the nature of social classes and of their evolution in modern industrial societies. There is therefore a great deal of published material on this issue, but, not unnaturally, in much of this we find only limited agreement on the principal issues in question. The main controversy surrounding the nature of workers' ideologies and values stems from the work of Marx and Lenin, both of whom had profound misgivings about the ability of the great majority of working people, at least on the basis of their own efforts alone, to develop any clear understanding of their relation to, and of the workings of, capitalist economic systems. In their view, long hours of work and the division of labour reduced the opportunities for contemplative thought and for other than a fragmented and pragmatic form of consciousness. To be sure, by virtue of considerable workplace deprivation, as well as authoritarian relationships at plant level and the hardships inherent in an uncertain and unplanned economic order, working people were aware of their obvious economic and political subordination. But their solution to this dilemma was through 'combination' and the development of a form of 'trade union consciousness' which enabled them to resist the 'encroachments of capital' and to achieve certain limited ends within the confines of the existing economic system. This, according to Marx and Lenin, would always fall short of a systematic, thoroughgoing critique of a given system of production and productive relations.[1]

Further debates on the nature of working-class consciousness have of course continued apace over the years, and, on the face of it, a number of lines of inquiry have arisen in this context which might suggest the need for some modifications of our proposition concerning the origins of values with regard to the question of workers' participation and control. Nevertheless, as we hope to demonstrate, the great majority of proposals here can ultimately be seen to relate to the cornerstones of our own model, for there are important economic and technical forces observable which help to shape the general value framework and in turn, therefore, to account for many important aspects of workers' attitudes and behaviour. Moreover, although community factors, for example, undoubtedly have an effect upon the perceptions of work and of plant-level labour relations by the employees concerned, these, too, are reciprocally influenced by economic and technical considerations. And finally, the important interplay between 'objective' and 'subjective' variables is in any event, as we shall see, particularly evident in the discussions which follow.

In general, investigations into workers' values have been channelled in four principal directions each having important implications for the orientations of employees to the issue of workers' participation and control. These have been: first, that of workers' attitudes to trade unionism and to the legitimacy accredited to various union activities; second, that of 'orientations' to work which reflect community as much as work influences; third, that concerned with workers' 'images of society', and finally, within educational sociology, that which has focused on linguistic codes and the link these provide between social class, power, and perception.

In so far as workers' attitudes to trade unionism are concerned, the majority of these are clearly consistent with employees seeking to establish a measure of control over decision-making processes at work. Indeed, although circumstantial and situational considerations may well affect the particular pressures that working people will, via their unions, exert upon management, five clusters of attitudes can still be recognized in relation to the appropriate functions of trade unions and, by inference, the members' judgment of legitimate forms of union activity. These can be seen to be 'ideological', 'revolutionary', 'conservative', 'instrumental', and 'political' in nature.[2]

A great many workers are undoubtedly ideologically committed to trade unionism, seeing it as an expression of collective class interest, and emphasizing the 'moral' duty of all workers to belong to an appropriate union. Moreover, their philosophy is most often of a socialist kind and, in the words of Spinrad, they view 'work, workplace, workmates and working class' as constituting 'a very meaningful part of the union member's life'.[3] It is usual to assume that such an approach to trade unionism reflects a traditional proletarian consciousness

7

which is being continually eroded by the development of collective, instrumental orientations in which concern for pay and other fringe benefits have become paramount. Nevertheless, it is of interest to note that recent research in Great Britain has shown that a moral commitment to trade unionism is far more frequently held than is generally appreciated: indeed, in a Liverpool study it was the most common perception recorded.[4]

This particular conception of unionism should be distinguished, however, from the revolutionary view that unions should be part of the vehicle for overthrowing the capitalist system of production, if necessary by violent means. For here the research evidence overwhelmingly supports the claim of Marx and Lenin that the worker's 'trade-union consciousness' does not as a rule extend to formulations of this type.[5]

Among craft workers especially, a 'conservative' viewpoint is common, for as Perlman has argued, union members seek job security and the control of whatever limited employment opportunities are available and value union activities in the promotion of these ends above all.[6] The factors underlying such a disposition are partly economic, partly technical. Thus, by virtue of continual subjection to uncertain employment prospects—especially during periods of economic depression—working-class consciousness has in Perlman's view become shaped by the reality of 'scarcity of opportunities', although only craft workers have been able traditionally to protect themselves from this situation (and then not universally) by controlling employment opportunities, restricting the supply of labour into their particular trade, and by practising what Perlman calls 'communism of opportunity' among the members of the craft itself.[7]

It is commonly argued, however, that following a sustained and lengthy period of affluence, the development and maintenance of craft practices gradually lose their primary rationale; workers thus tend to become increasingly 'instrumentally-oriented', and are prepared therefore to relinquish such controls so long as the economic rewards were considered sufficient for their purposes. But, in so far as workers' attitudes to the primary functions of unionism are concerned, it is important to note that far fewer instrumental approaches have been identified than would be expected if this pattern were now dominant and, indeed, this was true even of the reasons given by a particularly affluent sample of workers for joining trade unions in the first instance.[8]

And finally, of special interest from our point of view, many workers have been classified as 'political' unionists in the narrow sense of emphasizing, above all, their desire for a greater measure of control over decision-making processes at work in order to ensure greater equity and justice and protection from the arbitrary and capricious exercise of managerial authority. Again, in Great Britain and even in the USA, remarkably strong support for this proposition has been evident in existing research studies.[9]

Clearly, therefore, the majority of these orientations to union activities are consistent with seeking extensions in the decision-making power of employees at workplace level. But it is interesting that different types of participation may be expected to be consequent upon these various perceptions. After all, for the 'conservatively-minded' craft worker the main aim is to maintain and if possible to extend *job* control, the question of higher-level decision-making therefore being *potentially* secondary. And while both 'ideological' and to some extent 'political' unionists would be expected to favour rather more ambitious proposals for industrial democracy, the 'revolutionary' unionist, by contrast, would tend to perceive any limited forms of control as scarcely worth while and potentially deflecting the activities of workers from their primary goals. 'Instrumentally-oriented' unionists might well reject workers' participation in management unless it could be shown to enhance a more effective pursuit of monetary rewards. But, in any event, it is not necessarily reasonable to assume that an emphasis on one particular union function automatically involves the exclusion of others and in sum there is, therefore, a great deal of material on workers' perceptions of unionism which suggests a backcloth of values conducive to a concern for greater participation and control over workplace decision-making processes.

The second line of inquiry on workers' values is addressed to the question of whether employees develop general orientations to work, and if they do so, whether these originate from community rather than factory influences.[10] This approach is, of course, ultimately based on the so-called action frame of reference in which special prominence is given to voluntarism rather than determinism in human action and to the ability of particular groups of workers to construct their own meanings and understandings of work roles and relationships independently, say, of the acknowledged constraints of economic and technical variables. And more specifically:[11]

> The individuals in the enterprise . . . are not simply a random collection but share rather in certain values and goals to which their involvement may be attributed in the first place, and whose sources must then clearly be sought externally to the enterprise.

Of course an argument of this kind could accommodate the effect of general values and ideologies within particular societies on the incumbents' orientations but, more importantly, it diverts attention to the importance of family and community influences. Where these encourage the pursuit of instrumental goals to the exclusion of other satisfactions, the commitment of workers to participation would then be expected to be minimal. And, indeed, some support for this view is undoubtedly to be found in the first of the affluent-worker studies where, of all occupational groups, only the craftsmen were at all concerned with seeking a greater say in decision-making.[12]

But without in any way wishing to become involved in a rather peripheral argument there are, from our point of view, a number of relevant issues raised here. To begin with, the authors of the affluent-worker studies were themselves careful to point out that they regarded their sample as prototypical rather than inevitably typical of the British workforce as a whole. It is quite consistent, then, for certain workers with distinctive and marked instrumental orientations to eschew participation even when the majority of working people seek extensions of their decision-making power. Second, instrumental goals are not necessarily antithetical to the achievement of other conditions such as flexible and more interesting work and greater participation, but rather may be consistent with the pursuit by workers of a number of strategies depending on circumstance and situation.[13] And, above all, when a growth in their latent power enables them to achieve a number of hitherto unattainable goals we may expect equally the so-called 'revolution of rising expectations' to bring certain additional bargaining areas on to the agenda. Moreover, the evidence points more and more to the important interplay between work and community; thus, to regard either as the principal source of workers' values is to present only a partial picture.[14] And finally, it is in any event worth mentioning that communities are themselves shaped by certain structural forces, notably economic and technical, which at the very least extend the range of 'value' options open to working people. Thus it is, of course, precisely the main economic changes of the post-Keynesian era which have facilitated the continuous pursuit of material goals, while a number of technical changes have sharply reduced the potential for the development of local cohesive communities. Thus, with technical advance, the number of workers employed in mining, shipbuilding, textiles and so on (and in their attendant communities) have been abruptly reduced, while with the rapidity of technical change, labour mobility has been at a premium and therefore the opportunities for developing stable communities somewhat restricted. Moreover, economic changes in the post-Second World War period have served to promote the process of urban renewal and its concomitant consequences for family and community relations. In other words, consistent with the view expressed in this study that there is an important reciprocity of influence between objective and subjective variables, it is clear that wider structural factors have affected the fabric of local communities and in turn the attitudes of employees to work roles and relationships. People ultimately shape their own ideas and values but the external constraints on this social choice should never be underestimated.

In any event, the question of workers' orientations and any association of these with assessments of participation ties in closely with the third line of investigation which bears on the issue under review; namely workers' 'images of society'. Now, in the attempt to designate middle-range propositions about human attitudes and behaviour the question of social imagery has been especially significant. The most noticeable statement here was that of Lockwood who, it will be remembered, identified three principal forms of working-class social imagery—traditional–deferential, traditional–proletarian, and privatized—in which social differentiation was seen to be based on prestige, power and money respectively.[15] Moreover, underlying these variations was a complex interrelationship between economic, technical and community factors.[16]

The first two images were seen to be encouraged by stable community structures and work relationships, thus, traditional–deferential imagery accounted not only for a Conservative voting pattern among certain working people, but probably emerged from small-scale workplace operations in which close paternalistic ties between employer and employee were enhanced, and which were backed by a clear status hierarchy within restricted local communities. But, by contrast, the traditional–proletarian image was fostered by larger-scale operations in which a clear separation between employer and employee had taken place, by high job involvement among the workers themselves and by homogeneous workers' communities. However, accompanying rapid changes in technology and rising material standards of living, further developments in workers' social imagery are to be expected, characterized by high rates of geographical mobility, increasing 'pecuniary' consciousness and the break-up of extended family and kin networks.[17]

Again, it would not be relevant to enter into any detailed critique and discussion of theoretical and empirical problems raised by this classification but it is worth emphasizing that, if these categories are valid, only *one* would seem consistent with working people pursuing greater participation and control at workplace level. After all, the traditional–deferential image involves the legitimation of an established hierarchical order and the privatized form of consciousness would seem to imply the rejection of participation for two main reasons; firstly, workers of this kind are dominated by a pecuniary model of class differentiation and, secondly, because their emphasis is primarily on *extra-plant* considerations. And although the traditional–proletarian image involves placing the question of power and its social distribution at the centre point of any wider structural analysis of society (we would therefore expect workers with such an image to be particularly concerned with control issues), this is presumably not only experienced by a small part of the working population, but might even be of *declining* significance if privatized and pecuniary images become increasingly important.

Of course, it may be that such social imagery is quite distinct from the workers' own assessments of the desirability of a greater share in workplace decision-making, but to the extent that there is a connection, it would be difficult to account for the emergence of interest in participation and control in the late 1960s and early 1970s. By contrast, however, rising levels of expectation brought about by factors which have stimulated the latent power of working people and which in turn favoured the development of a host of socialist, democratic and libertarian ideals would appear to be far more significant here.

If we turn, then, to a consideration of the evidence on the effects of participation in decision-making on value structures themselves it is clear first of all that there are dynamic consequences which predispose workers to seek further advances in their decision-making power. Valuable work on the development of linguistic codes, hitherto mainly contained within the study of the sociology of education, is of great relevance in this context. For it has become fairly clear from Bernstein's work that social class and power intersect at the point of language use,[18] that is to say, the emergence of elaborated codes by which people gain awareness of 'the possibilities inherent in a complex conceptual hierarchy for the organization of experience' (i.e. the capacity to develop truly effective ideologies and values) may well be confined largely to the middle classes precisely because in their own work roles they have a greater ability to manipulate and control events and thereby are able to see connections between them.

And, by contrast, the tendencies to pragmatic forms of consciousness and to more context-specific particularistic forms of judgment by working people (which had of course been commented upon by both

Marx and Lenin) may well be the direct consequence of genuine obstacles which prevent them from controlling events within work situations. That is, the denial to working people of 'the cultural capital in the form of symbolic systems through which men can extend and change the boundaries of their experience',[19] could be amongst the most fundamental and far-reaching effects of current distributions of power and authority at workplace level and may further circumscribe their capacity to develop general forms of 'social imagery' itself. Indeed, if this argument is correct, the more workers participate in decision-making processes, the greater will be their chances of understanding the nature of social class relations and of developing distinct orientations to work. Furthermore, the emergence of diverse forms of social imagery within workers' ranks would also seem to reflect variations in degree of control over work tasks and over other areas of decision-making. In all, therefore, the question of workers' values and their relationship to a desire for greater control over decisions at workplace and societal levels is exceedingly complex, not least because of a certain circularity implied by our recognition that these attitudes are themselves shaped, in part, by a lack of effective power-sharing among all members of the enterprise.

Direct participation and control

In our examination of some of the forms of participation and control initiated by working people, these considerations will again be raised from time to time. But our main aim is still to demonstrate the inter-relationship between external 'objective' forces and reciprocal responses of workers in accounting for the emergence and the success or otherwise of various efforts to enhance their decision-making powers, and here we will find, not surprisingly, that most types of *direct* participation and control have been somewhat restricted, developing mainly among workgroups. At the same time, several noteworthy exceptions to this general pattern may again be ultimately understood within the broad framework of latent power and values.

(*1*) *Control by craft groups over hours and conditions of work*

We have of course argued that technology is one of the most important variables to have affected the latent power of working people, but the relationship is fairly complex and involves, in the main, the consideration of four factors; first, the levels of skill required of working people; second, the consequences for managerial structures; third, a recognition that the integration of disparate work processes may lead to the creation of strategically-placed workgroups, and, finally, the realization that with the fragmentation and isolation of certain workgroups, the maintenance of external supervision is jeopardized and the establishment of self-governing workteams is a frequent but by no means inevitable result. Now although there are clearly technological constraints of some significance here, the organizational forms developed by working people themselves reflect the dynamic interplay between external conditions such as these and the employees' own definitions of the situations in which they are engaged, as well as the variety of meanings they may attribute to these technical factors and working conditions resulting from them.

Industrial sociologists have commonly argued, of course, that a broad evolutionary trend may be detected in the development of technology, and further that this has had radical consequences for the levels of skill demanded of working people. In the early stages of the industrial revolution, therefore, although large numbers of labourers were required, an equally high premium was still placed on *skilled production work* and hence on craft workers. In an intermediary stage, however, machines began to take over a great many tasks previously performed by skilled workers and the demand therefore became increasingly marked for semi-skilled machine operators and for assembly-line workers. And then in a further stage, in high-automated industries, skilled workers are again essential and form a substantial proportion of the labour force but their work tends to be of a *maintenance* rather than directly productive character.[20]

The opportunities for task-based participation and control practices are of course greatly encouraged at the two extremes of the technical scale, partly because of the difficulties experienced by management in recruiting a skilled workforce but also on account of the expertise of workers in these areas which makes close monitoring and measuring of activities difficult to organize. But in any event managerial structures are also extremely sensitive to technology and loose, 'democratic' styles of decision-making are seemingly encouraged at either end of the scale. Indeed, these so-called 'organismic' patterns of managerial control contrast with the tight, authoritarian or 'mechanistic' forms which typify middle ranges of technology and especially assembly-line conditions.

Woodward's demonstration of such a connection is obviously outstanding in this field,[21] but it is worth mentioning that, notwithstanding these objective constraints within the social organization of work, values are of great importance in this respect as well. An important study in the mining industry by Trist and his colleagues shed light on the different ways of organizing work within a given technical system, each of which had radical consequences for workgroup autonomy.[22] Thus, while they discovered, as might be expected, that the middle ranges of the technical scale tended to reduce the opportunities for workgroup control over production processes, the work itself could still be reorganized to reduce the effects of these objective constraints quite substantially.[23]

A third technical factor which enhances the latent power of workgroups and their prospects of influencing managerial decision making is clearly the increasingly complex integration of tasks brought about by modern technology. As a result, many workers have found themselves strategically placed to exert considerable pressure on employers not only for greater control of a task-based kind but also on the 'wages front'. But again, whether or not workers decide to use the latent power available to them clearly depends on a number of values adhered to by the workgroups concerned.

And finally, within extraction industries and other primary forms of production, it is usual for self-governing workteams to emerge largely free of immediate managerial control. In the mining industry, particularly, then, a whole host of workgroup practices have emerged such as the 'butty' system which left the distribution of wages in the hands of the men, and 'cavilling' in which lots were drawn in a formal ceremony to ensure that each workteam had an equal chance of working in either good or bad mining conditions.[24]

Skilled workers above all have been the main beneficiaries in this respect, though, to be sure, their relatively favourable position *vis-à-vis* their less-skilled colleagues can be understood partly in terms of the *prior* organization and controls that they were able to develop in the first instance. Many writers have sought to demonstrate parallels between these craft unions and the medieval guilds which protected workers from external commercial competition.[25] Nevertheless, as the Webbs pointed out, there is a fundamental difference between guilds and trade unions in that while under the former system workers sold their labour *directly* to customers, under modern industrial conditions, whatever the level of skill involved, workers serve an employer who stands between producer and customer and who has to extract from this relationship not only the 'wages of management' but also other emoluments for private capital.[26] But even under these more recent structural arrangements in which management has always sought to control working conditions and other aspects of the labour contract whenever possible, many craft groups have successfully opposed these restrictions. Indeed, they have been able at times, especially in the last century, to determine a great many aspects of their working conditions, not least their hours of work.[27]

It is, however, a matter of some speculation whether craft workers have remained highly skilled because of their ability to control entry into their particular trades and to maintain demarcation lines between them, or whether underlying technical factors have formed the principal source of their power. In the past, the closed character of craft unions was very much consequent upon conscious activities and policies of the workers concerned: indeed, they were difficult to replace precisely because of the 'restrictionist' craft policies they had so successfully pursued.[28]

(2) Demarcation and control over 'job rights'

These points are particularly well illustrated when we turn to examine the better-known aspects of control by craft unions over technical decision-making processes at work, for the variety of craft practices involved here is clearly both cause and consequence of the greater participatory role traditionally enjoyed by skilled workers in contrast with their less-skilled colleagues.

Since the advent of industrialism, economic insecurity has been a persistent hazard for working people and although with rising living standards and social security provisions this danger has been partially allayed, in recent times the increasingly rapid pace of technical change has been a source of further concern. Under such circumstances the desire to control job opportunities has been paramount but, on the whole, only skilled sections of the labour force have been successful in instituting necessary controls. Among these has been the establishment of *job rights* to be defended not only against encroachments by managements but also by 'dilutee' labour. This has been achieved, of course, partly through the enforcement of the apprenticeship system, which by virtue of the long period of training involved provides a disincentive to membership, and partly by recourse to demarcation. Here, individual crafts have ensured that their members will perform only certain tasks and will not encroach on the territory of others. Moreover, by insisting on the 'closed shop', i.e. the stipulation that union membership is a *prior* condition of employment, any potential division within the ranks of a particular trade can be satisfactorily overcome.

Craft workers have thus traditionally sought to control a particular job territory. Nevertheless, it is worth pointing out at this juncture that demarcation disputes frequently stem from managerial rather than workers' initiatives. In other words, when management seeks changes in work practices which upset the delicate balance of job controls, the main defensive mechanisms of these unions are brought into play. But between craft unions, constant attempts are made to reach agreement over which tasks are the appropriate responsibility of which craft group. Moreover, demarcational controls have usually been interpreted by managements as a prime example of a 'restrictive practice'—one, in other words, which prevents them from ensuring labour flexibility, the direction of particular groups of workers to given tasks and, within the constraints of a given technology, from successfully measuring the work of employees and thus from being able to effect the pace of work, the sequence in which particular activities are carried out, and so on. Again, such demarcational controls have been a major target of productivity bargaining which, as we have seen, represents an attempt by management to extend its own 'frontier of control' over shop-floor decision-making processes. Clearly, therefore, the relationship between technology and the opportunities of workers to exert a measure of job control is a complex issue, for there are important reciprocal influences of workers' organization and values, as well as of the determination of management to prevent such control over 'on the job decisions' being of lasting character.

(3) *Workgroup practices*

But the controls of craft workers at shop-floor level by no means exhaust all examples of direct participation that have arisen as a result of employees' initiatives because, even under less obviously supportive technical conditions, many working people have struggled to control certain aspects of their immediate working lives. Certainly the literature in industrial sociology is replete with accounts of workgroup practices, some of which have been consciously designed to reduce alienation effects at workplace level and all of which testify to the complex relationship between the external determinants of human social action and their mediation through socio-cultural values and action.

Of all the workgroup practices which are involved here, however, three main forms are particularly worthy of mention; first, various forms of direct action against machinery and machine processes; second, individual and group practices which modify the experiences of extremely alienating technical environments; and third, control over output which is particularly evident under piecework systems of wage payment.

Undoubtedly the most extreme, if somewhat untypical, form of workgroup control here is the direct attempt at machine breaking and other forms of industrial sabotage. This, as Eldridge has argued, may be usefully understood as a form of traditional social action in which change is actively opposed.[29] The most colourful instance of all was, of course, provided by the Luddites, but what is less well known is the opposition, for example, to the introduction of machinery in agriculture and the widespread public sympathy that, at times, this enjoyed. In 1830, for example, there were machine-breaking riots in East Kent which gained a great deal of support on the grounds that unemployed agricultural workers simply had to seek relief from the parish and that therefore the community benefits from technical progress of this kind were basically nil.[30] Moreover, it is by no means unusual for workers to resort to other, rather more limited, forms of action against machinery, as Coates for instance, has usefully recalled:[31]

> I was sent to a conveyor-head on the coal-face which was rather
> difficult to operate, since the seam through which the face was
> running was very thin and rather badly faulted. I arrived to find a
> lad sitting by the gear-head, wielding a seven-pound hammer. He had
> stopped the belt from running, and was carefully whacking at the
> metal tie-rod which joined two long sections of belt together. Raw, I
> asked him what he was doing. 'Won't that break the belt?' I said.
> 'What the hell do you think I'm trying to do?' he replied.

But militant direct action of this kind is probably less common than the development of 'solidary' workgroups which are concerned to extend workers' control over immediate work tasks. In mining and steelworking, in particular, a strong awareness of the dependence of the individual on his workmates is encouraged by manifestly dangerous conditions and this, in turn, is reflected in a number of controlling practices instituted by the groups concerned. We have already mentioned the 'butty' system and other workgroup practices in mining but among steelworkers there is an interesting form of control exercised over promotion within shop-floor jobs, for these are not decided upon by management but are determined entirely by the principle of seniority.

However, although the existence of such workgroups is undoubtedly dependent on technical processes as well as on the values of the workers themselves, even under relatively unfavourable technical conditions a number of individual and group practices have been recorded which demonstrate the determination of working people to modify even thoroughly alienating work environments. And this can be seen despite the tendency in the middle-range technologies—especially assembly line industries—for limited task-based participation to be reinforced by especially authoritarian managerial practices.[32] Many informal group systems, well illustrated by Roy, can be seen to ameliorate some of the tedium and boredom which are apparently inescapable in grossly repetitive work.[33]

However, the best-known instances of workgroup controls which have come more clearly into conflict with managerial goals have undoubtedly been associated with control of output. This has been especially noticeable under 'piecework' systems of wage payment, and indeed, as Eldridge has shown, the works of Marx, Weber, Taylor and other classical references demonstrate that workers had recourse to such practices in earlier eras.[34] After all, it is obvious that if, by increasing his output, a worker would have his 'rate for the job' decreased, he has an incentive, on 'rational' grounds, to produce no more than would be necessary to prevent such a contingency. But of even greater interest are the strong *workgroup* controls determining norms of output. In these circumstances an individual worker does not make an isolated assessment as to a 'fair day's work' and produce to this level but co-operates with a collective group decision on output. This arrangement, however, is inevitably a major handicap for management who could otherwise use the 'rate-buster' as a yardstick in assessing efforts and earnings of other group members. There is therefore a tendency for such practices to be labelled as 'restrictive', and except in favourable economic circumstances, for management reaction to be hostile.

Nevertheless, it is easy to overstate the prevalence of 'restrictive' practices in British industry. Indeed, in an attempt to discover their frequency, Clarke and his colleagues found that most managements either reported no experience of such difficulties or regarded them as insignificant.[35] It is, however, very important in terms of our understanding of power relations in industry that firms in which a closed shop operated (and this is of course a good indication of the organizational power particularly of skilled workers) were more prone to restrictions of this kind than other firms in the sample.[36] In accordance, therefore, with the main tenets of our argument, it would appear that the *successful* introduction of a number of important workgroup practices aimed at exacting a measure of control over the workplace environment is largely explicable in terms of the latent power of employees themselves.

(4) Producer co-operatives

Producer co-operatives, of course, reflect far more ambitious aspirations than the workgroup practices examined so far and they spring not from spontaneous actions at shop-floor level but from coherent ideologies about industrial organization. And yet, as is our view expressed at a number of points in this study, idealistic forces alone are not conducive to lengthy and sustained periods of workers' participation and control. It is scarcely surprising, then, that producer co-operatives, which have been insufficiently grounded in the latent power of working people and further have had to operate in an economy dominated by market considerations, have seldom been of lasting significance.

The first attempt to join together consumers and producers was instituted by the Rochdale pioneers, but despite the undoubted success of consumer co-operatives and notwithstanding the world-wide diffusion of these ideals, the history of producer co-operatives has in the main been disappointing. To be sure, in Great Britain alone there are still about eighteen manufacturing societies affiliated to the Co-operative Productive Federation but these clearly represent only a small fraction of British manufacturing industry.[37] Indeed, it has been in agriculture rather than industry where co-operative principles have been applied with rather more sustained and lasting effect, a situation evident from examples in many parts of the world ranging from the Israeli kibbutzim to the Russian kolkhozes.

Co-operative productive manufacture is usually based on three main principles; first, employees are co-owners of the enterprise; second, they may be nominated for any management board; and third, they share in the profits.[38] Not only, therefore, is some provision usually made for decisions of a policy nature to be taken by employees, but also in so far as the questions of ownership and dividends are concerned, the employee is clearly the prime beneficiary.[39]

But despite their ability to dispense with non-working shareholders, the great majority of producer co-operatives have been small and restricted ventures. Moreover, since the Second World War, regardless of the possibilities of obtaining capital loans under generally buoyant economic conditions, very few societies have been initiated, the dominant reason for this being, according to one reviewer, that these societies 'have paid insufficient attention to managerial development'.[40] More strictly, it could be maintained that in a sea which is predominantly capitalist, islands of producer co-operatives have found it extremely difficult to expand or to develop

—indeed, they have been hard put to it to survive at all—for certain external market criteria have to be pursued above all other considerations if an expanding and thriving enterprise is to be preserved. Again, unlike the various workgroup practices examined in the previous sections, producer co-operatives bear little if any relation to the latent powers available to working people, and therefore there has been no real opportunity for the workers concerned to insist that particular practices be maintained despite managerial hostility or adverse market situations. And ideological conviction is, as we have argued, insufficient to sustain particular organizational forms—at least for any lengthy period—unless there is some pronounced supporting power base. This point, moreover, will be amply illustrated in the following examples, which cover a number of ambitious attempts by working people to direct and control their own working lives in ways which directly oppose the principles of capitalist ownership and the distribution of resources on the basis of market criteria.

Indirect or representative participation

More generally at this point, then, a review of the forms of representative participation initiated by working people brings to light a number of examples based on the highest of human ideals and founded upon a catalogue of embittered struggles. Throughout history, Utopian thinkers have argued passionately the feasibility of other forms of social and economic organization from those which commonly obtain, and have proposed that these be founded on mutual co-operation for the social good, with the respective talents of all men and women being released and developed to the full in an unconstrained and non-exploitative association with their fellows. To be sure, it has also been recognized that in large-scale complex societies with advanced organizational arrangements, some system of representative participation would be necessary to bring these ideals to fruition, but this being so, it has nevertheless been argued that the social distinctions within organizations could be minimal, the possibilities of accountability optimal, and the ratification of any policy decision still be subject to the 'will of the people'. Moreover, in the twentieth century, if technology were developed to assist in this process, advances in communications systems could promote participatory democracy to a hitherto unforeseeable stage.

(1) *Workers' control, syndicalism and industrial unionism*

The generic term 'workers' control' has been used to cover a number of different practices but common to them all has been the ideal of replacing 'the capitalist industrial system by a new industrial order in which the industries of the country will be controlled (partly or completely) by associations of the workers employed in those industries'.[41] Certain proposals therefore are clearly excluded by this definition, notably the suggestion of joint control within a predominantly capitalist industrial order and the relatively limited craft and work-group practices examined in our earlier sections. None the less, differences of opinion have arisen over the shape of workers' control; thus, while for some this is largely a revolutionary concept designating a system of workers' and soldiers' committees to be used as a basis for social transformation, others have sought more lasting ventures in which the scale of industrial operations has been limited to self-governing and largely headless or *acephalous* organizations by which to ensure that any representatives are *also* working people. Again, in other formulations the indispensability of *management* in any advanced industrial order has been argued but attempts have been made to ensure its ultimate accountability to the workers employed in any given concern. And finally, the precise role of State, consumer, and party systems within a given socio-political structure of this kind has been a perennial source of disagreement among those broadly committed to the workers' control movement itself.

Although the late 1960s and early 1970s have undoubtedly witnessed a re-awakening of interest in workers' control, the heyday of the movement was considerably earlier, in the years between 1910 and the beginning of the 1920s when a variety of schemes of this type were suggested and implemented. The underlying economic conditions at this time had varied effects. Thus, on the one hand, a war economy fuelled full employment which, in itself, stimulated the power of working people and, by encouraging workplace co-operation and organization, also served to enhance their bargaining strength. But the productive forces in the economy were distorted by the war effort so that, particularly towards the end of hostilities, there were chaotic production difficulties and major shortages of basic commodities, especially severe in Eastern Europe. This situation was thus conducive to the growth of workmen's organizations but at the same time provided no real means for satisfying their emerging demands. Moreover, widely-shared sympathy for the inevitable victims of the war itself gave rise to widespread mistrust of the political and economic orders which had spawned such a catastrophe. In short, people from many different social origins were disposed to look favourably on a rich variety of radical and revolutionary movements.

The events leading in 1917 to the success of the Bolshevik Revolution and to the similar but abortive attempt in Germany in 1918 are, of course, historically the most outstanding of the era. Moreover, the very success of the Russian revolution was seen as in some measure consequent upon the system of councils of soldiers, workers and peasants as a means for transferring all power in the State into the hands of the proletariat. Of course Marx's concept of 'the dictatorship of the proletariat' has caused a great deal of confusion in this context since it can be interpreted either as a support for authoritarian methods of government, or, and in view of Marx's own enthusiasm for the Paris Commune, perhaps more likely, the dictatorship of the proletariat over other classes in society while allowing for the democratic methods of organization within the working class itself. And, indeed, E. H. Carr in his review of the Bolshevik Revolution certainly suggests that the latter conception was usually held by the early revolutionaries:[42]

> The emotional overtones of the word 'dictatorship' as associated with the rule of the few or of one man were absent from the minds of Marxists who used this phrase. On the contrary, the dictatorship of the proletariat would be the first regime in history in which power would be exercised by the class constituting a majority of the population.

But whatever the correct interpretation, it is interesting to note the long history of the use of councils as organs of revolutionary movements. Around the time of the English Civil War, for example, the levellers' movement was based on an association of soldiers' and citizens' councils. Moreover, in the commune period in the French Revolution, councils of citizens were formed, though to be sure they revolved around working people less than in' the case of the Paris Commune of 1871.[43] Soldiers' and workers' councils, too, were formed in many parts of Germany in 1918, while a similar type of organization was adopted by republicans in the Spanish Civil War. Again, to take a more recent example, following the cultural revolution in China, the predominant mode of factory organization was for a time essentially of this character.[44]

Of course, although the distinction is not always plain, it is important to differentiate between workers' council systems used as a temporary measure during revolutionary societal transformation, from those envisaged as a permanent aspect of economic and industrial administration. Moreover, examples of the latter kind which may be usefully examined at this point had, as Pribićević has argued, at least

8

three main variants during the 1910s—syndicalism, industrial unionism and guild socialism[45]—although, because the third took a rather unusual position with respect to the role given to consumer interests, we have thought it preferable to include it under a separate heading.

The main aim of both syndicalists and industrial unionists was to organize economic production entirely on industrial lines:[46]

> The industrial organization would therefore become the foundation of the whole social structure, and industry would be under the full control of the workers' industrial organizations. This was the only way to obtain full economic freedom and equality. State ownership and control of industry was hardly less obnoxious to them than capitalist ownership and control.

Initially, syndicalism appeared to be synonymous with unionism but late in the nineteenth century in France it began to take on a new meaning under the guidance of Pelloutier,[47] and then became associated with the idea of producers' control and of a co-operative commonwealth built up from locally strong and self-governing productive units. Moreover, provision was made for conflicting interests among producers to be settled locally in the *Bourse du Travail*.[48] To be sure, the syndicalist movement was never so strong in Britain as in France but in the 1910s it nevertheless had considerable momentum. Indeed, this prompted the establishment of an influential journal *Industrial Syndicalist* under the guidance of Tom Mann, at this time the principal exponent of British syndicalism.[49]

While sharing the common assumptions of producers' control and the undesirability of all forms of bureaucratic State machinery, industrial unionists differed from syndicalists on a number of questions, particularly those directed towards existing trade unions and the use of political parties. Thus, whereas for the syndicalists party politics were considered a waste of time and even inconsistent with their ultimate ends, the industrial unionists thought it necessary to vote into power a socialist party to prevent the machinery of the State (and especially the armed forces) being used against working people. On the day, however, when the socialist party was elected, the industrial unionists planned to lock out the employers and take over industry, and, once this had been achieved, the need for Parliamentary political representatives would in their view be ended and the State would therefore wither away.[50] Moreover, industrial unionists defined the existing unions as reactionary organizations, and, by contrast with the syndicalists, sought quite new union structures outside the existing framework.

Industrial unionism was strongest in the USA, where the Industrial Workers of the World (the 'Wobblies') were effective from 1905 to 1924, directing their efforts towards the combination of the American working class and, ultimately, all wage earners into one trade union which would overthrow the employing classes and establish a workers' commonwealth. They never attracted more than 5 per cent of all trade unionists in America but between 1917 and 1918 their leading members were savagely dealt with in the American courts and the movement as a whole was to throw up a number of labour heroes, none greater than their leading poet Joe Hill whose immortal last words, 'Don't waste time mourning. Organize,' are of course legendary.[51] In Britain, however, industrial unionism was largely confined to the Glasgow area and a number of other Scottish centres and was far less important at this time than the shop-steward movement or, indeed, than syndicalism and guild socialism.[52]

The period from 1910 to the early 1920s thus witnessed some development of workers' control but, more recently, the issue of workers' control has yet again become a dominant theme in labour and trade-union circles. Again, this activity has its roots in a number of sources to which we have drawn attention throughout, notably the accretions in workers' power after years of depression and the escalation in the expectations of ordinary people on the fulfilment of 'lower order' needs. In some fundamental respects, however, recent proposals deviate from the doctrines current earlier in the century, and should be mentioned briefly here.

There are several schools of thought in circulation at the moment which bear on the question of workers' control but in terms of ownership, the role of trade unions, the nature of management, and the contemporary organization of industries which is increasingly in the hands of supra-national companies, many of the modern theories diverge from previous dogmas. Thus, most existing proponents of workers' control start with the assumption that the public ownership of the means of production is a necessary prerequisite for democratic industrial relations, but they are, on the whole, opposed to the wholesale ownership of modern industry by working people alone, for such an arrangement would be excessively atomistic in the complex economic system which prevails today. Moreover, trade unions are credited with a role far more central than that envisaged by industrial unionists. Thus, Coates and Topham in their work *The New Unionism*, have urged powerful democratic unions in Great Britain to press urgently for policies of workers' control, so that part of the impetus for such developments would stem from the official labour movement itself.[53]

To be sure, in certain cases, the prior democratization of the governing structure of unions might be seen to constitute a necessary preliminary, but workers' control is now seldom seen as the alternative to effective trade unionism. Furthermore—and this is the third important departure by modern theorists of workers' control from those of an earlier period—the term 'self-management' is customary in this context. Thus, within the parameters of a planned economic order it is envisaged that workers would control the general policies of the enterprise but that it would require a democratized managerial structure to bring this into effect. In short, in this conception, the notion of self-governing, acephalous institutions is incompatible with the large-scale organizations of the modern era. And lastly, present-day arguments for workers' control have had to pay regard to a situation in which many companies operate on a multi- or supra-national scale of operations. There is a growing recognition, too, that greater inroads into managerial prerogatives will, in these circumstances, have to rely on corresponding alliances between members of the labour movements of the countries affected by these multi-national activities.

Naturally, the ultimate fate of these contemporary movements remains to be seen, but for analytic purposes it is important to note that these emerged with fresh and increasing vigour in the late 1960s and 1970s and have been part of a general process of disenchantment with prevailing patterns of domination. In this climate it is hardly surprising that the conversion of some managements to participative arrangements should have also been a catalyst for radicals whose aims were rather more ambitious.

(2) Guild socialism

The theory and practice of guild socialism differed considerably from some of the other examples of workers' control which we have examined in this chapter so far. In some respects it was a more 'idealistic' movement, which was grounded in coherent humanitarian and socialist ideologies and was less a spontaneous outgrowth from the ranks of working people themselves. Moreover, because of the academic sophistication of its leading exponent, G. D. H. Cole, the precise influence of producer, consumer and societal interests within the guild-socialist system was carefully balanced and spelled out. But the guild movement, like many other forms of workers' control, was ultimately to meet the fate common to most of the 'idealistic' practices to have emerged from the womb of a predominantly capitalist economic order and, despite the temporary success of the building guilds in particular, it was not to be a lasting feature of the British industrial landscape.

The guildsmen attempted to marry syndicalism and socialism; thus on the one hand its exponents endeavoured to ensure that a collective State apparatus would not emerge, but on the other they sought to prevent consumer interests being threatened, a possibility, of course, if the means of production are controlled entirely by producers at local levels. Their ideal method for achieving these twin aims was through the development of national guilds and a series of representative bodies at regional and local levels built up from a basis of shop, works and district committees.[54]

Now G. D. H. Cole's work, *Self-Government in Industry* is, as Corina has argued, 'essentially a manifesto on the rights of man in industrial society',[55] and it is also the best-developed documentation of the guild socialist philosophy and is self-consciously passionate and idealistic in spirit. 'No movement,' wrote Cole, 'can be dangerous unless it is a movement of ideas.'[56] He went on:[57]

> Often as those whose ideals are high have failed because they have not
> kept their powder dry, it is certain that no amount of dry powder
> will make a revolution succeed without ideals. Constructive idealism
> is not only the driving force of every great uprising, it is also the
> bulwark against reaction.

Guild socialism in fact endeavoured to give workers control of the factories in which they were employed, but the State, in this view, should own the means of production and the guild should control the work of production.[58] Moreover, and this was critical to the theory, political and economic power had to be divided to protect individual freedom while, in addition, consumer interests had to be safeguarded. In other words:[59]

> The workers ought to control the normal conduct of industry; but
> they ought not to regulate the price of commodities at will, to
> dictate to the consumer what he shall consume, or, in short, to exploit
> the community as the individual profiteer exploits it today.

The guild socialist solution to these joint problems of central control and consumer exploitation was, then, division between the functions of the State as the representative of organized consumers and the trade unions as the representatives of the producers. Such a framework would, therefore, give workers considerable influence over general economic, political and social policies. Cole also spelled out the way in which the process of production could be administered at local levels, and did in fact anticipate the existence of managements but argued that they should be controlled by the workers employed in particular establishments. Thus foremen would be elected by ballot of all the workers in his particular shop and a similar procedure would obtain in clerical departments. Again, the works manager would be elected by ballot of all workers on the 'manipulative' side of the works with the same principle again holding within clerical departments. And finally, the general manager of the works would be selected by the works committee, which was in turn elected sectionally by ballot of the members in each shop.[60]

But despite the powerful idealism of the guild socialists, their successes were generally short-lived. To be sure, in the 1918–21 period in particular, the miners and railwaymen had adopted modified versions of guild socialism, and the builders and post-office workers were fully committed to this philosophy. At the outset, moreover, the building guilds met with a considerable measure of success despite obstruction from government officials and the tactics of 'profiteering employers'.[61] Indeed, building guilds became especially strong in the Manchester area where the municipal authority had been approached with an offer of building 2,000 houses.[62] The quality of work carried out by the guilds was also undeniably good.[63]

The guildsmen thus began to be confident of their ultimate success. They announced that 'the theory of the necessity of capitalism' had 'passed painlessly away' and in all they formed about sixty local building guild committees. The idea also spread to Ireland and to the USA and further attempts were made to form guilds in New Zealand.[64] But by 1922 the guild movement had virtually ended and the explanation for this, amply documented by Postgate, lay primarily in economic conditions and the effect that these had on the balance of power between the main industrial classes:[65]

> With the change in industrial conditions, the slump which again put the operative in a position of weakness as against the employer, the fair-weather Parliament and Guild disappeared. The first blow to the Guild was the cessation of the official support given to it by the Ministry of Health, and the abandonment of the Government housing scheme, which gravely affected building as a whole. As trade conditions got worse, the Guild found itself in financial difficulties, as all such experiments in time must, through business inexperience and its capital commitments being too small and its commitments and enterprises too large.

With the benefit of hindsight, G. D. H. Cole was later to re-analyse the experience of the guilds and to trace a number of problems which bear directly on the principal theoretical themes of this study. Thus, with respect to the theory of guild socialism, Cole considered that insufficient attention had been paid to the higher ranges of control in the economic system and especially to the problem of investment. But in so far as the lack of success of the guild movement was concerned, economic conditions apart, there were two further problems; the first, a question of values, and the second, a function of technology. In the first place, then, adherents of the doctrine of workers' control were very divided between the revolutionaries, who, following the success of the Bolshevik Revolution, sought a structural change in society on the Russian model, while the left-wing reformists wanted to build on existing institutions. The result was a great deal of confusion over both the means and the ends of the movement itself. But, in any event, in Cole's view the guild socialists were 'kicking against the pricks', since the development of large-scale organization—which was, of course, brought about by technical changes within the industrial system— tended to nullify the prospect of smaller productive operations envisaged by the leading advocates of this movement. That is to say, the guild socialists' weakness 'was that they never faced the funda- mental problems of power and of large-scale organization and planning'.[66]

Nevertheless, Cole was optimistic that future changes in techno- logy would provide a much more fertile environment for the construc- tion of new social relationships in industry, since with full automation smaller groups of people would be needed and this would make possible 'a more human kind of factory control'. Moreover, he cer- tainly kept his faith with a particular socialist vision which had provided the ideological basis for his commitment to industrial democracy and, indeed, argued that:[67]

> Socialism cannot be soundly built except on a foundation of trust in the capacity of ordinary people to manage their own affairs—which requires methods of management on a scale not so large as to deprive them of all possibility of exercising any real control over what is to be done.

(3) *Shop-steward movements and other plant-based systems of representation*

In British industry, the shop-steward system has undoubtedly been the most permanent and durable form of workers' participation using a representative framework. Once again, while economic, technical and governmental factors have had a role to play here, consistent with our own thesis, the *values* of stewards and their constituents can be seen to have been fundamental too, not only in shaping particular orientations to their own duties but also in their effects on the character of this distinctive and fascinating form of workers' participation in industry.

Of all the flirtations with workers' control in the 1910s and 1920s none was more fruitful than the shop-steward movement, and its subsequent evolution has indeed closely reflected the ebb and flow of economic and technical forces. The first movement was thus primarily associated with the engineers, those archetypal craftsmen who had built on the basis of a major technical power resource to establish a firm position among the aristocracy of labour. But the exigencies of wartime prompted the government to intervene in the munitions industry, to promote labour flexibility, and to pave the way for the 'dilution' of craft skills by employing semi-skilled and female labour. This was achieved via the Treasury Agreement and was to strike at the fundamentals of the engineers' power.[68] In such circumstances, some struggle to preserve the privileges of a craft position was to be expected, but there were also a great many craftsmen—notably J. T. Murphy—who saw the potential for building an entirely new type of bargaining structure which contained in it the germs of a revolutionary transformation of society.[69]

The First World War had stimulated a growth in union members but, for the most part, union structures remained firmly based on extra-workplace branches. This, however, was a most unsatisfactory arrangement for the engineers affected by the Treasury Agreement and therefore, once they recognized that a struggle against the dilution of craft privilege would be doomed to failure in a war economy, they began 'to break down divisions between craftsmen and less-skilled workers, to develop an industrial policy which united the interests of the two groups, and to construct all-grades organization in the workshops'.[70] In short, they realized that it was only through workplace-based organization that sufficient control over the new arrangements could be maintained at workshop level.

But in any power struggle the nature and the direction of any encounter are contingent to some degree on the values of the parties involved. Once their craft position had been challenged, the engineers might have found in the shop-steward system a device merely for maintaining craft privileges by ensuring that, at workshop level, any non-apprenticed workers were kept firmly in check by the skilled workers in the shop concerned. That it took a far more revolutionary course based on the ideal of workers' control was a reflection of the commitment of the participants in this particular struggle. Indeed, the ideological mainspring of the shop-steward system as it gradually evolved at this time was firmly 'based on the theory of class struggle, the abolition of capitalism, the complete re-organization of trade unionism and workers' control of industry.'[71] In *The Workers' Committee*, published in 1917 by the Sheffield Workers' Committee, Murphy advocated means for bringing these principles into effect. The basic unit of organization was the workshop committee composed of shop stewards elected by workers in specific workshops which were to be supplemented by local industrial committees in each district. The next step was to unite all the stewards in each firm by means of works or plant committees and at the same time to establish local workers' committees. And then the final tier was to consist of national industrial committees and the national workers' committee which would presage revolutionary societal change.[72]

But in the eventual evolution of the shop-steward movement, only the preliminary steps of this process were effectively accomplished: although the engineers none the less in this way laid the foundations for a new and lasting organization of the workshop which was distinct from the wider union hierarchy and, in particular, facilitated the collective action of workers in a number of different unions in a given workplace. However, only on the Clyde in 1915–16, and later in Sheffield, did truly effective local workers' committees become established.[73]

Moreover, it is obvious, in retrospect, that Murphy's ideas were industrial in character, and that his analysis largely ignored wider political issues. This having been said, it remains paradoxical that, on turning their attention away from industrial organization to political organization following the success of the Bolshevik Revolution, the shop stewards took a crucial step towards the weakening of their main power base at workplace and local levels. But the ultimate demise of the movement occurred later, in 1922, when, with worsening trade conditions, the employers were able to lock out the members of the AEU and to reassert completely the principle of the employers' 'right to manage their establishment'.[74] However, the early shop-steward movement did at least set the scene for an influential workplace representative structure which was to re-emerge with fresh vigour in the post-Second World War period.

The depression years witnessed a fall in union numbers and the development of a collective bargaining system in which the role of the full-time officer was again supreme. But by the 1950s the phenomenon of wages drift began to be understood: that is to say, full employment and a buoyant economy had meant that, at local levels, workers could obtain higher wage rates than those officially negotiated and the importance of the shop steward in this process of domestic bargaining began to be recognized. Thus, in the 1960s, a steady increase in the number of shop stewards was recorded, to the extent that in 1968 the Royal Commission inquiries suggested that there were probably about 175,000 stewards in British industry and that this represented an increase of about 14 per cent over ten years.[75]

But today the decision-making powers of shop stewards at work-place level vary considerably so that although the overall economic climate has provided a basis for augmenting workplace-based union activities, other factors help to explain differences in the degree of influence wielded by shop stewards *per se*; principal among these are technical circumstances and the values of the stewards individually and as a group.

Two technological characteristics have an effect on the workshop organization of stewards, namely the size of the undertaking and the levels of skill demanded by given technical processes. The strong association between the degree of industrial concentration and the propensity of workers to join unions has been well documented and requires little amplification here. But it is worth remarking again upon the greater propensity of skilled workers than their colleagues to join unions and to participate in decision-making processes at work-place level. Indeed, we have referred above to Goldthorpe and his colleagues' revelation that the majority of craftsmen in their sample sought greater control over decision-making by contrast with most of the less-skilled workers whose enthusiasm for participation was far more muted.[76] Further, skilled workers tend to have better shop-floor organization—the average constituencies of their stewards, the con-stituencies of senior stewards and the average number of hours expended on union activities all compare favourably with their colleagues in general unions which lack any firm craft basis.[77]

None the less, it is also evident that stewards themselves interpret their duties in a number of ways and that these orientations circum-scribe not only what they consider to be legitimate activities but also may affect the range and scope of issues with which they are involved in the bargaining process. In this respect, for example, our own small-scale research in the Sheffield region highlighted certain points of difference between the definitions adopted by stewards towards their duties. Broadly speaking, we were able to identify four principal types of steward in this context, namely the 'activist', the 'union man', the 'representative' and the 'dispute solver'. Each of these groups emphasized one aspect of the steward's responsibilities to the comparative neglect of others. Only activists were of the opinion that it was reasonable to promote the interests of their members to the full. The union men interpreted their role more in terms of the policing of union agreements; the representatives, on the other hand, recognized their responsibility as spokesmen for the shop, but only in circumstances which concerned their members; and finally, the dispute solvers were essentially management-oriented and understood their obligations in terms of 'smoothing-out' local difficulties and problems.[78] Moreover, the importance of the values of shop stewards in shaping their interest in particular types of issue has already been examined when the status of joint consultative machinery at workplace level was reviewed in some detail. And here, of course, it was noted that not only organizational strength but also the values of stewards were important in explaining the decline of formal consultative committees and their replacement by more fully participative, bargaining structures.

Naturally, several attempts have been made to map out the range and scope of issues with which shop stewards are concerned at workplace level and these clearly merit consideration of this point. The work of the Royal Commission, for instance, included an assessment of the stewards' range of bargaining in British industry and revealed that while nearly three-quarters of the sample discussed and settled working conditions as a standard practice, this proportion was reduced to just over one-half for wages questions and even less for discussions on hours of work, discipline and employment issues.[79] But these data have been supplemented by evidence from a more recent investigation in which the scope of shop stewards' decision-making powers were examined, and in which particular attention was paid to the areas where a degree of unilateral control was exercised by the stewards involved. In consequence, this study was able to disclose that over 70 per cent of managements included in the sample were not free to organize the workforce as they wished, and this is of course a good indication of the ability of shop stewards to encroach on so-called managerial prerogatives. But, in addition, the principal areas in which unilateral control was exercised included labour mobility, manning of machines, job demarcation, hampering work study, resistance to dilutees and union demarcation.[80] And this evidence undoubtedly helps to shed light on the precise impact of shop stewards on the decision-making processes of the firm as well as to confirm the extensive role played by shop stewards in British industry.

However, before concluding our section on shop stewards, it is worth tracing briefly the relationship between the shop-steward system, participation, collective bargaining and consultation since the terminology involved here has led to a great deal of confusion. To begin with, then, the growth in power of shop stewards has undoubtedly had marked effects on the system of collective bargaining in Great Britain, for, on the one hand, not only is a dual structure of collective bargaining now evident in which national agreements between full-time union officers and their counterparts in management and employers' associations are supplemented by domestic bargaining by shop stewards, but also, in the process, the range of issues over which it is considered appropriate to reach agreements has been extended.

By the same token, too, traditional distinctions between consultation, participation and negotiation have become somewhat irrelevant, although in the past their currency was beneficial to managements. Thus for a long time they were able to differentiate between bargaining and consultation, the former encompassing a rather limited range of circumstances in which conflicts of interest were recognized, and the latter being appropriate for a far wider group of common-interest questions which accorded with the principles of the so-called 'unitary frame' for the interpretation of workplace authority relations. Moreover, under these conditions, management was also able to separate consultation and participation, the first being an acceptable and even desirable aspect of workplace labour relations, but the second being rejected on the grounds that it eroded its decision-making authority. However, with the increasing power of shop stewards at workplace level these constructs have clearly been brought into question, first because the range of conflicting interests is obviously greater than was assumed under traditional definitions and, second, since the conspicuously participative role of shop stewards at plant level has raised doubts about the conception of a unitary source of authority in the workplace. What is required, therefore, is an acceptance of the participation by shop stewards in British industrial relations together with scrupulous measurement of their influence over decision-making processes and the levels, range and scope of issues entailed. This, too, should be supplemented by studies of an explanatory nature which would inquire into the grounds for significant deviations from normal procedures, and by progression towards an understanding of the nature of industrial conflict in which attitudinal as well as behavioural components are taken into account.

(4) Factory occupations, work-ins and takeovers

> UCS is part of our contemporary history, its story written by workers
> and their deeds. It is more than that—it is a portent of things to
> come. Workers will determine the future and in the process will write
> the most glorious pages in the history of our country.[81]

If the shop-steward movement has proved to be the main lasting
and influential form of representative participation in British industry, undoubtedly the most spectacular development has been the wave
of factory occupations, work-ins and takeovers which swept much of
western Europe in the late 1960s and early 1970s. In France, in May
and June 1968, above all, the events for a time seemed to herald the
revolutionary transformation of French society under workers' control, and in the years following, factory takeovers have been particularly common. Meanwhile, in Great Britain, of course, the events at
Upper Clyde Shipyards have opened a new chapter in the history of
industrial relations in this country.

Moreover, this special variant of workers' control is itself composed
of diverse elements, such as factory occupations and sit-ins which are
really conflict strategies on the one hand, and, on the other, work-ins
and factory takeovers during which, for a period of time, organized
groups of workers actually run the factory. And, indeed, the challenge offered to management in its capacity as representative of the
owners and the threat to the legitimacy of an existing pattern of control and domination is, of course, especially profound in a situation in
which workers are able to demonstrate their ability not only to produce but also to sell particular commodities.

Taking first of all the case of the uprising in France in the spring of
1968, the underlying causes of these events are still open to dispute.
Nevertheless, three factors are especially relevant here: first, general
economic conditions; second, the political restraints imposed during
the Gaullist period; and, third, the value climate of the time which not
only rested on strong syndicalist and revolutionary traditions but was
also affected by a number of wide-ranging tensions and frustrations of
the period.

Since the Second World War, of course, successive French governments have planned to expand at a minimum rate of between 4 and 5
per cent a year (which has been frequently exceeded), but, although in
these terms this has been conspicuously successful, growth itself has
been most uneven. Thus, the bulk of expansion has been concentrated
in modernizing sectors of the economy and, with the exception of
publicly-owned industrial enterprises which have been fundamental

to the process of development and which seem likely to have ensured the pre-eminence of France throughout Europe during the 1980s, other public provisions have remained sparse. Nowhere has this been more evident than in the higher education system where a huge influx of students has not seen commensurate increases of facilities and resources. These, then, provided important objective sources of student unrest which were exacerbated by other radicalizing forces of the period (and notably the war in Vietnam) which were conducive to the growth of anti-capitalist and anti-imperialist ideologies. Furthermore, in a political system which gave little opportunity for redressing these grievances a number of factors clearly combined to bring the students into open revolt against the regime and they were of course to form the catalyst for the general strike and the factory takeovers which followed.[82]

Moreover, despite an impressive and sustained rate of economic growth, the immediate gains of working people were again scarcely compatible with that deemed appropriate after such a period of economic expansion. And these traditional grievances were fused with far more radical elements which furnished the means for the creation of a new social order organized around workers' control. As Cohen has argued:[83]

> The traditional protests stemmed from, and were directed against, the failures of the plan *in its own terms*: an archaic and unproductive university system that frustrated the great mass of students in their efforts to prepare for a proper place in the new society; and long hours, low real wage increases, little job security and unacceptable working conditions that belied the promises of ever increasing affluence that the plan made to the mass of workers.
>
> The radical rebellion was a refusal to accept the tight limits the plan proposed for future social changes. The plan, and the political economy it represented, reached the limits of any idea of radical alterations of authority structures, and any attempt to redistribute power at every level of social organization in order to create fundamentally different social relations.

In Great Britain, attention during this period focused on the UCS work-in, when, for a time in 1971, shop stewards and workers effectively controlled the general policies of the company. The immediate provocation was the action of the Conservative government, but underlying economic factors were important here too, as was the high level of organization of the Clyde workers and their traditional rejection of capitalism as the most appropriate means of running an economic system. The economic backcloth to the work-in at UCS has been discussed at length by Thompson and Hart:[84]

> That the system of the 'mixed economy' pursued since 1945 was indeed in serious difficulties was a fact universally confessed, though not necessarily in these exact words. It had meant an economy mostly under private ownership run for private profit, but with considerable State backing in loans, subsidies and other forms of assistance, cheap inputs from the nationalized basic industries, free wage bargaining, combined however with a crippling armaments burden and massive financial speculation abroad. By the mid-1960s this was visibly breaking down, with roaring inflation, continual balance of payments crises and industrial stagnation.

The so-called 'lame-duck' policy was of course to be the principal solution offered by the incoming Conservative government in 1970: that is to say, State subsidies to private enterprise would be discontinued and any 'backward and inefficient' industries which had been subjected to substantial neglect and almost non-existent investment in new plant and machinery would as a direct consequence of this be rendered bankrupt. Little if any account would be taken, in the process, of the hardship which would be suffered not only by workers and their families but by dependent communities as a whole, nor was there to be any attempt to apportion blame among the parties involved in such an industry. Other than Rolls-Royce, UCS would surely have been one of the more spectacular victims of this policy had it not been for the decisive and sustained actions of the workers concerned. Immediately preceding their collective action to safeguard their livelihood the report by the specialist committee looking into UCS affairs recommended that any continuation of operations 'would be unjustified' and that, more specifically, the workforce should be reduced from 8,500 to 2,500 with what amounted to wage reductions for the remaining employees.[85] Subsequent events are, of course, a milestone in the history of British industrial relations, for not only did the work-in illustrate the great organizational powers of working people, but it successfully challenged the priority of property ownership over workers' rights to employment. Contemporary politics too were significantly altered, the government being obliged to shift away from its lame-duck philosophy.

The UCS drama was to be followed by a whole series of occupations and work-ins designed to prevent redundancies, notably at Plessey Alexandria, River Don works, Fisher Bendix and Allis-Chalmers.[86] Moreover, almost all were successful, so much so that this form of workers' action has since become an established industrial-relations practice.

Nevertheless, as we have argued, it is important to distinguish between occupations constituted solely as a temporary bargaining strategy from those in which workers have had an opportunity to manage the affairs of their company, if only through the medium of their stewards. To be sure, the occupation or sit-in has many advantages for workers by comparison with the traditional strike weapon. When they are in control of the machinery in the shop, workers can easily prevent 'blacklegging' and the use of white-collar and other staff by management in its attempt to keep up production. Again, chances are minimized of a direct clash with the police and of un-favourable public reactions, which are an inevitable risk during picket-line activities. But although, with the notable exception of March 1972 in the Manchester area, factory occupations have generally achieved beneficial results from the workers' point of view and are in consequence here to stay, their bearing on the formulation of workers' attitudes to participation and control is somewhat more questionable, in contrast with work-ins which are fundamental in this respect. After all, the ucs experience has served, above all, to demon-strate the ability of working people to undertake policy decisions in a self-management framework, and in championing this cause, the Clyde workers were able to provide further grist for the mill of the industrial democrat. Indeed, the significance of this contribution and this form of action towards the goal of greater self-determination by working people could hardly be overestimated.

It has been our intention in this chapter, then, to examine an extensive range of examples of workers' participation and control which, by contrast with the practices examined earlier, have risen on the basis of the initiatives of working people. What has been remark-able, of course, is the finding that, despite diversity of origins, of form and of content of these particular schemes, very similar causal elements can be adduced to explain their principal characteristics. And, in particular, we have been able to confirm once again the main elements of our own model and the more specific derivative argument that a rise in the level of latent power of working people does induce mount-ing expectations among them in the course of which questions about workers' participation and control attain a new significance.

5 Trade unions, their officials, and workers' participation

The leaders of particular labour movements and labour organizations have approached the question of workers' participation and control in markedly different ways. All have tended to support strong plant-based systems of union representation since these help to ensure that agreements are actually honoured at local levels, that non-unionized employees cannot severely impair union activities, and that arbitrary or capricious decisions of management are effectively opposed. But in practice only a rather narrow band of participation or control programmes has attracted the unreserved enthusiasm of officers who, to begin with, have been inclined to reject the majority of schemes initiated by management, largely on the grounds that these serve to duplicate channels of workers' representation and in consequence weaken workers' inclinations to join trade unions and to overcome problems by means of union procedural systems. But, second, in their concern to preserve their own position in the industrial system, trade union officers have frequently looked with suspicion on many of the more ambitious ideas for outright workers' control. Indeed, from time to time they have even resisted particular shop-steward and other plant-based representative systems formally linked to the union structure whenever these have threatened their own decision-making authority within the union hierarchy.

Officials of established labour organizations have an interest therefore in ensuring that workers' participation is clearly integrated into the established union structure. To be sure, many have been personally committed to democratic and socialist ideals and at times these have provided important ideological bases for acknowledging that a greater sharing of power within the ranks of the labour movement would be desirable. But in view of their concern over these matters it is scarcely surprising that their enthusiasm for particular forms of participation has been confined (by and large) to those clearly founded in union structures and that their own experimentation in this direction has been generally restricted to two principal types: union segments in enterprises and union ownership.

9

The attitudes of union officials on the question of workers' participation and control are of great importance, however, and would seem to be highly sensitive to the degree of democracy obtaining within any given trade union, which in turn depends a great deal on the latent power of the members themselves. Indeed, in Great Britain, an analysis of the assessment of leaders of the labour movement of workers' participation and control would in fact reveal two distinct alterations of opinion since the First World War. In the early part of this century, differentiation of functions within unions was somewhat more diffuse than is the case today, when trade unions have evolved comparatively 'mature' organizational forms. The growth of general unions from the 1890s onwards had brought to the fore trade union leaders of an idealistic rather than of an administrative outlook, and although the leaders of craft unions remained solidly 'conservative', other upheavals of the time of course resulted in the emergence of the powerful shop-steward movement. In consequence, as Clegg has argued:[1]

> During and after the First World War British trade unions were for the most part converted to doctrines of workers' control or joint control which held that in a socialist society industry should be run by unions or by a joint board half chosen by the unions and half by the government. Only if workers ran industry through their own organizations, held the proponents of these doctrines, could 'wage-slavery' be ended.

But the early 1920s witnessed a major retreat from this position. In the first place, with worsening employment conditions trade union officials were preoccupied in traditional bargaining areas and, then, in 1930 a change in emphasis was particularly evident in discussions of the London Passenger Transport Bill. This was a most important test case, for, in introducing the Bill, Herbert Morrison argued that board members in publicly-owned industries should be selected on the basis of competence for the job rather than as representatives of the workers concerned. When this view was ultimately upheld it set a major precedent for trade union attitudes to this question in the years to come. Indeed, Morrison's position was officially endorsed by the TUC in 1944 in their *Interim Report on Post War Reconstruction* and this very much affected the outcome of discussions on the main nationalization acts after the end of the Second World War.

Of course, in one view, this decision was one of the most unfortunate as far as the British trade union movement is concerned for although few developments in workers' participation could have been expected in the inter-war years when the unions were severely weakened by adverse economic circumstances, the underlying conditions were undoubtedly propitious at the end of the Second World War. At this time, following their role in that war, the esteem of trade-union officials had reached new heights, union recruitment had risen substantially and a Labour government had been elected on the basis of a deeply-felt desire for the introduction of an entirely new social order. In short, although the balance of power between the main industrial relations classes was favourable to extensions in participation, at the value level the birth of industrial democracy was sacrificed and displaced by the vision of 'managerialist' thinkers who anticipated the emergence of a meritocratic rather than a democratic industrial social structure.

Naturally, none of this is to suggest that the public sector of the economy is now largely run by persons who easily fit the stereotype of the managerialist thesis, but an important opportunity was undoubtedly missed at this time for developing workers' participation and this, in turn, has affected the attitudes of working people and the public at large to the question of public ownership itself. Of course, in retrospect, it is also easy to note a number of additional problems of the nationalization programme and particularly that it served to rescue certain industries from bankruptcy and that, by virtue of very generous terms of compensation, it unlocked a great deal of capital for investment privately in growth sectors of the economy. Moreover, later governments have failed to recognize that the publicly-owned sector could provide the basis for positive economic strategies and instead have enforced particularly stringent wages and prices policies, so that, although on the whole nationalized industries have actually had a remarkable record in terms of raising productivity,[2] many have perforce suffered financial losses and in so doing have of course subsidized the private sector of the economy. But, notwithstanding these additional difficulties, it is clear that the experience of workers in publicly-owned industries has not on the whole been significantly different from that of their colleagues in private firms, and this very much reflects the similar decision-making and control structures which obtain under both systems of ownership. Again, the consequent alienation experienced by employees in nationalized firms leads to a general disillusionment and at times fatal agnosticism among working people to the issue of public ownership, and they thereby offer only limited opposition to the more forthright opponents of nationalization itself.

Furthermore, the subordination of the public to the private sector of the economy is perpetuated too by the very composition of most corporation boards. As it happens *neither* democratic *nor* meritocratic criteria have necessarily applied in the appointment of key directors for, as Jenkins has demonstrated in *Power at the Top*, there is a preponderance of directors of private companies on the majority of these boards and they are, of course, able to ensure that decisions taken in nationalized industries are largely in accord with the interests of privately-owned industry.[3] But this state of affairs is to some extent a reflection of the unwillingness of the official labour movement to offer any decisive challenge on the question of control, which is in turn partly consequent upon its general approach to the issue of workers' participation up until the 1960s.

To be sure, at the end of the Second World War, public ownership was conceived as co-extensive with certain limited developments in workers' decision-making powers, but in the various nationalization acts this was confined largely to a dual structure of bargaining and consultative committees. Thus, the right of trade unions to negotiate on wages and conditions was secured and so, largely fortuitously, nationalization has been a positive stimulus for unionization especially among white-collar workers. But outside traditional bargaining areas, however, formal *consultation* was apparently considered sufficient means for involving workers in decision-making processes. This is not to imply, of course, that workers themselves necessarily share these assumptions, as is clear from the demise of formal joint consultation in so many nationalized industries, but, for our purposes, it is only important to note the limitations on experiments in workers' participation in the immediate post-Second World War period and to observe that these were in some degree a consequence of the official TUC position at the time.

But the latter years of the 1960s undoubtedly witnessed a major change in the official view of the labour movement towards industrial democracy, beginning in 1967 with the deliberations of a Labour Party working group headed by Mr Jack Jones of the Transport and General Workers' Union.[4] As it happens, the group was unable to recommend a blueprint for participation to fit all industrial situations and further considered that different issues were involved in the public and private sectors of the economy, but they were at least able to reach certain conclusions on points of principle. These were, first, that workers have the right to determine their economic environments by participating in a widening range of decisions within the firm and that the recognition of that right, and measures to secure it, must be a matter of urgency; second, that workers' participation must be closely identified with the trade-union organization and representation of workers; and third, that industrial democracy must be developed on the basis of a single channel of representation.[5]

These proposals would of course have been favourably received by the progressively-minded union official because they envisaged an important extension in the role of workers in affecting decisions in their day-to-day working lives but, at the same time, by virtue of being firmly grounded in the union structure, they offered no major threat to the authority of the officials themselves. And again, although it is patently logical to base the extension of participation on this powerful organizational structure, the preference of union officials for this framework is also consistent with their own particular interests in this matter.

Now these principles were reaffirmed and extended in 1973 in the TUC's interim report on industrial democracy which was prepared for the annual congress in September of that year, a further statement being in prospect for 1974.[6] This preliminary report was introduced by Mr Vic Feather who argued that the TUC had an 'emerging and developing policy for giving workers a greater amount of control over the industries in which they worked'.[7] In detail, the official trade-union view was that there should be 50 per cent direct trade-union representation at board level, and to facilitate this, the unions looked for a change in company law which would ensure that an emergent supervisory board could, if the necessity arose, overrule both the board of management and the annual general meeting of shareholders within any privately-owned firm. They also sought extensions in industrial democracy within publicly-owned enterprises via the union structure although here, by contrast with the TUC proposals of 1944, there was no suggestion that unionists on the board of directors be required to act in an individual capacity only and hence to sever connections with their respective unions. On the contrary, the principle of accountability was a major plank of the new policy.[8]

But why, it may reasonably be asked, did such a change of approach come about? Part of the explanation can doubtless be found in the general mood of the period but a principal factor, too, would appear to be the democratization of unions themselves. We have argued at many points in this study, that the general interest in participation from the late 1960s onwards was largely consequent upon the growing latent power of working people coupled with a rise in their levels of expectations brought about by a sustained period of 'affluence'. But whether or not union officials were accurately to reflect and even to lead developments along these lines depended greatly on their sensitivity to the wishes of the membership and this in turn was enhanced by the degree of democracy in any given union. Thus, in general, the more accountable the official to the membership the greater his enthusiasm for participatory democracy appeared to be, while in more bureaucratically-run unions official attitudes to workers' participation remained far more lukewarm.

It has of course long been acknowledged that the prior democratization of unions is an important foundation for building industrial democracy. Thus, as Fletcher has argued:[9]

> As experienced trade unionists invariably point out whenever 'workers' control' is under discussion, workers have little chance of controlling industry if they cannot control their own unions. Union democracy is therefore one of the prerequisites of industrial democracy.

And as some indication of this, it is scarcely coincidental that union officials who were at the forefront in debates on industrial democracy were also those who were relatively more responsive to democratic pressures within their own organizations. The TGWU for example, had, over many years, been plagued by problems of bureaucratic and oligarchic control but, nevertheless, in the late 1960s and early 1970s important structural changes were recorded in its organization, the outcome of which was to involve union activists far more in the decision-making processes of the union. A deliberate policy emerged to include ordinary members in the making of agreements largely by encouraging local collective bargaining, and shop stewards participated formally not only in the final decisions on particular agreements but also in the formulation of union claims.[10] To be sure, these developments were in part a *response* to local initiatives which had been encouraged in turn by the growing latent power of workers at plant level, but the fact that they were positively fostered undoubtedly suggests a sympathetic appreciation of the views and aspirations of the membership, which is reflected in the union's prominence in recent public discussions about industrial democracy.

The same general argument applies to the Amalgamated Union of Engineering Workers (AUEW). The organized power of shop stewards within this union may have generated a renewed interest in workers' participation and control, but, more importantly, the maintenance of a system of election for key officials has undoubtedly encouraged a greater affinity between officials and membership than is common among more flagrantly bureaucratic unions, and in turn fosters a corresponding commitment to industrial democracy. Both Hugh Scanlon and Ernest Roberts have written extensively on this issue, the latter having argued explicitly that workers' control cannot simply be directed against management but can only be founded on more democratic union and Labour Party organizations.[11] It is worth mentioning, however, that officials tend to envisage workers' participation and control in terms of their own organizations and may therefore still be disposed to place obstacles in the way of forms of workers' control in which the role of unions is limited.

Indeed, by way of illustration, though in a very different national and historical context, it is interesting to examine the response of union officials to the German Revolution of 1918, for here was a situation undoubtedly favourable to the development of a fully-fledged system of workers' control. The German Revolution broke out in November 1918 and for a time it appeared that it might follow the pattern of the Russian Revolution of the previous year. Moreover, the success of the latter seemed bound up with a councils system based on soldiers and workers and these therefore began to develop in many parts of Germany. But at this point there was a major cleavage of opinion within the ranks of German labour: the Independent Socialists wanted a thoroughgoing Soviet or Councils State on the Russian model, but the majority socialists in the Social Democratic Party, whose leaders were generally experienced trade unionists, preferred democratic parliamentary institutions of the British type. In the crucial Congress of Councils held in Berlin it was clear that the latter were in the ascendancy even though the Spartacists broke out into open revolt in an attempt to emulate the success of the Bolsheviks; and, in Guillebaud's words:[12]

> In the end victory lay, though by a narrow margin, with the parliamentarians, backed up as they were by the powerful and disciplined trade union organization. . . . By degrees they [the councils] lost all semblance of power and finally vanished without leaving any impress on local government.

Furthermore, the attitude of the official labour movement to workers' control came into sharp relief in Germany again, when legislation to establish a system of *works* rather than *workers'* councils was in prospect.[13]

> The old established Trade Union leaders gradually regained control over the bulk of their members, and thus found themselves able to steer the course of the new Works Councils measure into 'safe' channels—safe, that is, so far as the maintenance of the pre-existing Trade Union predominance in labour organization was concerned.

This arguably rather dated case nevertheless demonstrates that wholehearted support of union officials can only be expected for forms of industrial democracy which ultimately rest on the established organizational structure of unions, and this in turn is pertinent to any explanation of the very restricted range of participation practices which have received unreserved acclaim from *officials* of labour movements and of the limited number of experiments in workers' participation which have actually stemmed *directly* from their initiatives.

(1) Plant-based union segments

But full-time union officials have characteristically been inclined to favour and to assist in the promotion of union segments at plant level. In the USA, of course, where industry-wide bargaining is less usual than in Europe, a great many negotiations have always been carried out by the members of particular union 'locals' with their respective employers but early hostility to unions impeded wholesale international developments along these lines, and thus the branch, whose members were employed in a number of firms within a given locality, became the principal basis of union organization. However, with accretions in the latent power of working people which have been contingent on economic and technical change, a power void was created in the channels of communication in many firms, and this could have been filled by a number of agencies, including informal workers' organizations, shop-steward systems, personnel and other paternalistic managerial practices, and, of course, the one most favoured by the full-time officer, the plant-based union segment which is formally integrated into the wider union hierarchy.

In Great Britain, as we have seen, the most common development in this respect has been the shop-steward system, which owed far more to the initiatives of local workers than to official union policies. But in other countries, officials were especially anxious to support plant-based representative systems so long, once again, as these were integrated into the wider union hierarchy. Thus, in Italy, as in most of Western Europe, the post-Second World War period witnessed comparatively 'full' employment, rapid production growth, widespread labour shortages, an advance in real earnings and the increasing prominence of large corporations.[14] But traditionally here the unions were strong at the centre and comparatively weaker at plant level with the result that collective bargaining was highly centralized and the national or regional multi-employer agreement typical. However, as a consequence of the changing economic climate coupled with the increasing concentration of industry which facilitated the development of plant-based representative systems, such centralized bargaining structures became progressively obsolete and a 'power vacuum' at local levels began to be noticeable. In any event of course, dependence on a multi-employer collective agreement is a reflection of union weakness since it is clearly a union strategy used like a 'dyke' to ensure that those in more favourable circumstances are able to protect their less well-placed colleagues. But whenever the economic order is more opportune from the standpoint of the labour force, these agreements at best represent a *minimum* level which particular sections of workers can significantly advance through locally based activity.

None the less, immediately after the Second World War, the Italian unions, having no official status within the plant, were in no position to meet the challenge of changing economic circumstances. Moreover, any attempt to rectify this situation was severely hampered by the existence of 'internal commissions' (works councils) which 'anticipated' locally-based union organizations and the widespread attempt by Italian managements to develop paternalistic practices in order to weaken the intent of workers seeking effective union action. But, gradually, leading officials of Italian unions became dissatisfied with the position, and sought to amend it. The first step was a major assault on the 'internal commissions' and here the Confederazione Italiana Sindicati Nazional dei Lavoratori (CISL) took the lead in 1960 by advocating that unions must have a monopoly of bargaining functions within the plant. Meanwhile, parallel with this development, the three principal unions in Italy began to build 'factory unions'; the CISL set up various plant-based union segments called Sezione Aziendale Sindacale (SAS), the Unione Italiana del Lavoro (UIL) followed suit with their Nuclei Aziendali (NA) and, finally, the largest union, the Confederazione Generale Italiana del Lavoro (CGIL) established their Sezioni Sindacali di Fabbrica (SSF).[15] But these were, of course, developed as part of an *official* union strategy for, although on the one hand unions have been critical of various managerial practices, they have also at times disapproved of workers' actions (notably factory occupations and takeovers). Once again, then, consistent official support tends to be forthcoming only for those limited forms of workers' participation and control which are firmly based on the established union structure.

(2) Union ownership and workers' participation: the case of the Histadrut

Union ownership has also provided trade-union officials with an opportunity to promote participation by their members in the decision-making processes of the firm. The Histadrut (the General Federation of Labour in Israel) is by far the best example of this and highlights very well the central issues of the relationship between latent power, values and the success or otherwise of given forms of workers' participation and control.

Both ideological and economic stimuli may be identified in an analysis of the origins of the extensive arrangements for participation which were originally contemplated in Histadrut-owned plants. Indeed, the Histadrut itself was founded more as a movement than as an institution, and represented a manner of thinking which was directed by a powerful ideology which fused nationalist–Zionist, egalitarian–socialist and general–humanist elements.[16] But gradually the first-named ideology became dominant and so, in an attempt to resuscitate egalitarian forms of consciousness, the leaders of the Histadrut sought to develop workers' participation in firms within their jurisdiction. Moreover, this ideological background was augmented by economic pressures which were partly consequent upon general competition from foreign companies and other private firms in Israel but was also conditional on the close relationship between the Histadrut and the State, for it became imperative to increase productivity for nationalistic reasons. Again, in establishing operations in new immigrant areas, the Histadrut had at times failed to take full account of the true economic costs, and this further stimulated the concern for productivity.[17]

It is worth mentioning, too, that the Histadrut continues to be very influential in Israel's economy; in 1970, it was responsible for about 24 per cent of employment, 23 per cent of the national product and 19 per cent of the country's exports.[18] Furthermore, although in theory all economic activities are ultimately controlled by Hevrat Ovdim (the community of workers), in practice, decision-making at the executive level lies largely in the hands of salaried managerial personnel.[19]

Histadrut-owned firms have adopted four main solutions to the problem of involving workers in decision-making processes: first, workers' committees (which are really plant bargaining committees); second, joint production committees; third, plant councils; and fourth, the joint management programme. Workers' committees and joint production committees have only limited functions since they have no jurisdiction over work assignments and technical matters, over which management has authority, but the plant councils and the joint management programme have been more ambitious in terms of level, scope and range of decision making.

Plant councils owe their origins to a resolution passed by the Histadrut Convention in 1956. This provided in each plant for the establishment of a council with representatives of management and workers having equal voting powers, for the authority of the council to encompass all matters pertaining to the enterprise, for the JPCs to be integrated into the plant council, for decisions approved of by two-thirds of the members of each side to be considered binding, and for a twice-yearly general assembly in which management and council members would discuss problems with the workforce as a whole.[20]

Nevertheless, the plant-councils scheme was doomed to failure and by 1961 *all* councils had become inactive and this therefore led to the introduction of the system of joint management. In 1964, a special meeting of the Histadrut council was convened to endorse this programme although it was not until 1968 that this new phase in workers' participation became operational. The scheme provided for participation by Histadrut employees at two levels: first, on central management bodies; and second, in the individual plants. More precisely, one-third of all members of central management bodies were to be workers' representatives, while equal numbers of management and employee representatives were to control plant-level policies.

For all that, the very grave problems experienced in practice by these more ambitious participation programmes requires some explanation, particularly in view of the fact that surveys carried out in Israel have suggested that the bulk of rank-and-file employees as well as secretaries of workers' committees are generally enthusiastic about progress along these lines. Indeed, Tabb and Goldfarb reported that 54 per cent of the general workforce and nine out of every ten secretaries they interviewed were in favour of participation, with only 16 per cent of the former and none of the latter being completely antagonistic.[21] However—and this was ultimately to prove decisive in accounting for the demise of the councils in Israel— the attitudes of management were undoubtedly different. Only a minority were behind the scheme (although it must be said that on the whole their objections were conceived in terms of its impracticality and they were not generally opposed to participation in principle).[22]

In Israel's case, management's ability to subvert the councils' operations derived from the structure of power relations and workplace level:[23]

> The legal right to order managers was not, it seems enough. The managerial group, as one centre of power, had to be won over, no less than the worker group. However, the managers were not won over because they did not believe that it was in their interest or in the interest of the enterprise to involve the workers in management. They believed that the workers were only concerned with their narrow interests and, therefore, were in no position to be concerned with the overall problems of the undertaking. The little experience afforded them by the enterprise councils convinced them that workers' participation in management was a hindrance, not a help. Moreover, it was the opinion of the managers that 'management is a profession and must not be turned over to amateurs'.

The success of the argument deployed by Israel's managers can only be partly understood, however, in terms of their internalization of the main tenets of the 'managerialist' thesis. After all, had there been other competing power centres of any significance, these reforms would presumably have been achieved *despite* managerial hostility. But union ownership can be damaging to the power of shop-floor workers on two main counts. First and most obvious is that, since the union is both employer and bargaining agent, workers lack an organization designed exclusively to further their particular interests. To be sure, workers' committees do exist in Histadrut plants, but the loyalty of the secretaries of these committees tends to be divided between firm and members. Equally important, too, with the divorce of ownership from control in Histadrut enterprises, managerial authority must perforce rest almost entirely on technical and professional criteria which are, of course, called into question with every advance in workers' participation. Hence, by contrast with capitalist companies in which unification of interests between owners and top managerial personnel has been the general rule, there are fundamental divisions between policy and executive organs in union-owned firms and, under such circumstances, a hostile managerial reaction to participation would be expected.

In retrospect, then, the proposals for workers' participation in Histadrut enterprises appear flagrantly ill-adapted to the underlying structure of power and values. Managers, who had *de facto* control over decision-making processes, generally failed to identify with the aims of legal owners and were therefore unwilling to accept a curtailment of the primary source of their authority. Thus, the only centres of power which might have been thought likely to insist on such developments were the committee secretaries and the workers but, notwithstanding their general enthusiasm for workers' participation, a number of secretaries in particular had divided loyalties and saw the emergence of plant councils as potentially threatening to their own workplace authority and looked upon the practice if not the principle with a certain measure of suspicion. This left only the rank-and-file workers giving unreserved support for the participation programme, and they were divided and ill-organized: in short, they lacked sufficient latent power to ensure that their interests prevailed against entrenched managerial opposition. The outcome indeed was far from the ideal envisaged by the founders of the Histadrut; forms of unorganized conflict, for example, remained endemic, with the consequence that the number of working days lost through stoppages has been higher in Histadrut establishments than in other enterprises in Israel. And this is, of course, just what would be expected when workers are deprived of an effective local channel for resolving their disagreements with management.

More generally, too, the experience of workers' participation in Histadrut enterprises shows the limitations of those participation programmes imposed from above which bear little relation to the underlying structure of power and of values of the interested parties. This theme will be explored further in chapter 6, but it is one more indication of the problems which inevitably result when an attempt is made to establish effective methods for participation and control on idealistic grounds alone.

6 Politics and participation

In the foregoing chapters we have been able to establish support for the main propositions of this inquiry and, more specifically, to observe that, notwithstanding the aims of the initiators of any given form of participation, in practice the operation of any scheme can still be best understood by taking account of the latent power and values of the parties involved. But we conditioned our explanatory model of the genesis and the substance of a diverse collection of measures designed to advance workers' participation and control with the caveat that political parties had a role to play here, too, and it is with this that we deal in our penultimate chapter. Furthermore, a review of the relevant arguments offers an additional and a welcome opportunity to analyse a number of wide-ranging programmes for participation which have originated in government legislation and, at the same time, to comment on the function of cultural variables (as aspects of the ideological climate) which have facilitated or impeded the growth of workplace democracy.

It has long been obvious to followers of the labour movement that the institution of workers' participation on a permanent basis would not be achieved by industrial action alone. The demise of the work-in at the Lip factory in France in 1973 (when police were employed in the break-up of this experiment in workers' control) has provided a cogent as well as a recent example of this truism. Indeed, there are clearly certain general precepts involved here, notably, that locally-based actions may be frustrated by State intervention and by the passage of legislation which outlaws such actions, that a hostile government can ensure that a labour movement has a largely defensive approach to all industrial questions including that of participation, that 'right-wing' dictatorships have usually ensured the emasculation and even destruction of indigent labour movements and other independent organizations of working people (thereby inhibiting even limited forms of participation via collective-bargaining machinery), and that by virtue of their control of the police and the armed forces, totalitarian governments can inhibit even the most rudimentary moves towards workers' rights.

These negative aspects of State intervention are worth mentioning at the outset because they illustrate certain clear limits to what may be achieved on the question of workers' participation within the confines of a given nation state. Equally they highlight our view that the main activity of governments in the field of industrial democracy has lain not in legal enactments pertaining to workers' participation itself but in their effect on the balance of power between the main social classes of any society and in the creation therein of a constellation of general values which bear on the issue in question. Again, somewhat para-doxically, we could postulate that the types of participation and control which have been envisaged in government legislation are themselves readily intelligible in terms of underlying power balances (and values) within particular societies. In other words, governments clearly encapsulate and reflect (as well as influence and modify) prevailing class and interest-group formations.

To the extent that this argument is sound, certain practical observations may thence be in order, above all, that some legislation with respect to workers' participation in industry *may* be quite worthless if it bears no resemblance to the realities of power and values at local levels. Participation at board level is an outstanding example, for this—though generally instituted by an 'order of state'—may be unworkable if the arrangements are disregarded by determined employers or if, in a subtle manner, they are by-passed by an outcrop of supplementary, informal 'managerial' board meetings; or again, if in the absence of a truly effective power base, worker directors are unable to have any significant impact on the general policies of the firm. Consequently, given our assessment of the function of govern-ments on the question of industrial democracy, it is pertinent at this point to trace some of the principal by-products of the statutory process and by so doing elucidate certain conditions which have been beneficial, first for the latent power, and second for the values, of working people.

Concurrently with the emergence of industrial states, governments have taken on an increasing measure of control over economic affairs. Thus whereas in the nineteenth century *laissez-faire* principles dominated political and economic thinking resulting in the general rule that governments only assumed full powers in this field as an emergency measure in wartime, in the twentieth century, following the Keynesian 'revolution' (which was largely a response to large-scale unemployment and economic depression in the 1930s) the impact of the State in general economic planning has become noticeably more pronounced. Moreover, it has been appreciated that a substantial public sector is a necessary pivot upon which to build any general economic strategy and, indeed, there is evidence that those governments which have been most eager to take decisive steps in the overall planning and direction of industry have also experienced the most dramatic rises in their rate of economic growth.[1] Again, the apparently permanent role of government in economic management is reflected in the tendency for the well-being or otherwise of economic systems to be held as the responsibility of the ruling political party rather than, say, of the owners or managers of particular firms within industry itself. And of course the upshot of these developments is that in any country operating a two- or multi-party system of government, the primary precondition for the retention of office is the maintenance of full employment and economic growth, those principal economic pillars which inescapably signal a rise in the level of latent power of ordinary people.

But the impact of governments on the underlying power of the main industrial classes has not been confined to economic policies alone. Occasionally, for example, they have promoted the extension of unionism. Indeed, we have referred above to State recognition of unions in war-time, to the stimulus of nationalization to bargaining activities, and to a variety of government actions which have served to encourage white-collar unionism. Improved standards of education, too, have undoubtedly enhanced the power of some union members and any progress towards universal, comprehensive and egalitarian practices in education can only increase the ability of workers' representatives to argue their cases with clarity and skill. Again, the growth of, albeit inadequate, systems of social security must be favourable to the extension of freedom of action for workers who are no longer utterly dependent on wages which are, of course, cut off during a strike. Similarly, too, equality between the sexes and the sharing of responsibility for the upkeep of the marital home can be seen to offer one more solution to the financial hardships which a family might otherwise suffer in the furtherance of union activities.

Governments have other opportunities to promote or to stultify a concern for democratic processes of decision-making. To be sure, while they mirror the cultural, institutional and political values of historically-specific societies they also engender those same patterns of thought and behaviour in which certain modes of action are legitimized and widely upheld but in which others are derided and even outlawed. And although it would be naïve as well as sociologically unsound to assume that the values promoted by political leaders are in any sense commensurate with their actions, or indeed, to suggest that all groups and classes will adhere to such values, the overall backcloth may still be appreciated in so far as it is either favourable or otherwise to workers' participation in industry. And to the extent that governments are able to take a certain stand in one direction or another in this respect, they may clearly help to influence the attitudes and values of managers and workers at local levels.

However—and this proviso cannot be overemphasized—the policies of governing parties with respect to industrial democracy can be best understood not as innovations for their own sake but rather as reactions to other contemporary forces in society and, most noticeably, the distribution of power therein. To be sure, governments respond variously to roughly similar configurations of these underlying phenomena and, without doubt, many opportunities for extending workers' participation have been forgone in the wake of ineffective or inappropriate legislation. But unquestionably the balance of power in industry and the values relevant thereto have from one epoch to another formed the necessary perimeters for legislative forays towards industrial democracy.

In this chapter, then, we will focus attention on these themes which will be illustrated further by an analysis of a rich variety of government enactments on workers' participation and control. We shall note, too, that the genesis and operation of individual programmes in this respect have been moulded very clearly along the lines as suggested above, but first it is appropriate to pause for a figurative summary of the main patterns involved here (see Table 6).

TABLE 6 *Forms of workers' participation and control initiated by governments*

(1)	Works councils, joint consultative and negotiational committees at industry and plant levels
(2)	Co-determination and other 'worker director' schemes
(3)	Self-management and workers' councils' systems

(1) Works councils, joint consultative and negotiational committees at industry and plant levels

In chapter 1 we observed that governments of a great many countries have sought to institute works councils by legislative means, but undoubtedly the best example of intervention along these lines began in Germany prior to the Nazi era, when a succession of orders were enacted which made the establishment of such councils mandatory and so set the main precedent and tradition for other models which were to develop later not only in Germany but also in most other nations in western Europe. Thus even though we shall return again to the German case in our consideration of co-determination, this example of instituting works-council machinery properly occupies a great deal of our attention here.

For the purposes of our own inquiry, the German legislation in this respect can be best broken up into three historical periods, the first covering the years up to the end of the First World War, the second, the revolutionary upheavals following this war, and the third bearing on the decades after the Second World War.

The first germs of enthusiasm for works-council legislation could be detected in Germany as early as the 1830s and 1840s when a period of social unrest was recorded which provided a fertile soil for reformist measures directed at 'overcoming the divisive and negative effects of class antagonism and providing a basis for co-operation between employers and employees'.[2] Proposals for factory councils gradually filtered through to government levels and, during the Constitutional Convention in Frankfurt in 1848–9, plans for such councils were developed by the Committee on Economics. Even though these were never implemented, they prepared the foundation for workers' participation in decisions relating to personnel and social questions which were to be components of future legislation. In this conception the councils would be empowered 'to mediate disputes between the employer and his employees, to suggest and police factory regulations, to establish and administer health insurance plans, to supervise the morals and education of children employed in the plant, and finally, to select the branch delegates for district, regional and national economic councils also provided for'.[3] These proposals, too, were strongly advocated by the 'Fraternity of Labour', even though at this time only a few piecemeal experiments were instituted, but again this initial enthusiasm for the councils was 'engulfed by the tide of conservatism rising at mid-century'.[4]

Nevertheless, interest in works councils was reawakened in the 1870s in the aftermath of an ideology which was in turn grounded in the ascendancy of two powerful working-class movements (the trade unions and the Social Democratic Party). As Shuchman has argued, the projection of socialist ideals at this time was especially important with respect to workers' participation for they added a new dimension to the ongoing discussions, giving a moral impetus to an idea valued hitherto only as an expedient for uniting different classes during periods of acute and bitter social conflict.[5] It is worth mentioning, too, that Naumann, the founder of the Democratic Party, anticipated the work of the managerialist thinkers as well as Dahrendorf's thesis on the nature of industrial conflict by suggesting that large-scale enterprises would increasingly produce an owning class of *rentiers* who had no direct control and that, in consequence, the primary sources of conflict at work would arise progressively from problems of internal organization associated with control over decision-making processes.[6] And at all events, this controversy helped to fuel an ideological climate which was, by degrees, becoming more favourable to workers' participation in industry.

The first direct legislative action on factory councils in Germany came about in 1891 when the Law for the Protection of Labour provided for factory committees in almost all works employing twenty employees or over.[7] And yet, although much of public opinion would have sustained further evolution along these lines, the balance of power at factory level came to be heavily weighted on the employers' side, and therefore by 1906, notwithstanding the encouragement given to councils by this legislation, only one in ten of the establishments covered by the act had in the event installed a factory committee.[8] Not surprisingly, in this milieu, further inroads into managerial authority were postponed, to be formally sanctioned later when the country was in the throes of the First World War.

As in Britain, this war brought about a number of concessions on the part of the German government to the indigent labour movement by way of insuring that industrial production was not jeopardized at a time when the economy generally was strained by a concentration of effort in the military sector. Recognizing these pressures on the administration, the government responded, in part, by means of the Auxiliary Service Act, under which labour service was compulsory for all the adult population. Such a move was obviously most unpopular with the unions, and therefore the government was in a particularly conciliatory mood, being quite prepared, in the process, to countenance further and stronger legislation on works councils. But while these, too, were made compulsory, they were nevertheless bitterly resented by numerous employers who regarded them as an infringement of their decision-making rights. Certainly, in 1918, fines had to be imposed on several employers who had simply refused to comply with the order.[9] In a general context, then, if such managers are determined to frustrate legislation even during a period of national crisis, there can be no easy passage for such laws in peacetime, unless, that is, the labour movement is soundly organized at local levels and can thereby ensure that laws of this kind are respected.

Further progress for German workers towards a firmer footing in the decision-making structure of the enterprise was ostensibly furnished by the Works Council Act of 1920. The events leading up to this legislation, however, were revolutionary in character and the Act itself was born out of the ongoing struggles both between capital and labour and (within the ranks of the labour movement) between reformists and revolutionaries. To detail the German Revolution and its aftermath here would be superfluous in the light of chapters 4 and 5, but it is worth recording that the law of 1920 clearly reflected the political domination of the reformists who, by attending to the minutiae of council functions, ensured that the influence of trade-union officials (which, as we have observed, was decisive in the wider political context) was in no way circumscribed or prejudiced by the Act itself.[10]

The Works Council Act provided, then, for the election of factory councils in all German enterprises with twenty or more employees.[11] A large co-operative element was envisaged here but, aside from this, the councils were endowed with fundamental powers of decision, such as the execution of awards affecting employees as a whole, the making of joint agreements with employers on work rules, the defence of workers' rights of association, the reconciling of certain grievances, and the participation in the administration of works welfare schemes.[12] None the less, these functions were pale and limited by comparison with those of the independent workers' councils which had been set up by rank-and-file workers as revolutionary and administrative organs.

Moreover, the greatest care was taken in this enactment to prevent councils from encroaching on the responsibilities of trade unions in traditional bargaining areas. Similarly, a number of conciliation boards were requisitioned to control the councils at a higher level and, indeed, management was still accredited with the responsibility for effecting decisions in the enterprise as a whole, so that its executive functions were kept intact.[13] To be sure, at the scheme's inception, many revolutionaries who had served on workers' councils were elected on to the new bodies and were thus able to pursue radical policies, but gradually, with changing conditions and the 'abatement of revolutionary fervour', the electoral processes favoured fewer extremists and, in this way, there was a diminution in the struggle to maximize the opportunities available via the councils for the advancement of working people.[14]

The divisions within the ranks of German labour, which were exacerbated by the demarcation between union and council functions, were to prove disastrous for the movement. Certainly, works councils flourished along with unions in the 'fair weather period' of economic boom between 1920 and 1922, but following the German inflation and the ensuing slump and period of high unemployment, the latent power of working people suffered an abrupt demise, and the organizational divisions within the movement itself became an obvious embarrassment. Incredibly, at this juncture, one of the most important functions of works councillors was, thus, the selection of their constituents for dismissal and they, too, not infrequently suffered a similar fate for reasons which are by now familiar:[15]

> In practice, everything turns on the relative strength of employers on the one hand and of organized labour on the other. During 1924 and 1925, the evidence of the intimidation and victimisation of works councillors is so widespread, that it is quite plain that legal provisions, which may be adequate to protect the councillors in times of normal business activity, are largely ineffective when trade is depressed and there is much unemployment.

Moreover, although it would be quite wrong to ascribe the subsequent emergence of the Nazi movement to the weakness of working-men's organizations alone, to put it at its best, it cannot have helped the opponents of such a creed to have a labour movement, debilitated by economic circumstances, being further enfeebled by the organizational division between trade unions on the one hand and works councils on the other. And, at all events, for labour movements in general, this experience has demonstrated beyond doubt the urgent need to preserve a united oppositional base even during apparently favourable economic circumstances:[16]

> There can be no doubt that the existence of the Councils provided the opposition to the official labour movement with what it stood most in need of—a form of organisation distinct from that of the Unions. On the one side, this has reacted on the Trade Unions by lessening their control over the forces of labour and giving rise to disharmony and mutual recrimination within the ranks. On the other side, the Councils have often lost through their own actions the backing of the Unions and have exposed themselves to the danger, which to a considerable extent materialised in 1924, of being devoured piecemeal by the employers. Further, the short-sighted exploitation by some of the Councils of their power, in the first two or three years, consolidated the opposition of the employers to their pretensions and helped to bring the whole institution into discredit.

Furthermore—and of significance from our point of view—even in the prosperous years of the early 1920s, works councils were not universally instituted throughout German industry, partly because of the refusal of certain employers to entertain them, but also because the workers themselves by no means viewed them with uniform enthusiasm. And again, the demise of the councils was accelerated as economic and trade conditions worsened. Thus, as a contemporary commentator wrote:[17]

> Although the Works Councils are universal and compulsory, in the sense that a Council should be elected in every establishment above a certain size, there is no penalty attached to the failure of employees to elect a Works Council, other than the loss of any privileges that they would have enjoyed under the Act ... it is surprising that there should be such widespread evidence throughout the country of the absence of Councils where they should exist. It remains true that they are almost universally to be found in large undertakings, where employees are numbered by the thousand. But in establishments with less than 1,000 employees it is becoming increasingly common to find no works council.

Of course at a number of points in this inquiry we have suggested that a sizeable workforce is a potential stimulus to combination and, hence, leads directly to those participation practices which are usually expressed through the medium of a recognized trade union. But here we may note too that external constraints which arise from economic and technical conditions can, in effect, contribute to the subversion of the letter as well as the spirit of any law which threatens the delicate balance of power between the main industrial classes in a given socio-economic system.

Turning now to the decades following the Second World War, it is apparent first of all that much of West Germany's present industrial relations policy has been dominated by co-determination (to which we will return later), but, none the less, the reformist mood of this epoch has found expression in the re-introduction of the works councils system which was forfeited during the Nazi era. This was accomplished by the Works Constitution Law of 1952 which, if anything, ensured that the new councils spanned a broader spectrum of issues than those established by the 1920 Act. At the same time, however, council members are still exhorted to co-operate with management and cannot, in any event, 'interfere' in the execution of general policies. This apart, however, a wide range of general and social functions are entrusted to the councils; they can conclude plant agreements, supervise the implementation of laws and decrees, take up employee's grievances and participate in such matters as working schedules and rest periods, holiday schemes, accident-prevention measures, piecework rates and a great many social issues of this kind.[18] Their influence, however, is far less marked in other respects, especially on personnel matters (such as hiring and firing) and economic policy where their role is merely consultative. But by comparison with the earlier period when the unions sought to circumscribe and to restrict the councils' scope, the legislation is far-reaching and extensive and certainly more comprehensive than that envisaged for, say, joint consultative committees in Great Britain.

Now at many points in our inquiry, our attention has been focused on the interplay between broad 'structural' variables (such as economic and technical forces) and the possible reactions to them which owe much to differences of perspective at a value level. This reciprocity of influence is exceptionally well illustrated if we contrast the British and German legislation on consultative committees and works councils respectively and in so doing recollect the different cultural traditions which these formal institutions reflect. In Germany, as we have already seen, the government has a long tradition of direct intervention in industrial relations, but by comparison, British governments have, until recently, been reticent about using constitutional procedures in this field. Of course these differences may not amount to much as far as plant-level labour relations are concerned since, in Britain, shop stewards often carry out functions which are not infrequently *more* extensive than those of German works councils and, in any event, power and values can significantly modify the intended effects of any legislation. But, at the same time, they do indicate the range of responses possible within social situations which are otherwise roughly equivalent.

Nevertheless, while British governments have only lately become enthusiastic about the idea of comprehensive legislation on participation, it would be erroneous to suggest that such moves are unprecedented here, or indeed that governments in this country have been indifferent to initiatives in this direction. On the contrary, a positive enthusiasm by British governments in this respect can be traced to the deliberations of the Whitley Committee of 1917, when, as we have already noticed, the time was ripe for extensions of workers' participation and control both in Britain and in Germany. But whereas in the latter country the Auxiliary Service Act of the previous year had produced a compulsory system of works councils, in Britain, by way of contrast, no major legislation on the subject was forthcoming; but at least the Whitley Committee did establish the main guidelines, summarized by Clegg, which were to underpin voluntary as well as compulsory schemes for joint consultation in subsequent years:[19]

that there are many topics of concern to employers and trade unions, and to managers and men, which are not suitable for settlement by negotiation and collective agreement; that these topics should be handled by co-operation; and that relations within the plant should be predominantly or entirely confined to co-operation over issues outside the scope of collective agreements.

But it was some time later, during the Second World War, that this sort of reasoning began to be translated into governmental action. Trade-union membership and voluntary joint consultation had both declined appreciably during the depression years, but with the advent of fresh hostilities, the need to secure full co-operation and high productivity from the labour force was keenly felt, notably, of course, in industries directly associated with the war effort. Moreover, unlike the First, the Second World War had the universal backing of the Labour movement at least after the German invasion of Russia. At this time, therefore, political developments enhanced the bargaining power of working people and simultaneously promoted consultative practices based on consensual principles. In an atmosphere, then, in which government, employers and trade unions alike saw advantages in consultation, some progress was made towards its inscription in law. In 1942, the Director General of Ordnance agreed to the appointment of joint production consultative committees in all factories covered by the Ministry of Supply.[20] This was supplemented by an agreement in the engineering industry which established joint production, consultative and advisory committees and, furthermore, represented a major fillip to joint consultation in Britain as a whole. Indeed, by July 1943, there were over 4,000 committees of this type, extending to $2\frac{1}{2}$ million workers in the engineering industry.[21]

The next major step in the institution of formal participatory machinery was taken by the post-war Labour government as part of its nationalization programme. To be sure, in this period, as we have already recognized, many opportunities for industrial democracy were sacrificed on an altar of managerialism, but on the positive side, basic bargaining rights were established in all nationalized industries, and joint consultative machinery was also set up as part of the same process. The Coal Industry Nationalization Act, for instance, saw the creation of separate joint machinery for bargaining and consultation, the latter being catered for by the institution of colliery consultative committees at local levels.

Probably the best example of legislation in these respects, however, is that of the electrical supply industry, whose formal machinery for collective bargaining and joint consultation originated in the

Electricity Act of 1947 under which the industry was nationalized. This and other legislation applying to the industry led to the formation of a series of national, regional and local committees. At national level there are five main negotiating bodies, although the National Joint Industrial Council is by far the most important. All these bargaining committees (except that for higher management) have district-level negotiating bodies as well; but at local levels the procedures are more simple and usually consist of two negotiating committees covering works and staff employees separately. There is provision, too, for a parallel system of advisory (or consultative) machinery, which also operates on national, district and local levels.

But cultural variations apart, it must be recognized that the scope and efficacy of legislation is largely determined by the balance of power in industry itself and by perspectives current therein which, in their turn, spring from a commitment to different values and institutional arrangements. This having been understood, it becomes obvious that the status of advisory machinery, for example, fluctuates with the dispositions of shop stewards in particular sections of industry and depends especially on whether they see consultative machinery as an impediment to the emergence of appropriate bargaining systems. For wherever this feeling prevails, as in 1960 in London and south-east England, consultative committees may be immobilized by the emergence of a powerful and unofficial shop-steward movement.[22] Again, it is clear that activist-minded stewards tend to regard such consultative bodies with scarcely-concealed contempt and some, indeed, have nicknamed arrangements 'let's all cuddle'.[23] Moreover, even though in one electricity generating station involved in our own research, a local advisory committee not only flourished but in fact occupied a position of greater consequence than did the works committee, this was largely because none of the high-ranking stewards affected thought it appropriate to pursue a militant strategy, preferring to deal with health, safety and welfare matters rather than with wages and related issues.[24]

In other respects, too, the structure of power and values locally has mediated between legal principle and its application in practice; indeed, in some cases, committees which were made compulsory under nationalization acts have been found *non-operative*.[25] Moreover, in the coal industry the status of colliery consultative committees (CCCS) has been well researched, and the *Coal and Conflict* report disclosed that only 7 per cent of the workforce interviewed had ever asked a CCC representative to take up a problem of any kind, and only 28 per cent of this small fraction of employees experienced any reasonable measure of satisfaction from this intervention. Moreover, 46 per cent of the sample in one colliery and 61 per cent in another said they knew nothing about the CCC while 53 per cent in the first and 67 per cent in the second did not even know the names of their representatives.[26] There can therefore be little doubt of the obstacles faced by those who seek to impose committees of this type from above, unless they are prepared to include in their calculations the underlying realities of power in industry.

(2) Co-determination and other 'worker director' schemes

The background and the day-to-day operation of workers' participation in industry organized around works councils and allied machinery thus inevitably bears the stamp of the latent power and values of the main parties concerned. This argument will now be pursued further as we turn to participation at 'board' level where from time to time there has been experimentation on the part of governments. At the outset, however, it must be made clear that debates on this theme have usually been confined to predominantly capitalist economies (the issue of self-management being more apposite under socialist regimes) and that the situation has been confused as a result of the nature of company and corporation law in this respect.

Of course, as Fogarty points out, participation at board level can take on a number of guises, the following being the most usual: workers' participation in the control of enterprises *without* workers' ownership; workers' ownership of share capital *without* workers' control of enterprises; workers' ownership of share capital and workers' control of enterprise; and workers' ownership of share capital *as a basis* for control over enterprises.[27] And yet, however envisaged, participation at this level gives rise to uncertainties on the issue of accountability, for, in the absence of any special changes in company law, the prime function of the board will remain the protection of shareholders' and creditors' interests (in practice those of private and institutional owners of capital), so that any worker participating at this level must *de jure* take on a role indistinguishable from any other manager or company director. To be sure, a rather different situation may obtain *de facto*, since, in the nature of things, worker directors may well seek to pursue policies which accord more with employee than with shareholder interests, and although worker directors may appear to waver on this matter with the passage of time, they would initially be expected to perceive their functions in a way which deviates from the formal legal situation. Nevertheless, it would seem appropriate for modifications to be made in company law which would relieve the confusion of workers who participate in decisions at board level under current arrangements. Of great value here, too, would be the introduction of new accounting methods based not on profit and loss but on net value added:[28]

> which is as valid as the present system for ensuring that a company shall maintain its financial stability and avoid the wasteful use of resources, but has the advantage of taking such items as pay or contributions to community services out of the category of costs and expressing them like profit, as shares in the net proceeds of the enterprise.

But whatever the nature of the ultimate solution to the dilemmas inherent in the present formulation of company law and accounting methods in this respect, other fundamental questions remain which are more central to our main themes and it is to these that we now turn.

Interest in co-determination and other worker-director schemes have been aroused especially, of course, by the experiments in West Germany which (together with the Dutch system) have supplied the main European model for legislation to this end. It is therefore helpful at this point to look in some detail at the German experience, paying particular attention to co-determination laws since the Second World War but bearing in mind the important precedent of the 1920 Works Council Act which sanctioned the election of one (or sometimes two) council member(s) to the controlling board of the enterprise.[29]

During the period immediately after the Second World War, the workers and their trade unions in Germany were without doubt in a very strong position. A great many German managers had been openly discredited for the part they had played during the Nazi era and the principal industrial and commercial capitalists were similarly disgraced because it was appreciated that Hitler could not have come to power without their aid. In many districts, too, workers had on their own initiatives begun to rebuild the economy and had resumed the practice of electing their own works councils. Again, the power of the employers was further circumscribed by the controls of the occupying allied forces, by the intention to reduce the high concentration of the heavy sector of German industry and by the promise (which was unfulfilled) that previous owners would not be able to regain control of their firms. In short, a power vacuum was created in Germany at this time which was, to say the least, conducive to fresh thinking about the principles and practice of industrial organization in which the question of workers' participation in management loomed large.[30]

But circumstances as propitious as these could have been foregone had it not been for certain general ideological and political developments which were unique to West Germany in this period. Indeed, interest in co-determination was strengthened by three philosophical currents of a democratic socialist, religious and libertarian variety. The foremost was championed by leading trade unionists and by many members of the Social Democratic Party (SPD) who, as a consequence, sought as a point of principle, to ensure parity for labour in all economic and political bodies.[31] Then again, followers of Roman Catholicism, who were the best organized and most articulate of the Christian groupings which had come together in the Christian Democratic Union (CDU), had strong traditional interest in self-governing bodies and were to be important exponents of co-determination legislation.[32] And finally, there was a measure of support for this development from a number of libertarian reformers among managerial ranks.[33]

Simultaneously, the ongoing evolution in political institutions, itself in part a reflection of the thinking of the time, contributed further to the already favourable climate. Thus, in both the German Federation of Labour (DGB) and the SPD, co-determination and co-management were a useful rallying cry to bribe potential dissidents. Similarly, since both leading political parties (the CDU and SPD) were committed to reformist programmes in industry, it was clear that whichever party ultimately came to power, it would inevitably seek legislation with which to promote formal participatory rights for employees at the board level of the enterprise.[34]

For most of the post-war period in West Germany, then, it has been compulsory for workers to be represented on supervisory boards, but the legislation here is complex and its effects by no means uniform throughout West German industry. Thus, although yet further legislation is envisaged to ensure parity of representation throughout West German industry, it remains true that, whereas in the coal and iron and steel industries, 50 per cent of the members of supervisory boards are workers' representatives, in the rest of West German industry the proportion has been of the order of only one in three. Again, while in the aforementioned primary and manufacturing industries the labour director of the managerial board of the enterprise is also, in essence, a workers' representative, this 'privilege' does not extend on the whole to employees in other sectors of industry.[35]

Following the Second World War, the first step in the direction of co-determination was taken in 1947 within the confines of a group of steel companies in the Ruhr. These firms were to some extent prompted along this path by the British occupation authorities who were aiming to deconcentrate heavy industry in the area but, in any event, questions of power and its exercise were high on the agenda both in the drafting of the scheme and in its actual operation.[36] As one commentator has argued:[37]

> Political considerations, involving both hindsight and foresight, dominated the birth of the scheme, regardless of whether labour sired it on management, or the other way round. The newly unified German Trade Union Federation consciously made co-determination the main plank in its platform because this seemed the best means for unifying the politically diverse elements among its membership. The legislation which confirmed the procedures then existing in the steel industry and extended them to the iron and coal industries, and the later legislation about wider forms of co-determination for the rest of the economy, and for public services—all this legislation was supported or oppressed by people mainly on the basis of their political alignments.

The year 1951 saw the passing of the most notable piece of legislation on co-determination; this applied only to companies engaged in the production of iron and steel and the mining of coal and iron ore, and it was the offspring of a major power struggle. At the time the employers were willing to concede co-determination, but only at plant level on questions of a personnel and social nature, and they objected, furthermore, to giving parity of representation to workers on the supervisory board. In response, the DGB, who wanted equal controlling powers for workers' representatives, organized a referendum among the metal workers, 96 per cent of whom voted for the proposed strike action.[38] This threat of action alone was to prove successful enough, however, and the first co-determination law (to be supplemented in 1956) was thus inscribed on the Statute Book. But with the CDU in control at the political level, and with the unions becoming progressively less strong and militant in the industrial sphere, the Law on the Constitution of the Enterprise (or Works Constitution Law) of 1952 which made provision for the rest of West German industry, was much less generous to the workers' side: as we have previously mentioned, employees were entitled here to only one-third of the representatives of supervisory boards, and these were nominated by the trade unions rather than by the works councils.[39]

Legal action in this respect in West Germany has of course been facilitated by the 'double-decker' structure of authority within undertakings. Under this arrangement, there is a clear division between the supervisory board (*Aufsichtsrat*), which consists of shareholders and employee representatives, and the managing board (*Vorstand*), usually made up of commercial, technical and labour directors. This effectively distinguishes, too, between policy and executive organs within the firm. In the coal and iron and steel industries, moreover, the labour director is himself selected on the basis of nominations made by the metal or mine workers' unions which are then submitted to the works council and supervisory board of the company concerned. Indeed, in some respects, the labour director is, from the employees' point of view, a far more important consequence of co-determination legislation than the worker directors on the supervisory boards.[40] After all, he has administrative responsibility for a whole range of personnel and social policies including recruitment, hiring and firing, employee transfers, education of managerial personnel on human relations practices, pension and insurance funds, wages and salaries and so on. And although, of course, commercial and technical matters are outside his jurisdiction, he clearly has ultimate control over many areas of particular interest to shop-floor workers.[41]

But to what extent, it may be reasonably asked, is co-determination in practice affected by configurations of power and values within the workplace and the wider society? After all, this study has advanced the claim not only that factors such as these can make intelligible the generation of individual participatory programmes but also that they profoundly affect the day-to-day operation and success, or otherwise, experienced by any specific scheme. The first point to be made in this context is, then, that far-reaching economic and technical considerations have undoubtedly been instrumental in the working of co-determination at local levels. A major deficiency of co-determination as conceived within West Germany is that the powers of trade unions at supra-company level are somewhat limited and they therefore have had little impact on the wave of mergers in the coal and steel industries. To be sure, in the face of the consequent erosion of workers' power, the unions have fought a number of rear-guard actions with positive results; in one notorious case they were able to persuade a company to refrain from adopting a new industrial classification (which would have meant opting out of the category under law which offered the most scope for workers' participation via co-determination), the effect of which would otherwise have been a considerable reduction of workers' rights.[42] Again, an initial phase in the consolidation of the German coal industry led to the displacement of twenty-eight labour directors, but after some negotiation, unions and management were able to agree on a compromise which avoided these redundancies by internal reorganization and the erection of a hierarchy among the ranks of labour directors themselves. Thus, under this arrangement, a labour director who might otherwise have had to leave the company following a merger, would instead take a lower level, but related, post within the enterprise.[43]

In general, then, national developments on the economic front can have fundamental implications for labour relations in the plant. And above all, when these are potentially deleterious from the workers' point of view, the outcome so far as participatory and control practices are concerned is decisively influenced by the latent, organizational strength of the employees' own independent bodies and by the actions they consider it to be appropriate as well as legitimate to take.

Indeed, one of the traditional handicaps of German labour has been the demarcation between union and works-council activities, for although works councillors themselves are often members of the appropriate union, there is still, nevertheless, some rivalry between these two factions which has at times damaged the workers' cause. The 1952 Act on co-determination is a case in point, being seen in some circles as a Pyrrhic victory for the workers concerned:[44]

> Not only had political conservatives managed to keep these more recent demands well under the level of the Co-determination Law, but the unions also discovered that they had weakened their position by increasing the powers of non-union agencies. In particular, the strengthening of the works councils without parallel re-inforcement of formal union controls worked against the trade unions: now it was the councils rather than union officers which seemed to strive for and win concessions from management. Seeds were laid for rivalry between these two forms of employee representation, and some observers felt that the unions had pulled the rug out from under themselves.

Besides, in most of West German industry, supervisory boards have been dominated more by the banks than by ordinary workpeople, especially with respect to commercial and technical policies. Indeed, approximately one in three of the non-employee places are, in practice, held by bank representatives, and frequently the chairman or vice-chairman of the board is also a banker.[45] Again, in West Germany, a great deal of power is concentrated in three main banks which consequently exercise an unusual degree of control over investments throughout industry.

By contrast, the labour force is less well integrated nationally and far more fragmentary in its local organization, being divided, of course, along union and works-council lines. Thus, although the majority of workers are well disposed to co-determination, and despite the undoubted benefits stemming from the personnel and social policies of worker directors, co-determination has hardly had earth-shaking consequences for the social and industrial order. On the contrary, the impact of workers on West German industry through co-determination is clearly conditioned by their own solidarity and strength *vis-à-vis* other oppositional groups and 'stakeholders' within the enterprise, and the acquisition of labour directors and worker directors on supervisory boards, while far from irrelevant, is itself not a cause but a reflection of this underlying power.

Nevertheless, there were clearly fundamental ideological and political forces at work in West Germany in the post-Second World War period which contrasted with, say, the experience of Great Britain at the same time and which were to induce a reformist spirit to be directed towards the extension of workers' rights to participate at board-room level in industry. But there were some piecemeal developments in Britain in this respect as well and these, together with certain later experiments, should be outlined at this point.

Now we have from time to time recognized that, in seeking to extend public ownership, governments can prepare a fertile ground for the growth of industrial democracy. And yet, as we observed in chapter 5, the main post-war nationalization programme carried out by the Labour government between 1945 and 1951 was not on the whole used for this purpose at all, even though basic bargaining and consultative rights were, of course, formally established for all employees in the relevant industries. By the same token, a number of ex-trade-union representatives were generally co-opted on to the boards of nationalized industries, although there was no question of their being accountable to any trade union or to any constituency of workers. In other words, even if by virtue of temperament and of political conviction it would have been in character for such board members to steer a course in which employees' interests were to the forefront, they were most certainly robbed of any obvious power base which might have facilitated the successful pursuit of policies along these lines.[46]

But the election, in 1964, of a Labour government (which was committed at the very least to nationalization of the steel industry) was an opportune moment for further experimentation with employee participation on boards of directors and in due course gave rise to a limited worker-director scheme in the steel industry. This envisaged the appointment of up to four workers to directorships on each of the group or area boards which were brought into being by the initial nationalization act. Nevertheless, alongside the West German programme these were clearly timid proposals because: first, the boards had only advisory functions; second, worker directors were to act in only a personal capacity; and third, although they were nominated by the trade unions, the corporations were to ratify any appointments.[47]

To be sure, subsequent modifications of this early conception may yet make more provision for a satisfactory advance in the direction of co-determination, But in this event, union pressure allied with technical changes (which among other things seem a likely prelude to a major contraction in the labour force and which, in turn, have induced a conciliatory posture on the part of management) appear to be the main antecedent conditions. Thus, in 1970, following a major restructuring of the steel corporation, in the course of which the area boards were replaced by six product divisions, some rethinking of the worker-director scheme was inevitable. Moreover, as a result of persistent criticism from the unions concerned, a confidential report was requisitioned (which was undertaken by Alexander) and in the light of the recommendations therein, the BSC announced its intention to amend the worker-director scheme. In particular, it paid special attention to the promotion by these directors of a shop-floor point of view, to the strengthening of links between worker directors and trade unions and to the maintenance of trade-union office, where applicable, by the directors concerned. Nevertheless, there are at present only sixteen worker directors in the entire steel industry and, since the BSCs chairman can still make final appointments from the nominations made by unions, the scheme itself even now falls short of a fully-fledged co-determination programme on the West German model.[48]

(3) Self-management and workers' councils

No study of workers' participation and control would, of course, be complete without some reference to the Yugoslav self-management system, for, although this is not a unique experiment in that workers' councils have been established administratively in a number of other nations (and notably Poland,[49] Czechoslovakia[50] and Algeria[51]), it clearly supplies us with a general model from which certain conclusions about the operation of self-management systems may be drawn. Furthermore, since a great many investigations have now been carried out within Yugoslav factories, we have far more systematic information on the day-to-day workings of the scheme upon which to rely than is readily available for the other countries. But in order to illustrate the principal themes of the present study, it is pertinent to review the relevant material on the self-management system under three main headings: first, the background conditions; second, the principal legislation on the scheme itself; and third, its actual operation at enterprise level.

In contrast with co-determination, self-management is not founded on the premise of the potential unity of different class interests but upon the prior abolition of economic classes by means of the expropriation of individual capital holdings. In Yugoslavia, this move followed the Second World War when, although the system of agriculture was left in private hands, all existing industries were taken into public ownership. To begin with, during the so-called administrative period, the authorities set out to organize their economy on the Soviet model and, with this aim in view, they drew up a massive central plan which was designed to achieve rapid economic development via a system of production targets for individual enterprises. Indeed, targets for between 16,000 and 20,000 commodities were set out in minute detail.[52]

The ensuing clash with Soviet leaders precipitated a shift in Yugoslav thinking on these matters, and in the ensuing ideological controversy on the future of socialism, interest revolved around the classical writings of Marx and Lenin on the ultimate 'withering away of the State' and this in turn led to intense criticism of étatistic and bureaucratic forms of socialism. Again, Yugoslavia was in fact expelled from the Cominform in 1948 and then faced an economic blockade from Eastern European countries—two further circumstances which were to stimulate new ideas about the principles of economic administration.[53]

Nevertheless, if the prior abolition of private capital provided a necessary condition for the creation of a thoroughgoing self-management system and if this was precipitated by the emergence of fresh ideologies brought on by the break with Russia, there were yet other aspects of Yugoslav culture which, as Riddell has argued, tended to militate against 'the permanent establishment of a centralized state on the Soviet model'.[54] Thus, to begin with, although the country had been overrun by Axis forces, the partisans had succeeded in regaining parts of this territory without the immediate assistance of the Red Army and, in liberated areas, where autonomous administrative units were in operation, the idea of self-management became by no means foreign to ordinary people. Secondly, many of the communist leaders in Yugoslavia had become acquainted with anarcho-syndicalist ideas while fighting with Republican forces in the Spanish Civil War and this experience, too, kindled an ideology in which self-government was a principal component. And finally, since Yugoslavia was, in any event, made up of a number of contrasting and heterogeneous regions, it was hardly conceivable that such diversity could be easily united under the aegis of a centralized nation state.[55] This unique cultural configuration was thus an ideal framework for the development of ideologies in which democratic and socialist ideals were given approximately equal weight.

Now, in statutory terms, the Law on the Management of State Economic Enterprises, passed in 1950, laid the main foundations for the present system of administration in Yugoslav factories. In detail, the principal organs established by the Act were: first, the workers' council; second, the management board; and third, the enterprise director.[56] In each workplace, a workers' council, elected by the entire labour force, was to be given overall responsibility for policy and entrusted with the legal obligation to determine the general economic activity of the works. The council itself would be of a range of between 15 and 120 members, according to the size of establishment, and it in turn elected its own executive committee (the management board) to carry out policy and to settle a number of personnel and economic matters. Finally, the director was to be charged with responsibility for day-to-day administration of policies which stemmed from the decisions of the workers' council. Moreover, his own appointment and its termination was also to depend on the initiatives of the workers' councillors, albeit with the sanction of the commune people's committee (the decentralized political wing brought into being by the Yugoslav authorities).[57]

To be sure, since its inception, this Act has been supplemented on many occasions by government fiat and the formal character of Yugoslav enterprises has been modified accordingly. But two changes of particular note have accompanied these legal meanders, namely, direct participation has come to the fore as a supplement to the representative system and, at the same time, even greater autonomy is now being exercised in individual plants than was conceded by the initial legislation. Thus, in an attempt to promote the ordinary workers' involvement in decision-making, workers' councils were extended to middle management levels and, in 1961, so-called 'economic units' were spawned in an effort to ensure greater freedom of decision on the shop floor. Enterprise autonomy has been encouraged, too, by later measures, not least by the legislation of 1969, which carefully avoided any detailed provision for the organization of management at factory level.[58]

Any summary of the main characteristics of the councils' system in Yugoslavia, therefore, must of necessity recognize the pains which have been taken to distinguish between State and social ownership of production and should thence go on to describe the ideal–typical economic system there as follows. First, there is self-government in the sense that the process of management is formally based on democratic majority rule; second, a policy of income-sharing operates; third, the economy is decentralized and the deployment of resources depends on market mechanisms; fourth, employees have a right to use the assets of the enterprise but do not personally own the firms in which they work; and finally, there is 'freedom of employment' in the sense that there is no State direction of labour.[59] But, as Vanek has also pointed out, although such principles are incompatible with control and management by capital, they need not be socialist either:[60]

> In fact, the distinction between labor-managed and non-labor-managed is far more significant than the distinction between socialist and non-socialist. While the former involves a whole way of life bearing on every hour of a man's entire day, the latter, from an individual's point of view, may not mean much more than a different distribution of wealth and income.

Nevertheless, in our view, any scheme for workers' participation or control arising from the processes of government and law must inevitably run the gauntlet of the ongoing power relationships between the main parties involved at factory level. But before turning to the relevant evidence here, reference will be made to certain components of the macro-economic order which exercise a profound influence on the domestic economic scene in Yugoslavia.

The reliance on market mechanisms as the principal means of resource allocation is unquestionably the most significant in this respect. To be sure, some important economic advantages can accrue from the use of the market, not least that producers are thus relatively free from interference from external administrative authorities, that incomes, too, may be determined solely on the basis of output and productivity, and that the very independence of producers acts as an incentive for maximum productive effort and, thence, for general economic expansion.[61] But equally, as Bottomore also suggests, the operation of market criteria can be distinctly unattractive on social grounds largely because serious inequalities spring from variations in the level of technology, market situation, relative strength of different branches of the economy and other even 'accidental' factors which bear no relation whatsoever to any widely upheld ethical principles.[62] Furthermore, although nearly half the investment capital of Yugoslav firms is generated internally, the rest is derived from external sources (usually the banks) and, with the increasing tendency to borrow capital from abroad, there is a real danger that not only will the decisions of workers' councils be shaped by a consideration of market forces but that, in future, a growing dependence on privately-owned capital will have even more serious repercussions on the balance of power in the society and, in turn, could further constrain the processes of decision-making at local level.[63]

Given knowledge of these national and international economic factors the evolution of the Yugoslav system of self-management becomes readily understandable. Thus, although the Yugoslav economy has recorded a remarkable rise in its rate of economic growth (indeed, in the late 1950s it had the greatest increase in *per capita* gross national product in the world), at the same time persistent unemployment and substantial regional inequalities—for example, between 1947 and 1969 the income *per capita* of workers in Slovenia rose from 175 to 188 (using standard index numbers) while that of those in Kosovo actually fell from 50 to 35 during the same period—have produced an outcrop of nationalist sentiments.[64] Furthermore, the impact of external economic constraints, and particularly of the operation of market forces, on the power of participants in industry at local levels has been reflected in the progressive enhancement of the authority of top management and other senior grades of staff whose education and interests are more compatible with taking decisions on financial, marketing and technical issues. Indeed, the falling-off of influence by central government on plant level decisions has been so marked and its results so dramatic that, as Kolaja has argued:[65]

> Essentially, the new workers' council legislation has primarily
> benefited management, giving it more freedom and room for
> initiative. On the other hand, workers' labour unions have remained
> more dependent, not only upon management, but also upon direction
> from outside.

It is, however, important to present a balanced view of the gains and losses to Yugoslav workers of the self-management system and to offset the somewhat pessimistic account given so far by some of its obviously positive characteristics. To begin with, although major regional inequalities of income remain in Yugoslavia, social-class variations in material standards of living are minimal by comparison with those current in the west and, indeed, in predominantly capitalist societies as a whole.[66] This, too, is of particular significance in a market economy because the 'distortion-effects' of really large disparities of income and wealth on production priorities are correspondingly reduced because a sizeable percentage of firms are not engaged solely in producing for consumption by the rich. Again, while there is good reason to believe that, on technical and commercial questions, the views of workers and their representatives have been of only limited account, over a range of personnel and social issues (including hiring and firing, working conditions, fringe benefits and even wages) their influence has been noticeably more pronounced.[67] And, above all, since the remuneration of all employees is open to discussion and debate, the disparity of income between higher managerial staff on the one hand and unskilled labourers on the other is seldom of an order of more than approximately three or four to one.[68] In addition, the practice of rotation of membership has given large numbers of workers the opportunity to experience office-holding on workers' councils and management boards: indeed, between 1950 and the early 1960s, well over a million people served in these capacities.[69] Finally, although women and semi-skilled workers have had disproportionately unfavourable treatment in this respect, the chances for widespread participation are clearly extensive and appear especially so by comparison with those available to workers in any other west European country.[70]

But if we turn at this point to examine the role in practice of workers in a typical Yugoslav enterprise, two general conclusions may be drawn: that the influence of workers on decision-making processes is restricted by comparison with that exercised by higher management, and that it has declined progressively in the absence of external administrative pressures. Furthermore, since sophisticated measuring techniques have been brought to bear on such questions, we can be fairly confident of the validity of this assessment.

Two well-known approaches have been adopted in the cause of the measurement of the configuration of power in Yugoslav factories; the first using the 'control-graph' method, and the second relying on the careful observation of council meetings. The first is essentially a variant of the 'reputational approach' to power measurement in the course of which respondents are asked to judge the respective influence of prominent groups within the workplace. Rus has usefully summarized the results of seven separate studies in which the control graph method was employed and has come to the surprising conclusion that, if workers' council and local trade union are seen as interchangeable bodies, the pattern of influence is not to any significant degree different from that obtaining, say, in firms in the USA.[71] For, when questioned, men and women at different levels of the enterprise consistently ranked top management as having the most influence, followed by the management board, then the workers' council and, last of all, the unskilled workers in the plant, whose influence was judged to be even lower than that of trade unions and the Communist Party, even though both received low scores overall.[72] This evidence, too, tends to support the claim that management and administrative staff 'have power without responsibility' and the council 'responsibility without power'.[73] To be sure, this perceived pattern of influence was not legitimated by workers covered by these studies; on the contrary, they would have welcomed an increase in their own authority and that of their representatives.[74] But equally, investigations after 1968 betrayed some resignation among workers as to the role of higher management, and this suggested some weakening of the self-management ideology, for workers had begun to aspire not to an extension of their personal power, but to a state of parity between workers' councils and the upper managerial reaches.[75] On the other hand, the evidence pointed to the superiority in production of democratic forms of organization in industry, the most *efficient* enterprises being those in which management, in the view of rank-and-file workers, were responsive to the views of others.[76] Not surprisingly, too, workers were much more concerned over questions on personnel and social matters than over commercial and technical considerations.[77]

Supplementary material from observational studies of workers' councils in practice tends to corroborate these findings. Kolaja, in both the factories he investigated, discovered that managers were able to ensure that all measures in which they were interested were implemented by the workers' council, that those suggestions which were adopted by the council derived, in the majority of cases, from management, and that only the better-educated workers were effective in discussions.[78] Furthermore, although some influence of the council of producers and communes within the local district was detected (indeed, all the recommendations from these external groups were ratified by the workers' council), not only were the majority of shop-floor workers effectively excluded from the decision-making processes at council level but they were also largely ignorant of the details of its operation. In one shop, for instance, ten out of twenty-four employees knew nothing of a meeting concerned with the allocation of apartments for workers and managerial staff.[79] A valuable study by Obradovic went further and confirmed that technology has a conditioning effect on participation.[80] He demonstrated, too, that membership of self-governing bodies was reflected in expressions of satisfaction towards work, pay, working conditions and aspects of job control.[81] Moreover—and of central importance from the standpoint of this study—an opportunity for participation was of greater consequence for workers in repetitive work in highly mechanized plants than for those engaged in handicraft and automated industries. There was evidence, then, of the 'compensational effect of a social system in relation to the negative aspects of a technological system'.[82] In short, the opportunities for higher-level participation were undoubtedly appreciated in an intensely alienating work environment.

In conclusion, we must mention that, despite incontrovertible evidence of the influence of senior management on factory life in Yugoslavia, there are signs that 'countervailing tendencies' are emerging from the ranks of those working people who have found it most difficult to express their interests through workers' council machinery. Thus, although as Kolaja has argued, the role of trade unions has been overtly circumscribed by the workers' council legislation, there is increasing evidence that workers are turning to the trade-union movement as a means of expressing their grievances and of promoting their respective claims to the wealth produced by the enterprise as a whole. In the past, unions have often tacitly supported a number of unofficial stoppages but, in 1970, an important milestone was reached when the miners' union declared the first official strike in Yugoslavia since the passage of the initial councils' law in 1950.[83] And, of course, this is the logical and predictable consequence of a condition in which workers find that a political and industrial instrument, which is apparently geared to the fulfilment of their interests, fails, in its exercise, to meet their expectations in the face of a particular balance of power and values in the day-to-day operation of industry.

7 Conclusions and prospects

In introducing this volume we declared our intention to review the material pertaining to a highly interesting and significant subject in a somewhat novel light. With this end in view, we directed our attention both to our explanatory analysis of workers' participation and control and to the fundamental question of the exercise of power in industry and in society at large. It is now opportune to restate those conclusions to which we attach special significance and to assess the implications of our findings for the issues of power and participation.

It has been our main contention that workers' participation in decision-making may be best understood as one index of the exercise of power in industrial life. But to explain the genesis of the phenomena in question and, indeed, to account for the success or otherwise of the actual operation of any arrangement designed for this purpose, it was inevitable that we would delve rather more deeply into those components of industrial life which enhance or depress the latent power of the main social classes, parties or groups and which encourage, too, the formation of values specific to industrial participation. Or in short, and in accordance with the equation $P = f(L,V)$, we were able to deduce that workers' participation and control were a function of latent power and values.

In the course of this study we also expanded on the unsatisfactory presentation of the concept of latent power in the bulk of the relevant literature to date, and observed that the key indices here (numbers, organization and resources) had been employed, in essence, as descriptive categories only. Thus, in seeking their adoption in this study as explanatory constructs and to avoid an otherwise tautological argument, it was incumbent upon us to elucidate those forces (economic, technological and governmental—i.e. political) which seemed to be especially salient in such a framework.

More than once in the course of this study, in alluding to the conditioning role of these social factors, we have emphasized the importance of the values of the parties in question. These certainly made intelligible the otherwise erratic and inconsistent variations in types of participation arising from roughly similar balances of latent power. But equally central to our own understanding of the operation of workers' participation and control in industry was the realization that values favourable to these developments could not, in isolation, ensure the lasting success of any of the schemes under consideration. Furthermore, these values were not in our view confined to individual responses to specific social situations but had other origins as well. Indeed, many emanated from more comprehensive ideologies or from political actions, while others sprang from the practice of participation and from a rise in the level of latent power among workers themselves.

The validity of these propositions was established by an examination of a rich and interesting array of practices and programmes for extending workers' participation and control of decision-making processes. Moreover, this analysis was facilitated by a classification which replaced 'rule of thumb' categories by ones which differentiated between the initiators of the programmes in question.

Armed with this framework, we began by examining the variegated forms of participation stemming from managerial initiatives. Here we observed that, on balance, certain changes in managerial ideologies had worked against the expansion of participation, for although tradi-tional-ownership sentiments had been progressively abandoned they had been replaced by the idea that management has an expertise indis-pensable to the efficient organization of industry. This indeed has now become the main source of legitimacy of managerial authority. Fur-thermore, such a view, which is encompassed in the managerialist thesis and finds more specific expression in the assertion that modern managers are highly professional, technically proficient and largely non-propertied, clearly represents a fundamental obstacle to any fully-fledged system of workers' participation and control. Neverthe-less, it has been in the interests of many efficiency-conscious em-ployers to relinquish some of their decision-making prerogatives (especially where these are restricted to those of foremen and other lower-managerial personnel) in return for higher output and pro-ductivity, acceptance of change, flexible working arrangements and relatively conflict-free industrial relations. Moreover, in our view such developments are almost certain to multiply substantially in the years ahead, partly because of the competitive advantages to be gained by introducing experiments of this nature, but also because employees themselves are likely to demand greater control over decision-making processes at shop-floor level as expectations rise in this respect.

The discussion was given new direction at this juncture as we examined a wide range of participation and control practices which have emerged from the ranks of working people. These again varied greatly in scope from limited workgroup practices to those more ambitious programmes in which workers' control was a means for transforming an entire social order. But, somewhat remarkably, and despite the very diverse origins and ideals which precipitated them, the success or otherwise of these practices could be seen to depend in great measure on the same basic forces of latent power and values among the parties concerned.

We then examined the role of the trade-union officer and noted that only a narrow band of participation practices had as a rule attracted unreserved enthusiasm from this source. To be sure, whenever these have been rooted in the union structure, officials have supported them, but those initiatives of managements and workers which have failed to relate to union organization have met with some suspicion. Naturally, of course, all trade-union officials have not reacted in this way, for those with a strong personal commitment to socialist and democratic ideologies and those who are subject to democratic pressures in the internal organization of their union have usually been more positive in this respect. Again, the progressive advancement in the latent power of plant-based workers and lay officials is exerting a considerable pressure on those officials who are less favourably disposed to participation in the workplace.

Finally, in chapter 6, we turned to an examination of the function of governments and political parties in this regard. And here, although there was no intention on our part to suggest that no contribution could be made by legislation in this field, it was abundantly clear that while this type of action has served to foster a climate of opinion conducive to democracy and has impinged on economic forces and power balances which are fundamental in workplace relations, its *direct* relevance for participation is somewhat questionable. What is more, these statutory provisions can themselves be understood as specific responses to contemporary conditions and their success seen ultimately to hinge on those key elements which have been identified in this study.

From a specialist viewpoint, then, we have touched on many themes which are currently important in industrial sociology and industrial relations. We hope that our discussions on power will have added a certain measure of conceptual clarity to the arguments here and that we have provided a framework by means of which to make intelligible a number of otherwise disparate themes, studies and experiments. Again, on the question of industrial democracy, our approach differs from that of those who, in criticizing the untenable position that workers cannot participate in management, in their turn have advanced somewhat Utopian opinions about the genesis of effective participation, and in so doing have failed to recognize that it is precisely by augmenting the latent and oppositional power of workers (and stimulating the values conducive to experiments of this kind) that progress can be made towards the establishment of workers' participation in decision-making at every level.

But throughout this study we have also attempted to satisfy the interests of the general reader, and to this end it would seem reasonable here to assess some of the prospects ahead: first, by an estimate of the probable success of those schemes which are being suggested at present; second, by an analysis of those changes which might be efficacious in this respect; and finally, by relating these to the social and political climate of our time.

Contemporary politicians have commonly advocated four classes of participation: (1) profit sharing and co-partnership schemes; (2) works councils, whether based on the trade union structure or not; (3) board-level representation either through works councils or unions; (4) lower-level forms of participation at workgroup level to prevent job monotony, and so on. In the light of the evidence above, can these proposals be expected to meet with any success?

The main point to be made here, of course, is that since a great deal hinges on economic, technical and political variables and on the constellation of values current in any given time or place, a blanket answer to the question would be unrealistic. None the less, it is apparent that, while employees may superficially welcome profit-sharing and co-partnership schemes, their adoption is not likely to represent any major step towards genuine participation. Indeed, as we pointed out, profit-sharing arrangements are as a rule hardly more than ineffective bonus incentives since, by being insufficiently adapted to individual and workgroup efforts, they are too remote to have much effect on plant-level industrial relations. Similarly, although there is no doubt that co-partnership schemes can be compatible with commercial success and do make provision for participation, our information to date suggests that paternalistic practices tend to preclude fully-fledged participation in those firms in which such an arrangement is operative. One consequence of this, too, is that the formation of pressure groups from below, based usually on union organization, is effectively stifled.

Works councils, too, are unlikely to be an especially impressive medium for participation at plant level. After all, they tend, like trade unions, to make progress in fair-weather periods of full employment and economic boom but to founder in less opportune circumstances. What is more, compulsory works councils unconnected with trade unions have at times operated against the interests of workers. In all probability, of course, any eventual Act of Parliament would respect those works councils already in existence if these were in strongly unionized plants and were thus organized round a single channel of representation. Moreover, it is doubtful whether the compulsory institution of works councils would be of much avail in those, usually small, firms which are characterized by strong paternalistic ties between management and men, except perhaps as an additional, rather cumbersome procedure for the diffusion of information. In practice, too, management would almost certainly dominate meetings and rank-and-file workers would be left with a clumsy instrument for dealing with minor disputes which might have been more speedily settled by less formal methods. And in any event, what happens if management refuses to grant workers' requests or even to set up a works council? The current draft proposals make little if any provision for employee redress, and therefore, in such events, and in the absence of trade-union organization, we must surely anticipate the persistence of those well-tried but rather negative and individualistic solutions of absenteeism, resignation from the firm, and so on.

Furthermore, the establishment of non-unionized works councils, whatever the ideals behind them, could be a divisive force among the ranks of workers in yet other firms where union organization is embryonic, or weak, or both. What is more, although the resemblance is tempered by fundamental variations in cultural, political and institutional conditions, the German inter-war experience, in which the gulf between trade unions and works councils contributed at least in part to the demise of the labour movement in that country, is testimony enough to the dire consequences of such divisions in unfavourable economic circumstances.

The success of board-level representation, too, turns as much on the latent power of constituent parties in industry as on the legal niceties of any Act itself, although without a measure of compulsion in this field it is almost certain that management hostility to participation at this level would impede other than piecemeal moves in this direction. None the less, without the support of powerful unions, representatives of workers on boards of directors will almost certainly be constrained and ineffective. Similarly, an openly hostile atmosphere between management and workers is unlikely to be abated by legislation of this type; rather, the imposition of compulsory arrangements would probably lead to an outcrop of informal managerial meetings designed to by-pass official procedures. And in general, once again, there is the perennial problem that under depressed economic conditions these schemes would either be put into cold storage or cease to function altogether. Therefore, although government action along these lines might well be necessary if workers are to make inroads into decision-making processes at board level, it should be seen once more as a dependent rather than as an independent condition of the distribution of industrial power.

If, however, the main aim of legislation is to enhance industrial efficiency rather than to extend the rights of working people, lower-level forms of participation will probably be most requisite in this respect. Certainly, managerial opposition will be far less evident here, since these projects involve only a slight adaptation of the formal authority-structure of the firm. At the same time, however, where unions are strong, they may evoke a negative reaction and induce industrial conflict if they are not introduced via union channels as a natural extension of collective-bargaining machinery. Furthermore, being particularly susceptible to technological variations, such participation is likely to be correspondingly ineffective in reducing the ravages of workplace alienation under assembly-line and other intermediary-range technologies.

On the positive side, however, and to the extent that the main propositions contained in our model have been substantiated, a number of additional inferences are legitimate. First, it is our considered opinion that the law in this field is of marginal importance compared with economic buoyancy and full employment which are the true guardians of workers' rights to decision-making. By the same token, the growth of conglomerate corporations and the parallel accretions in workers' support for unions provides a foundation for employee participation far more solid than that envisaged in legislation to date. To be sure, the emergence of such supra-national combines conveys an element of danger for labour movements, and in the face of this, some defensive strategy will be unavoidable, ranging from autonomous actions of trade union combine committees to co-operative efforts between workers separated by national frontiers. But, at least, the age of the multi-national company has served to implement the collapse of paternalistic ties which have, over generations, been detrimental to independent trade-union organization and action. Moreover, from our own survey it seems clear that personal freedom on the job is affected less often by job-enrichment programmes than by the proscription of assembly-line manufacture. Far-reaching structural transformations such as these could revitalize the lives of working people but piecemeal modifications of the traditional framework are by comparison a poor alternative. And lastly, in this context, government involvement in economic planning, the extension of public ownership and the subordination of market forces to social criteria must surely offer great scope for the promotion of workers' participation in industry.

Turning, then, more specifically, to the question of values, the contribution of legislation in the field of attitude formation and change could be considerable, and yet values could perhaps be more susceptible to other influences. If, for instance, humanistic doctrines were to gain general currency, the consequent elevation of the minimum conditions deemed tolerable at work could, in the most favourable circumstances, serve as an insistent pressure for the equalization of rights in the workplace. Furthermore, the maintenance and enhancement of a high material standard of living, being generally conducive to rising expectations for autonomy, creativity and involvement, could further stimulate this demand. And if participation were demonstrably effective, it would come to be received with enthusiasm from many additional quarters.

But if, however, we now look ahead to the medium- and long-term development of industrial societies, there seems some likelihood that industrial democracy could be sacrificed in the wake of ecological catastrophe. Ironically, though, if this diagnosis is valid, participation itself may represent one preventative of this incipient malaise, for workers previously equipped with the power of direction in their own working lives might well proceed to recognize the natural and physical realities surrounding human existence and thus accommodate, rather sooner than later, the unavoidable constraints which these ultimately impose on individual freedom.

It is conceivable, too, that the sharing of industrial power will similarly induce a long-overdue change in the organization of industrial society and pave the way for a post-industrial culture. Representation of the views of rank-and-file workers at local and higher levels of industry, coupled with public accountability from those in control of key sectors of the economy could, indeed, herald a new era. Moreover, the contributions of ordinary people with detailed experience of the operation of industry could be an invaluable asset in overall economic planning; public funds could be made available for new projects employing advanced technologies and arising from local as well as national discussions about what should be produced within any given social order. And this would not only ensure a sound and expanding economy, but would also assist the solution of environmental and regional problems while offering new opportunities for experimentation in democratic methods of management and control. If we have helped to clarify the issues at stake and suggested a path towards a future which holds the promise of the actualization of human potentialities, our purpose will be satisfied.

Notes

Chapter 1 **Point of departure**

1 A. Dawe, 'The two sociologies', *British Journal of Sociology*, 21, pp. 207–18, 211.
2 C. W. Mills, *The Sociological Imagination*, New York, 1959, p. 3.
3 Dawe, *op. cit.*, p. 214.
4 *Ibid.*, p. 213.
5 J. A. Schumpeter, *Capitalism, Socialism and Democracy*, London, 1943.
6 T. B. Bottomore, *Elites and Society*, Harmondsworth, 1964, p. 115.
7 P. Blumberg, *Industrial Democracy*, London, 1968; C. Pateman, *Participation and Democratic Theory*, Cambridge, 1970.
8 H. Marcuse, *Reason and Revolution*, London, 1954.
9 H. Barakat, 'Alienation: a process of encounter between Utopia and reality', *British Journal of Sociology*, 20, p. 1.
10 For a well-developed summary see Pateman, *op. cit.*, chapter 2.
11 A. H. Maslow, *Motivation and Personality*, New York, 1954; R. Likert, *New Patterns in Management*, New York, 1961; D. McGregor, *The Human Side of Enterprise*, New York, 1960.
12 This is evident especially in J. H. Goldthorpe *et al.*, *The Affluent Worker: Industrial Attitudes and Behaviour*, Cambridge, 1968.
13 S. L. Andreski, *Military Organization and Society*, London, 1954, p. 217.
14 *Ibid.*, p. 218.
15 F. Musgrove, *The Migratory Elite*, London, 1963.
16 *Ibid.*, pp. 116–17.
17 Blumberg, *op. cit.*, p. 123.
18 There are many relevant studies; see e.g. G. Hespe, and A. Little, 'Some aspects of employee participation', in P. B. Warr (ed), *Psychology at work*, Harmondsworth, 1971; H. Holter, 'Attitudes towards employee participation in company decision making processes', *Human Relations*, 18, pp. 297–322; C. J. Lammers, 'Power and participation in decision making in formal undertakings', *American Journal of Sociology*, 73, pp. 201–16; N. C. Morse and E. Reimer, 'Experimental change in a major organizational variable', *Journal of Abnormal and Social Psychology*, 52, pp. 120–9; A. K. Rice, *Productivity and Social Organization*, London, 1958; E. Thorsrud and F. E. Emery, *Form and Content in Industrial Democracy*, London, 1969; E. Thorsrud and F. E. Emery, 'Industrial democracy in Norway', *Industrial Relations*, 9, pp. 187–96.

19 S. Abbott, *Employee Participation*, London, 1973.
20 J. Schregle, 'Forms of participation in management', *Industrial Relations*, 9, pp. 117–22.
21 Abbott, *op. cit.*, p. 4.
22 For more details of the proposals see B. Cassidy, *Workers on the Board*, London, 1973; Abbott, *op. cit.*
23 Labour Party, *Industrial Democracy*, London, 1968, p. 1.
24 *Ibid.* and 'Industrial democracy', *Labour Weekly*, 8 June, 1973, p. 6.
25 Liberal Party, 'Evidence and memorandum on EEC proposals on supervisory boards and worker participation', 1973, p. 8.
26 *Ibid.*

Chapter 2 **Power in industrial relations**

1 G. Wallas, 'On syndicalism', *Sociological Review*, 5, pp. 247–57.
2 M. E. Olsen, *Power in Societies*, London, 1970, p. 2.
3 T. Parsons has been the main exponent of this approach; see T. Parsons, *Structure and Process in Modern Societies*, Chicago, 1960; T. Parsons, 'On the concept of influence', *Public Opinion Quarterly*, 27, pp. 37–62; A. Giddens, ' "Power" in the recent writings of Talcott Parsons', *Sociology*, 2, pp. 257–72.
4 C. W. Mills, *The Power Elite*, New York, 1956; R. Dahrendorf, *Class and Class Conflict in Industrial Society*, London, 1959.
5 T. Parsons, 'On the concept of political power', in R. Bendix and S. M. Lipset (eds), *Class, Status and Power*, London, 1967, p. 240.
6 C. W. Mills, 'The structure of power in American society', *British Journal of Sociology*, 9, pp. 29–41.
7 M. Weber, *Economy and Society*, New York, 1968, p. 53.
8 K. Davis and W. E. Moore, 'Some principles of stratification', *American Sociological Review*, 10, pp. 242–9.
9 P. Worsley, 'The distribution of power in industrial society', in P. Halmos (ed), *The Development of Industrial Societies*, Keele, 1964, pp. 22–3.
10 R. K. Kelsall, *Higher Civil Servants in Britain*, London, 1955.
11 D. G. Clark, *The Industrial Manager*, London, 1966; T. Nichols, *Ownership, Control and Ideology*, London, 1969.
12 C. B. Otley, 'The educational background of British Army officers', *Sociology*, 7, pp. 191–209.
13 L. Paul, *The Deployment and Remuneration of the Clergy*, London, 1964.
14 A. H. Halsey and M. A. Trow, *The British Academics*, London, 1971.
15 P. Mattick, *Marx and Keynes*, London, 1969, p. 339.
16 J. K. Galbraith, *The New Industrial State*, Harmondsworth, 1969, chapter 5.
17 D. Mechanic, 'Sources of power of lower participants in complex organizations', *Administrative Science Quarterly*, 7, pp. 349–64.
18 F. Hunter, *Community Power Structure*, Chapel Hill, 1953.
19 See R. E. Wolfinger, 'Reputation and reality in the study of community power', *American Sociological Review*, 25, pp, 636–44; N. W. Polsby, 'How to study community power: the pluralist alternative', *Journal of Politics*, 22, pp. 474–84.

20 R. Dahl, *Who Governs?*, New Haven, 1961.
21 C. J. Friedrich, *Constitutional Government and Democracy*, Boston, 1950, pp. 48–9.
22 H. A. Simon, 'Notes on the observation and measurement of political power', *Journal of Politics*, 15, pp. 500–16, 505.
23 R. Bierstedt, 'An analysis of social power', *American Sociological Review*, 15, pp. 730–8, 733.
24 K. Marx, *Capital: A Critical Analysis of Capitalist Production*, London, 1946, p. 325.
25 K. Marx, *Selected Writings in Sociology and Social Philosophy*, T. B. Bottomore and M. Rubel (eds), Harmondsworth, 1963, p. 198.
26 D. Lockwood 'The distribution of power in industrial society', in P. Halmos (ed) *The Development of Industrial Societies*, Keele, 1964, p. 36.
27 Bierstedt, *op. cit.*, p. 737.
28 *Ibid.*
29 K. Marx, *Value, Price and Profit*, London, 1899, p. 94.
30 Dahrendorf, *op. cit.*
31 Parsons, *Structure and Process in Modern Societies*.
32 Weber, *op. cit.*, p. 212.
33 *Ibid.*
34 *Ibid.*
35 *Ibid.*, p. 213.
36 *Ibid.*
37 *Ibid.*, p. 215.
38 D. H. Wrong, 'Some problems in defining social power', *American Journal of Sociology*, 73, pp. 673–81, 673.
39 N. W. Chamberlain, *Collective Bargaining*, New York, 1951, p. 121.
40 J. Child, *The Business Enterprise in Modern Industrial Society*, London, 1969, p. 89.
41 *Ibid.*, pp. 89–92.
42 A. Shuchman, *Co-determination*, Washington, 1957, p. 6.
43 S. Verba, *Small Groups and Political Behaviour*, Princeton, 1961, pp. 220–1.
44 Shuchman, *op. cit.*, p. 8.
45 D. H. Meadows *et al.*, *The Limits to Growth*, London, 1972, pp. 18–19.
46 For a general discussion of the dynamic effects of participation see C. Pateman, *Participation and Democratic Theory*, Cambridge, 1970, esp. chapter 3.
47 C. W. Mills, *The Sociological Imagination*, New York, 1959, p. 3.
48 G. A. Almond and S. Verba, *The Civic Culture*, Boston, 1965, p. 294.
49 S. Cotgrove, *The Science of Society*, London, 1967, p. 57.
50 H. A. Clegg, *A New Approach to Industrial Democracy*, Oxford, 1960.
51 S. and B. Webb, *Industrial Democracy*, London, 1897.
52 Actually the 'classical' work on the so-called 'modern theory' of democracy had been developed somewhat earlier by J. A. Schumpeter, *Capitalism, Socialism and Democracy*, London, 1943.
53 Clegg, *op. cit.*, p. 23.
54 *Ibid.*, p. 21.
55 The most sustained critique is by P. Blumberg, *Industrial Democracy*, London, 1968, but many of these ideas can be traced to R. Harrison, 'Retreat from industrial democracy', *New Left Review*, 4, pp. 32–7.

56 Dahrendorf, *op. cit.*
57 *Ibid.*, p. 249.
58 *Ibid.*, p. 106.
59 *Ibid.*, p. 257.
60 *Ibid.*, p. 265.
61 Wrong, *op. cit.*, p. 673.
62 E. Mandel 'Workers' control and workers' councils', *International*, 2, pp. 1–17, 6–7.
63 *Ibid.*, pp. 9–10.
64 G. S. Bain, *The Growth of White-Collar Unionism*, London, 1970, conclusions.
65 *Ibid.*, pp. 72–81.
66 J. A. Banks, *Marxist Sociology in Action*, London, 1970, p. 290.
67 L. R. Sayles, *The Behaviour of Industrial Work Groups*, New York, 1958.
68 J. Woodward, *Industrial Organization—Theory and Practice*, London, 1965.
69 R. Blauner, *Alienation and Freedom*, Chicago, 1964.
70 Bain, *op. cit.*, esp. chapter 9.
71 Lockwood, *op. cit.*
72 A. H. Maslow, *Motivation and Personality*, New York, 1954.
73 W. W. Daniel, 'Understanding employee behaviour in its context', in J. Child (ed), *Man and Organization*, London, 1973, p. 61.
74 S. and B. Webb, *Methods of Social Study*, London, 1932.
75 *Ibid.*, p. 4.
76 *Ibid.*, pp. 25–30.

Chapter 3 **Proposals by management**

1 P. Worsley, 'The distribution of power in industrial society', in P. Halmos (ed), *The Development of Industrial Societies*, Keele, 1964, p. 23.
2 *Ibid.*, p. 19.
3 A. Bevan, *In Place of Fear*, London, 1952, p. 21.
4 T. Nichols, *Ownership, Control and Ideology*, London, 1969, chapters 6, 7 and 8.
5 *Ibid.*, pp. 72–3.
6 *Ibid.*, pp. 78–9.
7 *Ibid.*, p. 83.
8 *Ibid.*, p. 80.
9 *Ibid.*, chapter 8.
10 R. O. Clarke, *et al.*, *Workers' Participation in Management in Britain*, London, 1972, p. 179.
11 A. Fox, *A Sociology of Work in Industry*, London, 1971, p. 126.
12 J. Child, *The Business Enterprise in Modern Industrial Society*, London, 1969, p. 48.
13 Fox, *op. cit.*, p. 126.
14 Clarke *et al.*, *op. cit.*, p. 174.
15 F. J. Roethlisberger and W. J. Dixon, *Management and the Worker*, Harvard, 1939.

16 P. Blumberg, *Industrial Democracy*, London, 1968, p. 34.
17 F. G. Lesieur, *The Scanlon Plan*, New York, 1958.
18 L. Coch and J. R. P. French Jnr, 'Overcoming resistance to change', in D. Cartwright and A. Zander (eds) *Group Dynamics*, London, 1959.
19 *Ibid.*, p. 329.
20 *Ibid.*, pp. 329–32.
21 J. R. P. French Jnr *et al.*, 'An experiment on participation in a Norwegian factory', *Human Relations*, 13, pp. 3–19.
22 *Ibid.*, p. 17.
23 *Ibid.*, p. 18.
24 S. F. Cotgrove, *et al.*, *The Nylon Spinners*, London, 1971.
25 *Ibid.*, pp. 111–12.
26 H. Sallis, 'Joint consultation and meetings of primary working groups in power stations', *British Journal of Industrial Relations*, 3, p. 328.
27 W. W. Daniel and N. McIntosh, *The Right to Manage?*, London, 1972, p. 15.
28 J. H. Goldthorpe *et al.*, *The Affluent Worker: Industrial Attitudes and Behaviour*, Cambridge, 1968.
29 Daniel and McIntosh, *op. cit.*, p. 4.
30 *Ibid.*, pp. 51–2.
31 W. J. Paul and K. B. Robertson, *Job Enrichment and Employee Motivation*, London, 1970.
32 *Ibid.*, chapter 5.
33 R. N. Ford, *Motivation through the Work Itself*, New York, 1969.
34 Philips, *Work Structuring*, Eindhoven, 1963–8.
35 Daniel and McIntosh, *op. cit.*, p. 49.
36 Clarke *et al.*, *op. cit.*, p. 164.
37 C. C. Gorfin, 'The suggestion scheme', *British Journal of Industrial Relations*, 7, pp. 368–84, 383–4.
38 *Ibid.*, p. 378.
39 *Ibid.*, pp. 379–83.
40 G. Copeman, *The Challenge of Employee Shareholding*, London, 1958.
41 *Ibid.*, p. 10.
42 R. Sawtell, *Sharing Our Industrial Future*, London, 1968, p. 27.
43 Copeman, *op. cit.*, p. 28.
44 Sawtell, *op. cit.*, pp. 27–8.
45 A. Flanders *et al.*, *Experiment in Industrial Democracy*, London, 1968.
46 *Ibid.*, chapter 3.
47 J. S. Lewis, *Partnership for All*, London, 1948; *Fairer Shares*, London, 1954.
48 Flanders *et al.*, *op. cit.*, p. 129.
49 *Ibid.*, Conclusions.
50 *Ibid.*, p. 14.
51 F. H. Blum, *Work and Community*, London, 1968.
52 P. Derrick and J. F. Phipps, *Co-ownership, Co-operation and Control*, London, 1969, p. 35.
53 Blum, *op. cit.*, p. 20.
54 *Ibid.*, p. 94.
55 *Ibid.*, p. 162.
56 *Ibid.*, chapter 16.

57 *Ibid.*, p. 203.
58 National Institute of Industrial Psychology, *Joint Consultation in British Industry*, London, 1952.
59 H. A. Clegg, *The System of Industrial Relations in Great Britain*, Oxford, 1972, pp. 185–92.
60 W. E. J. McCarthy, 'The role of shop stewards in British industrial relations', Research Paper 1, Royal Commission on Trade Unions and Employers' Associations, London, 1967, p. 36.
61 M. Derber, *Labour–Management Relations at the Plant Level under Industry—Wide Bargaining*, Urbana, Illinois, 1955, pp. 79–80.
62 A. I. Marsh, *Industrial Relations in Engineering*, Oxford, 1965, p. 183.
63 Clarke *et al.*, *op. cit.*, p. 95.
64 M. J. F. Poole, 'A Power Approach to Workers' Participation in Decision Making', unpublished PhD dissertation, Sheffield University, 1969.
65 M. J. F. Poole, 'Towards a sociology of shop stewards', *Sociological Review*, 22, pp. 57–82.
66 R. Collins, 'Trends in productivity bargaining', in K. Coates *et al.*, (eds) *Trade Union Register*, London, 1970, p. 86.
67 A. Flanders, *The Fawley Productivity Agreements*, London, 1964.
68 *Ibid.*, p. 199.
69 *Ibid.*, pp. 202–3.
70 For a detailed analysis of the close connection between productivity bargaining and wider economic variables see P. Neville, 'Productivity Bargaining', unpublished undergraduate dissertation, Sheffield University, 1973.

Chapter 4 **Workers' initiatives**

1 The most important contributions to this debate being by K. Marx, *Value, Price and Profit*, London, 1951 especially p. 94; and V. I. Lenin, 'What is to be Done?', in Lenin, *Collected Works*, Vol. 5, Moscow, 1961, p. 384.
2 See M. Perlman, *Labor Union Theories in America*, Illinois, 1958; and H. Beynon and R. M. Blackburn, *Perceptions of Work*, Cambridge, 1972, pp. 117–22.
3 W. Spinrad, 'Correlates of trade union participation: a summary of the literature', *American Sociological Review*, 25, pp. 237–44.
4 Beynon and Blackburn, *op. cit.*, p. 118.
5 Marx, *op. cit.*, and Lenin *op. cit.*, for empirical work see footnote 9.
6 S. Perlman, *A Theory of the Labor Movement*, New York, 1949, pp. 3–10.
7 *Ibid.*, p. 6.
8 J. H. Goldthorpe *et al.*, *The Affluent Worker: Industrial Attitudes and Behaviour*, Cambridge, 1968.
9 See A. Flanders, *Management and Unions*, London, 1970, pp. 239–40; H. Rosen and R. A. H. Rosen, *The Union Member Speaks*, Englewood Cliffs, 1955; T. Purcell, *Blue Collar Man*, Cambridge, Mass., 1960.
10 See Goldthorpe *et al.*, *op. cit.*, especially Conclusions.
11 *Ibid.*, p. 184.

12 *Ibid.*, p. 109.
13 W. W. Daniel, 'Industrial behaviour and orientation to work—a critique', *Journal of Management Studies*, 6, pp. 366–75; W. W. Daniel, 'Understanding employee behaviour in context', in J. Child (ed), *Man and Organization*, London, 1973.
14 Beynon and Blackburn, *op. cit.*, p. 24.
15 D. Lockwood, 'Sources of variation in working class images of society', *Sociological Review*, 14, pp. 249–67.
16 *Ibid.*, pp. 249–50.
17 *Ibid.*, especially pp. 257–62.
18 B. Bernstein, *Class Codes and Control*, London, 1971; M. J. F. Poole, 'Towards a sociology of shop stewards', *Sociological Review*, 22, pp. 57–82.
19 Bernstein, *op. cit.*, p. 172.
20 Especially J. Woodward, *Industrial Organization: Theory and Practice*, London, 1965; W. H. Scott *et al.*, *Technical Change and Industrial Relations*, Liverpool, 1956.
21 Woodward, *op. cit.*, chapter 7.
22 E. L. Trist *et al.*, *Organizational Choice*, London, 1963.
23 *Ibid.*, the general thesis of the study.
24 *Ibid.*, p. 34.
25 See e.g. F. Tannenbaum, *The Labor Movement*, New York, 1921; and H. C. Adams, 'An interpretation of the social movements of our time', *International Journal of Ethics*, 2, pp. 32–50, 45–6.
26 S. and B. Webb, *A History of Trade Unionism*, London, 1902, p. 10.
27 H. A. Clegg, *A New Approach to Industrial Democracy*, Oxford, 1960, pp. 120–1.
28 H. A. T. Turner, *Trade Union Growth Structure and Policy*, London, 1962, p. 242.
29 J. E. T. Eldridge, *Sociology and Industrial Life*, London, 1973, pp. 45–9.
30 *Ibid.*, p. 45.
31 K. Coates, 'Wage Slaves', in R. K. Blackburn and A. Cockburn, *The Incompatibles*, Harmondsworth, 1967, p. 62; see also L. Taylor and P. Walton, 'Industrial sabotage: motives and meanings', in S. Cohen, (ed) *Images of Deviance*, Harmondsworth, 1971.
32 Woodward, *op. cit.*
33 For example, D. Roy, 'Quota restriction and goldbricking in a machine shop', *American Journal of Sociology*, 57, pp. 427–42; D. Roy, 'Efficiency and the "fix": informal inter-group relations in piecework machine shops', *American Journal of Sociology*, 60, pp. 255–66.
34 Eldridge, *op. cit.*, pp. 50–1.
35 R. O. Clarke *et al.*, *Workers' Participation in Management in Britain*, London, 1972, p. 105.
36 *Ibid.*
37 R. Sawtell, *Sharing our Industrial Future?*, London, 1968, pp. 32–3.
38 *Ibid.*
39 J. Leonard, *Co-operative, Co-partnership Productive Societies*, Leicester, 1965.
40 Sawtell, *op. cit.*, p. 32.

41 B. Pribićević, *The Shop Stewards' Movement and Workers' Control*, Oxford, 1959, p. 1.
42 E. H. Carr, *The Bolshevik Revolution*, Harmondsworth, 1966, p. 160.
43 C. W. Guillebaud, *The Works Council*, Cambridge, 1928, p. 5.
44 E. L. Wheelwright and B. McFarlane, *The Chinese Road to Socialism*, New York, 1970.
45 Pribićević, *op. cit.*, pp. 10–24.
46 *Ibid.*, p. 11.
47 G. D. H. Cole, *Self-Government in Industry*, London, 1972, p. 235.
48 *Ibid.*, pp. 249–50.
49 Pribićević, *op. cit.*, p. 16.
50 *Ibid.*, p. 14.
51 P. Renshaw, *The Wobblies*, London, 1967, chapter 7.
52 Pribićević, *op. cit.*, p. 13.
53 K. Coates and T. Topham, *The New Unionism*, London, 1972.
54 Pribićević, *op. cit.*, pp. 21–4.
55 J. Corina, Introduction to G. D. H. Cole, *op. cit.*, p. xi.
56 Cole, *op. cit.*, p. 30.
57 *Ibid.*
58 *Ibid.*, p. 39.
59 *Ibid.*, p. 38.
60 *Ibid.*, 'Freedom in the Guild', chapter 6, pp. 156–210.
61 M. B. Reckitt and C. E. Bechhofer, *The Meaning of National Guilds*, London, 1918, pp. 278–87; reprinted in K. Coates and T. Topham, *Workers' Control*, London, 1970, p. 55.
62 *Ibid.*, p. 54.
63 *Ibid.*, p. 57.
64 *Ibid.*, p. 55.
65 R. Postgate, *The Builders' History*, London, 1923; reprinted in Coates and Topham, *Workers' Control*, p. 64.
66 G. D. H. Cole, Foreword to B. Pribićević, *op. cit.*, p. viii.
67 *Ibid.*, p. viii.
68 Pribićević, *op. cit.*, p. 34.
69 J. T. Murphy, *The Workers' Committee*, London, 1972.
70 J. Hinton, Introduction to Murphy, *op. cit.*, p. 3.
71 Pribićević, *op. cit.*, p. 85.
72 Murphy, *op. cit.*, pp. 19–26.
73 B. Pribićević, *op. cit.*, chapter 6.
74 *Ibid.*, p. 40.
75 W. E. J. McCarthy and S. R. Parker, 'Shop stewards and workshop relations', Research Paper 10, Royal Commission on Trade Unions and Employers' Associations, London, 1968, p. 15.
76 Goldthorpe, *et al.*, *op. cit.*
77 McCarthy and Parker, *op. cit.*, pp. 16–17.
78 Poole, *op. cit.*
79 McCarthy and Parker, *op. cit.*, p. 83.
80 E. O. Evans, 'Cheap at twice the price?', in M. Warner (ed), *The Sociology of the Workplace*, London, 1973.
81 J. Reid, Foreword to W. Thompson and F. Hart, *The U.C.S. Work-in*, London, 1972.

82 S. S. Cohen, *Modern Capitalist Planning*, London, 1969.
83 *Ibid.*, p. 251.
84 Thompson and Hart, *op. cit.*, p. 12.
85 *Ibid.*, pp. 36–43.
86 J. Gretton, 'To sit or not to sit?', *New Society*, 20, pp. 564–6.

Chapter 5 **Trade unions, their officials, and workers' participation**

1 H. A. Clegg, *The System of Industrial Relations in Great Britain*, Oxford, 1972, p. 189.
2 R. Pryke, *Public Enterprise in Practice*, London, 1971.
3 C. Jenkins, *Power at the Top*, London, 1959.
4 The Labour Party, *Industrial Democracy*, London, 1967.
5 *Ibid.*, p. 7.
6 *Guardian*, *Report on the TUC Annual Congress*, London, 1973, pp. 26–7, 35–6.
7 *Ibid.*, p. 26.
8 *Ibid.*, pp. 26–7.
9 R. Fletcher, 'Trade union democracy—structural factors', in K. Coates *et al.* (eds), *Trade Union Register*, London, 1970, p. 83.
10 J. Jones, 'Unions on the board', *New Statesman*, 6 July 1973, pp. 3–4.
11 H. Scanlon, 'Workers' control and the threat of international combines', in Coates *et al.*, *op. cit.*; E. Roberts, *Workers' Control*, London, 1972.
12 C. W. Guillebaud, *The Works Council*, Cambridge, 1928, p. 8.
13 *Ibid.*, p. 12.
14 A. M. Ross, 'Prosperity and labour relations in western Europe: Italy and France', *Industrial and Labour Relations Review*, 16, pp. 63–85.
15 *Ibid.*, p. 72.
16 J. Y. Tabb and A. Goldfarb, *Workers' Participation in Management*, Oxford, 1970, p. 284.
17 *Ibid.*, pp. 62–3.
18 E. Rosenstein, 'Histadrut's search for a participation program', *Industrial Relations*, 9, pp. 170–86, 171.
19 *Ibid.*, p. 171.
20 *Ibid.*, pp. 173–82.
21 Tabb and Goldfarb, *op. cit.*, pp. 155–7.
22 *Ibid.*, p. 157.
23 *Ibid.*, p. 127.

Chapter 6 **Politics and participation**

1 These general themes are pursued more fully in J. K. Galbraith, *The New Industrial State*, Harmondsworth, 1968; France is an outstanding example of the relation between positive government planning and economic growth.
2 A. Shuchman, *Co-determination*, Washington, 1957, p. 11.
3 *Ibid.*, p. 12.
4 *Ibid.*

5 *Ibid.*, pp. 13–14.
6 *Ibid.*, p. 15.
7 *Ibid.*, p. 18.
8 *Ibid.*
9 *Ibid.*, p. 19.
10 C. W. Guillebaud, *The Works Council*, Cambridge, 1928, chapter 1, and Shuchman, *op. cit.*, chapter 5.
11 For further details of elections see Shuchman, *op. cit.*, pp. 77–9.
12 *Ibid.*, pp. 79–83.
13 Guillebaud, *op. cit.*, chapter 2.
14 *Ibid.*, chapter 3.
15 *Ibid.*, p. 176.
16 *Ibid.*, p. 215.
17 *Ibid.*, p. 244.
18 For details of the works council legislation see Shuchman, *op. cit.*, chapter 10.
19 H. A. Clegg, *The System of Industrial Relations in Great Britain*, Oxford, 1972, p. 186.
20 *Ibid.*, p. 187.
21 *Ibid.*, p. 188.
22 *Ibid.*, p. 395.
23 W. E. J. McCarthy, 'The role of shop stewards in British industrial relations', Research Paper I, Royal Commission on Trade Unions and Employers' Associations, London, 1967, p. 33.
24 M. J. F. Poole, 'A power approach to workers' participation in decision making', unpublished PhD dissertation, Sheffield University, 1969.
25 W. D. Rees, 'The practical functions of joint consultation, considered historically and in the light of recent experiences in South Wales', unpublished MSc dissertation, London University, 1963.
26 W. H. Scott *et al.*, *Coal and Conflict*, Liverpool, 1963, pp. 171–4.
27 M. P. Fogarty, 'Company and corporation reform and worker participation: the state of the debate', *British Journal of Industrial Relations*, 10, pp. 1–11, 9.
28 *Ibid.*, p. 3.
29 Guillebaud, *op. cit.*, pp. 18–19.
30 H. Hartmann, 'Codetermination in West Germany', *Industrial Relations*, 9, pp. 137–47; H. J. Spiro, *The Politics of German Co-determination*, Cambridge, Mass., 1958, chapters 1 and 2; A. Sturmthal, *Workers' Councils*, Cambridge, Mass., 1964, chapter 3; Shuchman, *op. cit.*, chapters 7 and 8.
31 Spiro, *op. cit.*, p. 31.
32 *Ibid.*, pp. 57–60.
33 Hartmann, *op. cit.*, pp. 140–2.
34 Shuchman, *op. cit.*, chapter 7.
35 For further and fuller details of the legal mechanics of co-determination see Shuchman, *op. cit.*, chapter 9, and Spiro, *op. cit.*, chapter 3.
36 Spiro, *op. cit.*, pp. 31–5.
37 *Ibid.*, p. 5.

38 Shuchman, *op. cit.*, p. 136.
39 *Ibid*, chapter 10.
40 Hartmann, *op. cit.*, pp. 138–40.
41 Shuchman, *op. cit.*, pp. 150–5.
42 Hartmann, *op. cit.*, p. 139.
43 *Ibid.*, p. 140.
44 *Ibid.*, p. 139.
45 K. Coates and T. Topham, *The New Unionism*, London, 1972, p. 205.
46 Clegg, *op. cit.*, pp. 189–93.
47 Coates and Topham, *op. cit.*, pp. 52–3.
48 *Ibid.*, pp. 8–9.
49 J. Kolaja, *A Polish Factory*, Lexington, 1960; and A. Sturmthal, *op. cit.*, chapter 5.
50 D. W. Douglas, *Transitional Economic Systems*, New York, 1972.
51 I. Clegg, *Workers' Self-management in Algeria*, London, 1971.
52 D. S. Riddell, 'Social self-government: the background of theory and practice in Yugoslav socialism', *British Journal of Sociology*, 19, pp. 47–75, 51–4.
53 T. B. Bottomore, 'Comment on Dr Pašic's paper', in M. J. Broeckmeyer (ed), *Yugoslav Workers' Selfmanagement*, Dordrecht, 1970, pp. 30–41.
54 Riddell, *op. cit.*, p. 51.
55 *Ibid.*, pp. 50–1.
56 International Labour Office, *Workers' Management in Yugoslavia*, Geneva, 1962; J. Obradovic, 'Participation and work attitudes in Yugoslavia', *Industrial Relations*, 2, pp. 161–9, 161–2; Sturmthal, *op. cit.*, chapter 4.
57 International Labour Office, *op. cit.*
58 F. Singleton and T. Topham, *Workers' Control in Yugoslavia*, London, 1968; Broeckmeyer, *op. cit.*
59 J. Vanek, *The General Theory of Labor-Managed Economies*, Ithaca, 1970, chapter 1; see also J. Vanek, *The Economics of Workers' Management: A Yugoslav Case Study*, London, 1972.
60 J. Vanek, *The General Theory of Labor-Managed Market Economies*, p. 397.
61 Bottomore, *op. cit.*
62 *Ibid.*, p. 30.
63 Coates and Topham, *op. cit.*, chapter 15.
64 Kamušič, 'Economic efficiency and workers' selfmanagement', in Broeckmeyer (ed), *op. cit.*, pp. 76–116.
65 J. Kolaja, *Workers' Councils*, London, 1965, pp. 75–6.
66 J. Tinbergen, 'Does Selfmanagement approach the optimum order?', in Broeckmeyer (ed), *op. cit.*, pp. 117–27.
67 Even Kolaja recognized this to a point and it has been frequently mentioned in the literature; see Obradovic, *op. cit.*, for one interesting contribution.
68 Tinbergen, *op. cit.*, pp. 118–19.
69 C. Pateman, *Participation and Democratic Theory*, Cambridge, 1970, p. 98.
70 *Ibid.*, p. 99.

71 The 'control-graph' method has been particularly used, of course, by A. Tannenbaum, but see V. Rus, 'Influence structure in Yugoslav enterprises', *Industrial Relations*, 9, pp. 148–60.
72 *Ibid.*, table I.
73 *Ibid.*, p. 151.
74 *Ibid.*, pp. 154–7.
75 *Ibid.*, p. 157.
76 *Ibid.*, pp. 157–8.
77 *Ibid.*, pp. 158–9.
78 Kolaja, *Workers' Councils*, p. 71.
79 *Ibid.*, p. 58.
80 Obradovic, *op. cit.*, pp. 161–9.
81 However, in a footnote it is also important to note that, although there were problems of measurement involved here, Obradovic found those who had participated on councils to be more alienated than their fellow workers, probably because of the gap between expectations and reality.
82 R. Supek 'Problems and perspectives of workers' selfmanagement in Yugoslavia', in Broeckmeyer (ed), *op. cit.*, pp. 217–41, 233.
83 For documentation see Coates and Topham, *op. cit.*, chapter 15 and for the role of unions in a self-management system see Z. Vidaković, 'The functions of the trade unions in the process of establishing the structure of Yugoslav society on a basis of selfmanagement', in Broeckmeyer (ed), *op. cit.*, pp. 42–60.

Bibliography

ABBOTT, S. *Employee Participation*, Old Queen Street Paper, Conservative Research Department, London, 1973.

ADAMS, H. C. 'An interpretation of social movements of our time', *International Journal of Ethics*, 2, 1891–2, pp. 32–50.

ALMOND, G. A. and VERBA, S. *The Civic Culture*, Little Brown, Boston, 1965.

ANDRESKI, S. L. *Military Organization and Society*, Routledge & Kegan Paul, London, 1954.

BAIN, G. S. *The Growth of White-Collar Unionism*, Oxford University Press, London, 1970.

BANKS, J. A. *Marxist Sociology in Action*, Faber, London, 1970.

BARAKAT, H. 'Alienation: a process of encounter between utopia and reality', *British Journal of Sociology*, 20, 1969, pp. 1–10.

BENDIX, R. and LIPSET, S. M. (eds) *Class, Status, and Power*, Routledge & Kegan Paul, London, 1967.

BERNSTEIN, B. *Class, Codes and Control*, Routledge & Kegan Paul, London, 1971.

BEVAN, A. *In Place of Fear*, Heinemann, London, 1952.

BEYNON, H. and BLACKBURN, R. M. *Perceptions of Work*, Cambridge University Press, 1972.

BIERSTEDT, R. 'An analysis of social power', *American Sociological Review*, 15, 1950, pp. 730–8.

BLACKBURN, R. K. and COCKBURN, A. *The Incompatibles*, Penguin, Harmondsworth, 1967.

BLAUNER, R. *Alienation and Freedom*, University of Chicago Press, 1964.

BLUM, F. H. *Work and Community*, Routledge & Kegan Paul, London, 1968.

BLUMBERG, P. *Industrial Democracy: The Sociology of Participation*, Constable, London, 1968.

BOTTOMORE, T. B. 'Comment on Dr Pašic's paper', in M. J. Broeckmeyer (ed), *Yugoslav Workers' Selfmanagement*, Reidel, Dordrecht, 1970.

BOTTOMORE, T. B. *Elites and Society*, Penguin, Harmondsworth, 1964.

BOTTOMORE, T. B. and RUBEL, M. (eds) *Karl Marx: Selected Writings in Sociology and Social Psychology*, Penguin, Harmondsworth, 1963.

BROECKMEYER, M. J. (ed) *Yugoslav Workers' Selfmanagement*, Reidel, Dordrecht, 1970.

CARR, E. H. *The Bolshevik Revolution*, Penguin, Harmondsworth, 1966.

CARTWRIGHT, D. and ZANDER, A. (eds) *Group Dynamics*, Tavistock, London, 1959.

CASSIDY, B. *Workers on the Board*, Conservative Political Centre, London, 1973.

CHAMBERLAIN, N. W. *Collective Bargaining*, McGraw-Hill, New York, 1951.

CHILD, J. *The Business Enterprise in Modern Industrial Society*, Collier-Macmillan, London, 1969.

CHILD, J. (ed) *Man and Organization*, Allen & Unwin, London, 1973.

CLARK, D. G. *The Industrial Manager: His Background and Career Pattern*, Business Publications, London, 1966.

CLARKE, R. O., FATCHETT, D. J. and ROBERTS, B. C. *Workers' Participation in Management in Britain*, Heinemann, London, 1972.

CLEGG, H. A. *A New Approach to Industrial Democracy*, Blackwell, Oxford, 1960.

CLEGG, H. A. *The System of Industrial Relations in Great Britain*, Blackwell, Oxford, 1972.

CLEGG, I. *Workers' Self-management in Algeria*, Allen Lane, London, 1971.

COATES, K. 'Wage slaves', in R. K. Blackburn and A. Cockburn, *The Incompatibles*, Penguin, Harmondsworth, 1967.

COATES, K. and TOPHAM, T. *The New Unionism*, Owen, London, 1972.

COATES, K. and TOPHAM, T. *Workers' Control*, Panther, London, 1970.

COATES, K., TOPHAM, T. and BARRATT-BROWN, M. *Trade Union Register*, Merlin, London, 1970.

COCH, L. and FRENCH, J. R. P. JNR 'Overcoming resistance to change', in D. Cartwright and A. Zander (eds), *Group Dynamics*, Tavistock, London, 1959.

COHEN, S. (ed) *Images of Deviance*, Penguin, Harmondsworth, 1971.

COHEN, S. S. *Modern Capitalist Planning*, Weidenfeld & Nicolson, London, 1969.

COLE, G. D. H. Foreword to B. Pribićević, *The Shop Stewards' Movement and Workers' Control*, Blackwell, Oxford, 1959.

COLE, G. D. H. *Self-government in Industry*, Hutchinson, London, 1972.

COLLINS, R. 'Trends in productivity bargaining' in K. Coates *et al.*, *Trade Union Register*, Merlin, London, 1970.

COPEMAN, G. *The Challenge of Employee Shareholding*, Business Publications, London, 1958.

CORINA, J. Introduction to G. D. H. Cole, *Self-government in Industry*, Hutchinson, London, 1972.

COTGROVE, S. F. *The Science of Society*, Allen & Unwin, London, 1967.

COTGROVE, S. F., DUNHAM, J. and VAMPLEW, C. *The Nylon Spinners*, Allen & Unwin, 1971.

DAHL, R. *Who Governs? Democracy and Power in an American City*, Yale University Press, 1961.

DAHRENDORF, R. *Class and Class Conflict in Industrial Society*, Routledge & Kegan Paul, London, 1959.

DANIEL, W. W. 'Industrial behaviour and orientation to work— a critique', *Journal of Management Studies*, 6, 1969, pp. 366–75.

DANIEL, W. W. 'Understanding employee behaviour in its context: illustrations from productivity bargaining', in J. Child (ed), *Man and Organization*, Allen & Unwin, London, 1973.

DANIEL, W. W. and MCINTOSH, N. *The Right to Manage?*, MacDonald, London, 1972.

DAVIS, K. and MOORE, W. E. 'Some principles of stratification', *American Sociological Review*, 10, 1945, pp. 242–9.

DAWE, A. 'The two sociologies', *British Journal of Sociology*, 21, 1970, pp. 207–18.

DERBER, M. *Labour–Management Relations at the Plant Level under Industry -Wide Bargaining*, University of Illinois Press, 1955.

DERRICK, P. and PHIPPS, J. F. *Co-ownership, Co-operation and Control*, Longmans, London, 1969.

DOUGLAS, D. W. *Transitional Economic Systems*, Monthly Review Press, New York, 1972.

ELDRIDGE, J. E. T. *Sociology and Industrial Life*, Nelson, London, 1973.

EVANS, E. O. 'Cheap at twice the price?', in M. Warner (ed), *The Sociology of the Workplace*, Allen & Unwin, London, 1973.

FLANDERS, A. *The Fawley Productivity Agreements*, Faber, London, 1964.

FLANDERS, A. *Management and Unions*, Faber, London, 1970.

FLANDERS, A., POMERANZ, R. and WOODWARD, J. *Experiment in Industrial Democracy*, Faber, London, 1968.

FLETCHER, R. 'Trade union democracy—structural factors', in K. Coates *et al.* (eds), *Trade Union Register*.

FOGARTY, M. P. 'Company and corporation reform and worker participation: the state of the debate', *British Journal of Industrial Relations*, 10, 1972, pp. 1–11.

FORD, R. N. *Motivation Through the Work Itself*, American Management Association, New York, 1969.

FOX, A. *A Sociology of Work in Industry*, Collier-Macmillan, London, 1971.

FRENCH, J. R. P. JNR, ISRAEL, J. and ÅS, D. 'An experiment on participation in a Norwegian factory', *Human Relations*, 13, 1960, pp. 3–19.

FRIEDRICH, C. J. *Constitutional Government and Democracy*, Ginn, Boston, 1950.

GALBRAITH, J. K. *The New Industrial State*, Penguin, Harmondsworth, 1968.

GIDDENS, A. ' "Power" in the recent writings of Talcott Parsons', *Sociology*, 2, 1968, pp. 257–72.

GOLDTHORPE, J. H., LOCKWOOD, D., BECHHOFER, F. and PLATT, J. *The Affluent Worker: Industrial Attitudes and Behaviour*, Cambridge University Press, 1968.

GORFIN, C. C. 'The suggestion scheme', *British Journal of Industrial Relations*, 7, 1969, pp. 368–84.

GRETTON, J. 'To sit or not to sit?', *New Society*, 20, 15 June 1972, pp. 564–6.

'GUARDIAN' *Report on the TUC Annual Congress*, Guardian, London, 1973.

GUILLEBAUD, C. W. *The Works Council*, Cambridge University Press, 1928.

HALMOS, P. (ed) *The Development of Industrial Societies*, Sociological Review Monograph No. 8, University of Keele, 1964.

HALSEY, A. H. and TROW, M. A. *The British Academics*, Faber, London, 1971.

HARRISON, R. 'Retreat from industrial democracy', *New Left Review*, 4, 1960, pp. 32–7.

HARTMANN, H. 'Codetermination in West Germany', *Industrial Relations*, 9, 1970, pp. 137–47.

HESPE, G. and LITTLE, A. 'Some aspects of employee participation', in P. B. Warr (ed), *Psychology at Work*, Penguin, Harmondsworth, 1971.

HINTON, J. Introduction to J. T. Murphy, *The Workers' Committee*, Pluto Press, London, 1972.

HOLTER, H. 'Attitudes towards employee participation in company decision making processes', *Human Relations*, 18, 1965, pp. 297–322.

HUNTER, F. *Community Power Structure: A Study of Decision Makers*, University of North Carolina Press, 1953.

'INDUSTRIAL DEMOCRACY', *Labour Weekly*, 8 June 1973.

INTERNATIONAL LABOUR OFFICE, *Workers' Management in Yugoslavia*, International Labour Offices, Geneva, 1962.

JENKINS, C. *Power at the Top*, MacGibbon & Kee, London, 1959.

JONES, J. 'Unions on the board', *New Statesman*, 6 July 1973, pp. 3–4.

KAMUŠIČ, M. 'Economic efficiency and workers' selfmanagement', in M. J. Broeckmeyer (ed), *Yugoslav Workers' Selfmanagement*, Reidel, Dordrecht, 1970.

KELSALL, R. K. *Higher Civil Servants in Britain*, Routledge & Kegan Paul, London, 1955.

KOLAJA, J. *A Polish Factory*, University of Kentucky Press, 1960.

KOLAJA, J. *Workers' Councils*, Tavistock, London, 1965.

LABOUR PARTY, *Industrial Democracy*, Labour Party, London, 1967.

LABOUR PARTY, *Industrial Democracy*, Labour Party, London, 1968.

LAMMERS, C. J. 'Power and participation in decision making in formal undertakings', *American Journal of Sociology*, 73, 1967, pp. 201–16.

LENIN, V. I. 'What is to be done?', *Collected Works*, Foreign Languages Publishing House, Moscow, 1961.

LEONARD, J. *Co-operative, Co-partnership Productive Societies*, Co-operative Productive Federation, Leicester, 1965.

LESIEUR, F. G. *The Scanlon Plan*, Wiley, New York, 1958.

LEWIS, J. S. *Fairer Shares*, Staples, London, 1954.

LEWIS, J. S. *Partnership for All*, Kerr-Cros, London, 1948.

LIBERAL PARTY 'Evidence and memorandum on EEC proposals on supervisory boards and worker participation', Liberal Party, London, 1973.

LIKERT, R. *New Patterns in Management*, McGraw-Hill, New York, 1961.

LOCKWOOD, D. 'The distribution of power in industrial society: a comment', in P. Halmos (ed), *The Development of Industrial Societies*, University of Keele, 1964.

LOCKWOOD, D. 'Sources of variation in working class images of society', *Sociological Review*, 14, 1966, pp. 249–67.

MCCARTHY, W. E. J. 'The role of shop stewards in British industrial relations', Research Paper 1, Royal Commission on Trade Unions and Employers' Associations, HMSO, London, 1967.

MCCARTHY, W. E. J. and PARKER, S. R. 'Shop stewards and workshop relations', Research Paper 10, Royal Commission on Trade Unions and Employers' Associations, HMSO, London, 1968.

MCGREGOR, D. *The Human Side of Enterprise*, McGraw-Hill, New York, 1960.

MANDEL, E. 'Workers' Control and Workers' Councils', *International*, 2, 1973, pp. 1–17.

MARCUSE, H. *Reason and Revolution*, Routledge & Kegan Paul, London, 1954.

MARSH, A. I. *Industrial Relations in Engineering*, Pergamon, Oxford, 1965.

MARX, K. *Capital: A Critical Analysis of Capitalist Production*, Allen & Unwin, London, 1946.

MARX, K. *Selected Writings in Sociology and Social Philosophy*, T. B. Bottomore and M. Rubel (eds), Penguin, Harmondsworth, 1963.

13

MARX, K. *Value, Price and Profit*, Allen & Unwin, London, 1951.

MASLOW, A. H. *Motivation and Personality*, Harper & Row, New York, 1954.

MATTICK, P. *Marx and Keynes*, Merlin, London, 1969.

MEADOWS, D. H., MEADOWS, D. L., RANDERS, J. and BEHRENS, W. W. *The Limits to Growth*, Earth Island, London, 1972.

MECHANIC, D. 'Sources of power of lower participants in complex organizations', *Administrative Science Quarterly*, 7, 1962–3, pp. 349–64.

MILLS, C. W. *The Power Elite*, Oxford University Press, New York, 1956.

MILLS, C. W. *The Sociological Imagination*, Oxford University Press, New York, 1959.

MILLS, C. W. 'The structure of power in American society', *British Journal of Sociology*, 9, 1958, pp. 29–41.

MORSE, N. C. and REIMER, E. 'Experimental change in a major organizational variable', *Journal of Abnormal and Social Psychology*, 52, 1956, pp. 120–9.

MURPHY, J. T. *The Workers' Committee*, Pluto Press, London, 1972.

MUSGROVE, F. *The Migratory Elite*, Heinemann, London, 1963.

NATIONAL INSTITUTE OF INDUSTRIAL PSYCHOLOGY, *Joint Consultation in British Industry*, Staples, London, 1952.

NICHOLS, T. *Ownership, Control and Ideology*, Allen & Unwin, London, 1969.

OBRADOVIC, J. 'Participation and work attitudes in Yugoslavia', *Industrial Relations*, 2, 1970, pp. 161–9.

OLSEN, M. E. *Power in Societies*, Macmillan, London, 1970.

OTLEY, C. B. 'The educational background of British Army officers', *Sociology*, 7, 1973, pp. 191–209.

PARSONS, T. 'On the concept of influence', *Public Opinion Quarterly*, 27, 1963, pp. 37–62.

PARSONS, T. 'On the concept of political power', in R. Bendix and S. M. Lipset (eds), *Class, Status, and Power*, Routledge & Kegan Paul, London, 1967, pp. 240–65.

PARSONS, T. *Structure and Process in Modern Societies*, Free Press, Chicago, 1960.

PATEMAN, C. *Participation and Democratic Theory*, Cambridge University Press, 1970.

PAUL, L. *The Deployment and Remuneration of the Clergy*, Church Information Office, London, 1964.

PAUL, W. J. and ROBERTSON, K. B. *Job Enrichment and Employee Motivation*, Gower, London, 1970.

PERLMAN, M. *Labor Union Theories in America*, Row, Peterson, Illinois, 1958.

PERLMAN, S. *A Theory of the Labor Movement*, Kelley, New York, 1949.

PHILIPS, *Work Structuring: a summary of experiences at Philips* 1963–8 Philips, Eindhoven, 1963–8.

POLSBY, N. W. 'How to study community power: the pluralist alternative', *Journal of Politics*, 22, 1960, pp. 474–84.

POOLE, M. J. F. 'A power approach to workers' participation in decision making', unpublished PhD dissertation, Sheffield University, 1969.

POOLE, M. J. F. 'Towards a sociology of shop stewards', *Sociological Review*, 22, 1974, pp. 57–82.

POSTGATE, R. *The Builders' History*, NFBTO, London, 1923.

PRIBIĆEVIĆ, B. *The Shop Stewards' Movement and Workers' Control*, Blackwell, Oxford, 1959.

PRYKE, R. *Public Enterprise in Practice*, MacGibbon & Kee, London, 1971.

PURCELL, T. *Blue Collar Man*, Harvard University Press, 1960.

RECKITT, M. B. and BECHHOFER, C. E. *The Meaning of National Guilds*, Palmer, London, 1918.

REES, W. D. 'The practical functions of joint consultation, considered historically and in the light of recent experiences in South Wales', unpublished MSc dissertation, London University, 1963.

REID, J. Foreword to W. Thompson and F. Hart, *The U.C.S. Work-In*.

RENSHAW, P. *The Wobblies*, Eyre & Spottiswoode, London, 1967.

RICE, A. K. *Productivity and Social Organization*, Tavistock, London, 1958.

RIDDELL, D. S. 'Social self-government: the background of theory and practice in Yugoslav socialism', *British Journal of Sociology*, 19, 1968, pp. 47–75.

ROBERTS, E. *Workers' Control*, Allen & Unwin, London, 1972.

ROETHLISBERGER, F. J. and DIXON, W. J. *Management and the Worker*, Harvard University Press, 1939.

ROSEN, H. and ROSEN, R. A. H. *The Union Member Speaks*, Prentice-Hall, Englewood Cliffs, 1955.

ROSENSTEIN, E. 'Histadrut's search for a participation program', *Industrial Relations*, 9, 1970, pp. 170–86.

ROSS, A. M. 'Prosperity and labour relations in western Europe: Italy and France', *Industrial and Labour Relations Review*, 16, 1962, pp. 63–85.

ROY, D. 'Efficiency and the "fix": informal inter-group relations in piecework machine shops', *American Journal of Sociology*, 60, 1954, pp. 255–66.

ROY, D. 'Quota restriction and goldbricking in a machine shop', *American Journal of Sociology*, 57, 1952, pp. 427–42.

RUS, V. 'Influence structure in Yugoslav enterprises', *Industrial Relations*, 9, 1970, pp. 148–60.

SALLIS, H. 'Joint consultation and meetings of primary working groups in power stations', *British Journal of Industrial Relations*, 3, 1965, pp. 328–44.

SAWTELL, R. *Sharing our Industrial Future*, The Industrial Society, London, 1968.

SAYLES, L. R. *The Behavior of Industrial Work Groups*, Wiley, New York, 1958.

SCANLON, H. 'Workers' control and the threat of international combines', in K. Coates *et al.*, *Trade Union Register*.

SCHREGLE, J. 'Forms of participation in management', *Industrial Relations*, 9, 1970, pp. 117–22.

SCOTT, W. H., BANKS, J. A., HALSEY, A. H. and LUPTON, T. *Technical Change and Industrial Relations*, Liverpool University Press, 1956.

SCOTT, W. H., MUMFORD, E., MCGIVERING, I. C. and KIRKBY, J. M. *Coal and Conflict*, Liverpool University Press, 1963.

SHUCHMAN, A. *Co-determination, Labor's Middle Way in Germany*, Public Affairs Press, Washington, 1957.

SCHUMPETER, J. A. *Capitalism, Socialism and Democracy*, Allen & Unwin, London, 1943.

SIMON, H. A. 'Notes on the observation and measurement of political power', *Journal of Politics*, 15, 1953, pp. 500–16.

SINGLETON, F. and TOPHAM, T. *Workers' Control in Yugoslavia*, Fabian Society, London, 1968.

SPINRAD, W. 'Correlates of trade union participation: a summary of the literature', *American Sociological Review*, 25, 1960, pp. 237–44.

SPIRO, H. J. *The Politics of German Co-determination*, Harvard University Press, 1958.

STURMTHAL, A. *Workers' Councils*, Harvard University Press, 1964.

SUPEK, R. 'Problems and perspectives of workers' selfmanagement in Yugoslavia', in M. J. Broeckmeyer (ed), *Yugoslav Workers' Selfmanagement*, Reidel, Dordrecht, 1970.

TABB, J. Y. and GOLDFARB, A. *Workers' Participation in Management*, Pergamon, Oxford, 1970.

TANNENBAUM, F. *The Labor Movement*, Putnam, New York, 1921.

TAYLOR, L. and WALTON, P. 'Industrial sabotage: motives and meanings', in S. Cohen (ed), *Images of Deviance*, Penguin, Harmondsworth, 1971.

THOMPSON, W. and HART, F. *The U.C.S. Work-In*, Lawrence & Wishart, London, 1972.

THORSRUD, E. and EMERY, F. E. *Form and Content in Industrial Democracy*, Tavistock, London, 1969.

THORSRUD, E. and EMERY, F. E. 'Industrial democracy in Norway', *Industrial Relations*, 9, 1970, pp. 187–96.

TINBERGEN, J. 'Does selfmanagement approach the optimum order?', in M. J. Broeckmeyer (ed), *Yugoslav Workers' Selfmanagement*, Reidel, Dordrecht, 1970.

TRIST, E. L., HIGGIN, G. W., MURRAY, H. and POLLOCK, A. B. *Organizational Choice*, Tavistock, London, 1963.

TURNER, H. A. T. *Trade Union Growth Structure and Policy*, Allen & Unwin, London, 1962.

VANEK, J. *The Economics of Workers' Management: A Yugoslav Case Study*, Allen & Unwin, London, 1972.

VANEK, J. *The General Theory of Labor-Managed Economies*, Cornell University Press, 1970.

VERBA, S. *Small Groups and Political Behaviour*, Princeton University Press, 1961.

VIDAKOVIĆ, Z. 'The functions of the trade unions in the process of establishing the structure of Yugoslav society on a basis of selfmanagement', in M. J. Broeckmeyer (ed), *Yugoslav Workers' Selfmanagement*, Reidel, Dordrecht, 1970.

WALLAS, G. 'On syndicalism', The Sociological Society: Annual Meeting, *Sociological Review*, 5, 1912, pp. 247–57.

WARNER, M. (ed) *The Sociology of the Workplace*, Allen & Unwin, London, 1973.

WARR, P. B. (ed) *Psychology at Work*, Penguin, Harmondsworth, 1971.

WEBB, S. and WEBB, B. *A History of Trade Unionism*, Longmans, Green, London, 1902.

WEBB, S. and WEBB, B. *Industrial Democracy*, Longmans, London, 1897.

WEBB, S. and WEBB, B. *Methods of Social Study*, Longmans, Green, London, 1932.

WEBER, M. *Economy and Society*, Bedminster Press, New York, 1968.

WHEELWRIGHT, E. L. and MCFARLANE, B. *The Chinese Road to Socialism*, Monthly Review Press, New York, 1970.

WOLFINGER, R. E. 'Reputation and reality in the study of community power', *American Sociological Review*, 25, 1960, pp. 636–44.

WOODWARD, J. (ed) *Industrial Organization: Theory and Practice*, Oxford University Press, London, 1965.

WORSLEY, P. 'The distribution of power in industrial society', in P. Halmos (ed), *The Development of Industrial Societies*, University of Keele, 1964.

WRONG, D. H. 'Some problems in defining social power', *American Journal of Sociology*, 73, 1968, pp. 673–81.

Index